Capital Wars

Capital Wars

The New East-West Challenge
for Entrepreneurial Leadership
and Economic Success

Daniel Pinto

B L O O M S B U R Y
LONDON · NEW DELHI · NEW YORK · SYDNEY

First published in France in 2013 by Odile Jacob as *Le Choc des capitalismes: Comment nous avons été dépossédés de notre génie entrepreneurial et comment le réinventer*
Original French copyright © ODILE JACOB, 2013

First published in Great Britain 2014

Copyright © Daniel Pinto, 2014

Bloomsbury Publishing Plc
50 Bedford Square
London
WC1B 3DP

www.bloomsbury.com

Bloomsbury Publishing
London, New Delhi, New York and Sydney

A CIP record for this book is available from the British Library.

ISBN: 9-781-472905055

10 9 8 7 6 5 4 3 2 1

Design by Fiona Pike, Pike Design, Winchester
Typeset by Hewer Text UK Ltd, Edinburgh
Printed and bound in Great Britain by CPI Group (UK) Ltd, Croydon CR0 4YY

For Isaac Jack Pinto

in loving memory

Contents

Introduction

Why speak out? Why not 'keep dancing'? to paraphrase Chuck Prince, former boss of American banking giant Citigroup, when describing Wall Street's state of mind just minutes before the Titanic of finance hit the iceberg of economic reality.

These were the questions going through my mind more than a year ago when, already caught up in the maelstrom of an over-filled professional life, I set about writing this book. After years spent building up Stanhope Capital, the financial group I co-founded a decade ago, and trying to move the boundaries in a sector which through no will of its own became the Achilles heel of Western capitalism, the need to bear witness struck me as evident.

How could one remain a powerless spectator in a world where the CEOs of our largest corporations have turned themselves into public relations officers, more concerned with pleasing fund managers who never set foot in the real business world, than with preparing their groups for the challenges of the future? Why keep quiet and carry on when our major banks, despite a barrage of reforms, are still powder kegs liable to catapult the economy into chaos at any moment? Why simply accept the status quo as European governments exhaust themselves to preserve moribund social models while sacrificing entrepreneurs on the altar of their politicians' promises? In truth, five years after a crisis which threatened to take us all down, not much has changed. We are still addressing the symptoms of the last crisis, not its root cause.

Having experienced the continued failings and short-sightedness of business and political leaders on both sides of the Atlantic first-hand, I certainly did not want to write yet another eulogy for our ailing capitalist system. My aim with this book is not to talk of decline but of recovery and reconstruction. However, this process can only start in earnest once we have countered two prevailing attitudes. On one hand, the fifth column of defeatists who, the minute they hear the word change, look at you with a resigned smile and reply, 'What's the point? What could we possibly do?' On the other, the ayatollahs of legislation and regulation who fail to see that as long as our capitalist societies have not undergone a cultural revolution of some sort, brilliant minds will always find ways around the rules. And the merry go round of booms and busts will eventually finish off whatever is left of our civilisation. By putting forward new and concrete ideas aimed at putting the patient back on its feet, my ambition, as quixotic as it might seem, is to widen the public debate on ways of reinventing our brand of capitalism before it is relegated to the history books.

The debt crisis can certainly be blamed for bringing down the mighty 'twin towers' of American and European capitalism and, with them, two centuries of Western dominance on the global economic and political stage. But restricting the analysis to the immediate causes of the last crisis is completely missing the point. The decay of Western capitalism started well before 2008. Commentators, along with politicians of all stripes, are quick to point fingers at the supposed culprits: the Wall Street banker, the City speculator, the Chinese manufacturer, the Indian entrepreneur, or the Russian oligarch. The convenient wisdom is that disease is always caused by others. In fact, they are trying to deny a much harsher reality. For the past three decades, it is us that planted the seed of our own demise by killing the Western entrepreneur, thus condemning ourselves to anaemic growth, and at the same time setting up our main competitors to succeed.

In fact, hiding behind a seismic realignment of the global economy lie two opposing forms of capitalism locked in an existential struggle. The incumbent Western capitalism has managed in recent decades to suffocate its very heroes – the captains of industry who once upon a time created world-leading companies which brought prosperity and clout to their nations. Today, the entire system seems to be suffering from a chronic decision-making illness; it is mired in a deep crisis of governance in which the main stakeholders are all too often motivated by the lure of immediate results and personal gains.

While Asian and Latin American firms have largely remained in the hands of owner-managers who are natural empire builders, Western companies are now run by professional CEOs who operate like unadventurous 'administrators-in-chief'. The apparatchiks of modern capitalism, these executives are able to amass vast fortunes when successful but have little to lose personally when they fail. Disinclined to make the heavy investments required to ensure the leadership of their companies in the long term, they have learned to manage their own careers more skilfully than the future of their businesses and have become the vassals of nomadic financial shareholders for whom the enterprise is but a line item in an investment portfolio. The relative passivity of these Western CEOs is endorsed by their corporate boards where the cult of independence and 'accepted standards' of good governance have sanitised the decision-making process and turned our largest companies into bastions of business conservatism. By contrast, the foreign competitors which only yesterday were disdained by Western businesses continue to exhibit dynamism and ingenuity. It is in this contrast we can find the primary cause of our decline.

In the East and the South an authentic brand of entrepreneurial capitalism has prevailed; one fuelled by audacity and patience inspired, ironically, by the very model which once built the economies of the West. In these 'emerging' societies, what drives decision-making are not quarterly results or the threat of shareholders' lawsuits but rather the urge to build for the long term, in a determined and premeditated manner. Whether in China, where the entire state apparatus turned itself into an entrepreneurial force alongside a booming private sector, or in India where dynasties of entrepreneurs reign supreme, decision-makers only have one question in mind: what can they do today to steer their companies to the top five 10 years from now?

This kind of time horizon no longer exists in the West. It has vanished both from the business sphere and the political arena. And so it seems the emerging powers are now using our very recipes to beat us at our own game. By stifling our entrepreneurial drive, we in the US and Europe have set our own path towards economic misery, a situation which has led to the implosion of the prevailing social models painstakingly maintained since the Second World War. Ultimately, it is the geopolitical legitimacy of the West which is at stake.

Western myopia has had deep and long lasting consequences. By mid-2013 emerging markets were already accounting for the majority of global GDP for the first time, with the lion's share of global growth in the next five years set to take place in these economies[1]. Even with an annual growth rate of approximately 7 per cent – much less than the 10 per cent achieved during much of the last decade – China should be able to take over from the US as the world's biggest economy in the course of the next 10 or 15 years at most. By 2050, only two European countries – Germany and the UK – will still feature amongst the top 10 economies in the world[2] but they will be bringing up the rear. Contrary to the view held by many doomsayers, the somewhat slower growth experienced by China, India, and Brazil over the last couple of years will not materially affect this reality. The BRICS undoubtedly have to implement substantial economic, social, and political reforms to make their success more sustainable and broad-based. However, it would be a mistake to assume that the difficulties they have been experiencing of late, along with the prospect of America becoming energy self-sufficient in the next 20 years, are signalling a return to the old world order. The die is cast.

Incapable of getting back on the road to real growth, the US and Europe have become largely financially dependent on emerging powers, drip-fed on credit to maintain their standard of living. The trade surpluses have enabled the emerging economies to accumulate more than 6.8 trillion dollars in currency reserves[3], with China alone having almost half of this amount at its disposal. It is the old colonial powers who are begging for funds, cap in hand, amongst countries they regarded just yesterday with a mixture of condescension and resentment.

Both the engines of global growth and the number one creditors of the West, the emerging powers are now entering the last stage of economic domination by becoming the largest investors in European and American companies. From China to Saudi Arabia, through to the Gulf Emirates and Russia, emerging countries have accumulated a war chest of close to five trillion dollars[4], managed by their all-powerful sovereign wealth funds. These are the funds that saved some of the biggest Anglo-Saxon banks (Morgan Stanley, Barclays) during the financial crisis of 2008 and will probably be there once more over the coming months and years to recapitalise the big European banks. The private sector is also on the move.

Major family groups from India, China, Brazil, and Russia are carving out the lion's share of entire sectors of industry and services for themselves. In just a few years, leading Indian entrepreneurs have captured sectors such as the steel and car industries or information technology services. Brazilian family groups have taken strategic positions in the aeronautics and raw materials industries. Russian groups, who operate at the seam of the public and private sectors, have become powerhouses in energy and mining. As far as Chinese groups are concerned, a comprehensive list of the sectors in which they have taken the prime slot would be lengthy indeed. One by one, big Western firms seem to be caving in to the onslaught of smart competitors, determined, patient and capable of placing long-term bets while our own bosses' eyes are riveted on their company's day-to-day stock price.

But what has happened to Western nations which, until so recently, remained at the height of their glory? How can nations which remain at the cutting edge of knowledge and creativity in so many areas lose their competitive advantage so rapidly? How did the dream of the 'shining city on the hill', to quote President Reagan, the perfect incarnation of the American belief that everything and anything is possible, turn into a nightmare where 43 million individuals – one in seven – live on food stamps? And how can the Europe of Jean Monnet allow member-states like Spain to reach a point where over one quarter of the workforce is unemployed and where one in two young people can't find work?

The world's centre of gravity has shifted decidedly eastward. Over the last two decades as financial advisor to governments, CEOs of large corporations, entrepreneurs, and wealthy families both in the Old World and the New, I have been a privileged and intimate witness of this process. My observation is simple: entrepreneurial capitalism has changed hands. It is now easier to find entrepreneurs and visionary captains of industry in China, India, or Brazil than in the US, Great Britain, or France. With the decline of entrepreneurs and family-owned businesses in the West, the courage to start new ventures and the emotional connection between an enterprise and its shareholders has slowly withered away. By locking stakeholders into a system plagued with divergent interests and obsessed with immediate results, Western capitalism is effectively committing suicide.

In a way, the failure of Western governments to handle chronic debt and reinstate the necessary conditions for growth parallels the governance crisis we see in business today. On one hand, short-term financial gain is pursued compulsively and financial markets are fed a diet of figures that never satisfy. On the other, electoral gain is pursued at any price; hollow promises are made within time-frames that have no relation whatsoever to longer economic cycles. And because we cannot afford to deliver on these promises, we borrow again and again until inevitable financial disaster ensues. In both cases, lack of patience and the valorisation of personal short-term interests lead to disaster.

Repairing the world of finance is a prerequisite to the reconstruction of Western capitalism. Operating in a sector dominated by huge banks which have more than contributed to recent market chaos, I have always respected the basic principles of one of the last century's great financiers, Siegmund Warburg. Even in his day, Warburg already sensed the dangers of the radical financialisation of the economy. His belief was that finance should remain an enabler for the real economy rather than being an end in itself; that business should remain at the centre of the system and that the banker should be honoured simply to pass on the plates.

Having trained at the prestigious institution Warburg created in London, I made these values my own when I established Stanhope Capital. At a time when the traditional partnerships of Wall Street and the City have turned into listed behemoths, permitting an unlucky or dishonest trader to lose in seconds the equivalent of 10 years of profits for institutions which have often been saved by the taxpayer, I longed to return to a somewhat outmoded practice of a profession whose contribution to the vitality of our economies has long since been forgotten.

But economic fragility and decline has not been caused by the radical financialisation of our economies alone. Our business leaders, too, while not lacking in intelligence, have demonstrated extraordinary complacency in the face of upheavals. During the nineties I advised a major European information technology firm whose CEO explained to me that Indian companies in no way constituted a threat in the field of software as 'our' engineers were unmatched. We know all too well what followed. In other sectors, I have seen such icons of American capitalism as General Motors and Kodak file for bankruptcy, victims of their own convictions. At a time when Western heads of state fight for the honour of an audience with the Chinese President, we have no choice but to accept the central role that self-delusion has played in bringing about the downfall of the West.

The tragic irony of our situation is that this brand of entrepreneurial capitalism – all conquering and open to the world – which has propelled the emerging countries to the forefront of the political and economic world stage, used to belong to us. The subtle but powerful alliance between the entrepreneur, the state, and capital markets serving the economy, and not the opposite, was in fact invented by us. Too focused on the instant satisfaction of our needs, we in the West have preferred to sell our birth right for a mess of pottage. . .

The only good news in this gloomy picture, and the thrust of this book, is that it is still possible for us to claim it back. We will have to show courage, patience, and creativity, but it is up to us to reinvent the values and methods that made our economies great, and to adapt our societies to the new challenges of a multi-polar world.

---

1 Source: "Emerging Power: Developing Nations Now Claim The Majority of World GDP", The Atlantic, 4 June, 2013

2 PWC 2011 report "The World in 2050"

3 Source: IMF

4 "Sovereign Wealth Funds", CityUK, February 2012

Part One

From the capitalism of creators to the capitalism of apparatchiks: the rise and fall of the West

Chapter 1

The end of our illusions

Illusions, the drivers of our decline

Looking out from the top floor window of a conference room in the headquarters of Usinor in the Parisian business district of La Défense, I could almost imagine, on a clear day, making out on the horizon the columns of smoke rising up from the steel mills of Lorraine, the birthplace and industrial heart of the group. That steel and glass tower was a monument to the power of a company whose roots went back to the first masters of the furnace, 19th-century ironworkers who, through continual restructuring, had adapted themselves so well to the environment of fierce competition of the mid-nineties.

It was the summer of 1994. As a young merchant banker mandated to privatise Usinor, an industrial icon if ever there was one, my team from SG Warburg and I were to meet with one of the group's senior executives to begin preparing a market flotation. This was as eagerly awaited by the markets as it was by public authorities, who had been their major stockholder since the wave of French nationalisations in 1981.

The meeting began warmly enough and after covering the technical aspects of the flotation, we set about the essential issue of the competition. 'How can we explain Usinor's market positioning vis-à-vis your main competitors in such a fragmented industry?' asked one of my colleagues before qualifying his question with: 'the massive overcapacity affecting the industry is putting considerable pressure on margins and investors will legitimately expect to hear how you are planning to improve your group's profitability'.

This promoted a relaxed smile from our interlocutor. 'Our strategy is to focus on quality', he responded, with all the supreme self-confidence that comes from having jumped through every hoop on the way to a brilliant career at the cusp of the public and private sectors. He nevertheless confessed that Usinor, at the time the fourth largest steel producer in the world, had to address tough competition from rival groups such as the UK's British Steel and Germany's Thyssen who had already managed to snatch big deals from under his nose.

Having read an article on the dynamism of steel producers in the emerging countries, I chanced a question about the Indian company ISPAT run by the then relatively unknown Mr Mittal. Our majestic host's conference room was suddenly plunged into silence, as he stared at me with a look somewhere between astonishment and irony. After the most pregnant of pauses he responded: 'My good fellow, ISPAT is not a competitor'. Noting my surprise he added, 'the quality of Mr Mittal's steel products is well below the standards expected by our major automotive customers'. He clearly seemed insulted by the comparison.

The rest, as they say, is history. Ten years later, the entire Usinor group by then rebaptised as Arcelor and the world's leading steel producer having made a series of acquisitions including Cockerill Sambre, Arbed, and Aceralia, would end up falling into the clutches of the very same Mr Mittal.

And what an exceptional fate was in store for Lakshmi Mittal, a man who launched his group in 1976 from just a simple steel plant in Indonesia. Through his own operational genius and timely acquisitions throughout the world, he moved from the world's 29th steel producer in 1995, the year of Usinor's IPO, to the top slot in 2005 with an annual production of 63 million tons. This was the year in which he was to make his move on Arcelor[1]. In spite of his acknowledged talent and doggedness, it is safe to say that he wasn't welcomed with open arms by Arcelor's management team. In an interview that has since become infamous, the CEO of the time dared to explain to his shareholders that they should reject Mittal's advances if they didn't wish to be 'fobbed off with *monnaie de singe*[2]'.

This inappropriate outburst is a telling indication of the superiority complex which has for decades prevented many Western corporate giants from adapting to the new world order of international competition. The decade separating Arcelor's market flotation and Mittal's buyout was a period of intense disruption amongst the industry's major players. The rapid industrialisation of the emerging countries and the growth in their steel consumption had put local producers, particularly the Chinese and the Indians, in a position of strength. In 1995 not a single Chinese company figured in the list of the world's top 10 steel producers; now there are no fewer than four Chinese companies amongst the leaders. Lakshmi Mittal built his company from the ground up without hindrance from past paradigms. He was thus in an infinitely stronger position than Arcelor to conquer an industry that had, in many respects, got stuck in a time warp.

One would have thought that such profound changes should have prompted our leaders to become more lucid or, at the very least, more humble. The opposite happened. In 2006, the French Minister of the Economy, himself a former CEO, spoke of Mr Mittal with disdain stating he should learn 'the grammar of business'. Again, in 2012, when Mittal proposed to close down two antiquated blast-furnaces in Florange, thereby making the only economically rational decision available to him, he was faced with the threat of nationalisation. The French political establishment closed ranks against him, united in its hatred of everything he represented: wealth, outstanding professional success, and, above all, globalisation.

But beyond the steel industry, which found itself in the eye of the storm brought on by the competition from the emerging countries, whatever happened to the other Western companies whose brands made up our day to day existences and which became shadows of their former selves? The Bulls, Kodaks, Marconis, and the Thomsons? All became victims of a complacency that blinded them to the disruption rife in their respective industries. With their extinction, millions of jobs went up in smoke, not through a lack of intelligence but through a lack of foresight and flexibility.

Macro-economic figures, however, conceal this truth from us. We speak of weak growth and deindustrialisation as if they were inevitable; an ongoing disaster we are powerless to counter. GDP figures seem to be produced by a machine gone mad when they are in fact the result of our own – we, the main economic stakeholders – decisions, or rather, our indecision. In fact the West's entire economic 'ecosystem' is living in delusion. First, the delusion of the individual who still considers his right to a state pension at 60 to be God-given when increased life expectancy and mass unemployment clearly rule it out. Then, the delusion of many a multinational who instead of reinventing their business models remain wedded to the production of goods and services which are in decline. And finally, the delusion of our States who continue to spend and borrow beyond all reason and choose to hide this reality from us in order to keep the social peace.

No, we are not victims of the emerging countries; we are victims of our own delusions. But before we broach the subject of a wake-up call, one which is vital for the survival of our model, we should first size up the opposing forces and dynamics that have brought our economies to the state they find themselves in today.

The opposing forces

Over the last 30 years the growth gap between Western and emerging countries has reached hitherto unseen proportions. While, between 1980 and 2011, the US, Great Britain, and France have seen their respective GDPs grow by 2.63 per cent, 2.16 per cent and 1.82 per cent on average, China has achieved average annual growth rates of just over 10 per cent and India 6.26 per cent[3]. Although in the recent years growth has slowed in some of these emerging countries, the trend is nevertheless worrisome, particularly since the financial crisis of 2008 which affected Western countries much more than the rest of the world.

Since 2013, emerging countries are accounting for more than half of global GDP[4], bringing us back to a balance of economic forces that we hadn't experienced since the end of the eighteenth century.

If we extrapolate these trends to imagine what the world will be like by 2050, the G7 countries who are still at the height of their economic and political powers will together boast a GDP that will be scarcely half of that generated by the seven largest emerging economies.[5] According to these projections, Brazil will have overtaken Great Britain's GDP by 2013; Russia will have outstripped Germany by 2014; China will take the top slot in the world economy from the US in 2018. Naturally, the purchasing power parity method somewhat distorts the analysis, although even if we use GDP figures calculated to take into account exchange rate fluctuations, the Chinese economy will have outgrown America's within the next 20 years.

China's dazzling growth over the last few decades has been chiefly fuelled by exports, although domestic consumption has also risen steadily. In 2012, China's total trade amounted to 3.87 trillion dollars, with a trade surplus of 231 billion dollars.[6] By comparison, in that period, the US experienced a trade deficit of 727 billion dollars. The image of a China that manufactures low value-add products using a cheap labour force is already old hat. In general, high value-add products have made up an ever-increasing share of emerging countries' exports, particularly in high-tech industries. Sixteen per cent of exports of manufactured goods from high-income OECD countries are 'high-technology'. By contrast, 25 per cent of China's manufactured goods fall into this category, while Brazil is closing on the OECD countries with just under 10 per cent.[7] The myth of the West being attacked where it hurts the most, in sectors where the high cost of the workforce would make competition from emerging countries insurmountable, has clearly had its day.

Exports from emerging countries have allowed them to build up vast currency reserves. At the end of 2012, the BRIC countries alone accounted for over four trillion dollars of currency reserves, roughly 40 per cent of the total available globally. China alone has amassed a war chest of over three trillion dollars[8]. On the basis of these figures, we can easily understand how emerging countries can no longer be overlooked in settling today's global financial crisis, whether it be the US who could no longer dispose of its treasury bills without China's huge purchases, or the euro zone countries who would no longer find salvation without emerging countries agreeing to finance them directly or via the IMF.

'You have the growth, we'll have the debt!'

Noting the apparent inability of their private sector to stimulate growth in their economies and take on the challenge of the emerging countries, European States chose simply to soften the blow for their people by considerably increasing public expenditure. Rather than tackling the apathy and uncompetitiveness of their businesses head on, they chose to turn themselves into nanny states and maintain their populations' standards of living as best they could. Little did it matter that the measures taken were artificial or temporary. The most important thing was to avoid the collapse of a social model supposedly based on equity and solidarity.

Even in Great Britain, where the free-market is still king, public spending accounted for 45 per cent of GDP in 2012[9], a huge increase on the previous decade. Although Great Britain benefits from a substantial inflow of foreign investments, especially from emerging countries, the government has been unable, or unwilling, to resist the temptation to use taxpayers' money to bring the economy in on a soft landing. The question of how to get airborne again has yet to be asked.

On the Continent, the situation is even more dire. In France for instance, public spending amounted to 56 per cent of GDP in 2012[10]. At these levels, the State is no longer simply an enabler of the economy, it *is* the economy. It becomes the nerve centre of the system and is perceived by citizens and businesses alike as the ultimate arbiter and guardian of their interests. Unfortunately, this approach only makes matters worse as it allows the economy's main participants to labour on under the illusion that it is possible to escape the harsh realities of globalisation.

The US has proven to be no exception to the rule. Seeing GDP growth peter out and plateau at relatively low levels several years in a row, and observing the extinction of entire sections of American industry, the US also ended up resorting to increases in public spending to protect their economy. Total US government expenditure was just under 40 per cent of GDP in 2010 and 2011. By 2012, it had dropped slightly to 35 per cent.[11]. If this level is lower than in Europe, it is because for years now the State could count on private debt to artificially keep the American dream alive, with the disastrous consequences we saw in 2008. In 2007, household debt in the US represented around 130 per cent of their available income, more than twice the levels of debt reached in the 1980s. At the end of 2012, this had declined to 105 per cent as households attempted to de-leverage their immense debt load[12]. The culture of dependency on home loans and consumer credit enabled Americans to continue to fill up their shopping trolley at Walmart, the retail chain, despite the fact that 80 per cent of the products sold there are made in China. Evidently, the addiction to debt has not been bad news for everyone.

This explosion in public spending throughout the Western world has acted like a hard drug. Citizens can no longer do without it and States can find no other way back. Growth was dwindling, fiscal revenues were insufficient, and deficits could only be financed through an unfathomable debt burden. National debt had reached almost 102 per cent of US GDP during 2012 and is approaching the record levels of 120 per cent reached in 1946[13], just after the Second World War. In mid-2013, public debt in the euro zone was 92 per cent[14] of GDP.

If the contrast between Western and emerging countries growth rates were not enough to highlight the new economic world order, comparisons of public finances sadly leave no room for doubt.

The irony of it all is that, taken globally, growth forecasts for 2014 remain satisfactory, but we forget that they are calculated based on two extremes. On one hand, the emerging countries are set to experience budget surpluses and decent growth even though it will be somewhat weaker than that experienced over the last decade, while on the other hand, Western countries look likely to stagnate, sagging under the weight of abyssal debt and with no real hope of paying it back in the near future. The tragedy is that we seem to have accepted this ungracious recasting of roles: 'Let them have the growth, we'll have the debt!' seems to be our unspoken motto.

Banks and States: both arsonists and fire-fighters

Prior to the last financial crisis, had we carried out a Europe-wide survey to determine who were considered the ultimate guardians of our economy and, in particular our savings, the chances are that the overwhelming majority of respondents would have pointed to the State and the banks. With their historical mistrust of the Federal Government, the American people would no doubt have formulated a less predictable response. However, for an entire generation of Europeans who reached adulthood after the last World War, the belief that the State, and to a large extent, the banks, should together form the last bulwark of the economic system was deep-rooted. When reality caught up with us, the psychological impact was all the more unsettling.

I recall the experts' words of wisdom during the Asian debt crisis of 1997, and the subsequent crises in Russia the following year, and in Argentina in 2002. They knowledgeably held that the lack of rigour in the budgeting process and the fragility of the banking system in those countries were the root causes of the ensuing chaos. We were happy sermonising, as we were so sure of ourselves and of the professionalism of our civil servants and bankers. It didn't for one second come to mind that we, too, were sitting on a time bomb just waiting to explode, and that we would end up being betrayed by those very same professionals in whom we had placed our trust and our savings.

It was during a conversation a few years back with the most senior of our clients at Stanhope Capital, a highly educated man who had lived through the Great Crash of 1929 and the tragedy of the thirties, that I began to understand that we were experiencing something very different. Something for which our generation would be fully unprepared. Well before the sovereign debt crisis reared its ugly head, he would call me almost every week to taunt me with, 'Remember the debt moratoria during the thirties!' then, 'believe me, I experienced all that first hand and neither the States nor the banks will hold out'. An economic history buff myself, I entered into heated debates with him during which I tried to explain that the world had changed, that the Gold Standard was no longer around to suffocate our economies, and that our central banks had learned their lessons in 1929 and would be there to pump money into the economy as and when required, and before it was too late. I argued that if all else failed the IMF would come to the rescue and that he was wrong to over-dramatise the situation.

Today I am not so sure. Our fire-fighters have become arsonists. We have seen Western States get into such debt that interest charges are often the first line item in national budgets, even before education, health, and defence. Countries' servicing of these debts over time is based on a masterful piece of sleight of hand; the conviction that yesterday's spiralling debt can be paid back with tomorrow's spiralling borrowing. However we have seen how quickly the machine grinds to a halt when the interest rates expected by the market become too high or when, regardless of the rate, international investors simply lose their appetite for securities they consider too risky. This is how several southern European countries have lost sight of traditional money markets and can now rely only upon the European Central Bank. Even States such as France or Germany can sometimes find themselves forced to perform difficult balancing acts to refinance their debt.

The banks are even worse off. Who would have thought before the current crisis that major banking groups in America and Europe would borrow up to 50 times their equity? Establishments of the very highest order, trusted with collecting and investing household savings, could – and still could now – have found themselves technically bankrupt because of the slightest market glitch.

This is how the top 10 European banks entered the crisis of 2008: with a debt ratio of over 42 times their equity. To get some perspective on this figure, it is easy to imagine a commonplace example from the daily lives of millions of people. If a middle ranking executive knocks on the door of his bank to get a mortgage on the home of his dreams, he may be offered a loan amounting to twice the equity he puts up as a deposit. Even this is subject to the good humour of his bank manager and conditioned by the stability of his own employment. But regarding its own affairs, this very same establishment considers it perfectly accept-able to take on a debt burden representing more than 40 times its own equity. . .

The new regulatory requirements, as stipulated in the Basel III accord, have certainly improved the situation by forcing banks to increase their minimum capital from 2 per cent of their so-called risk weighted assets to 7 per cent[15], and in certain cases, as high as 9.5 per cent but these levels remain manifestly inadequate. The problem is that banks have become expert in cooking the books through financial innovation which allows them to inflate their equity while underplaying asset risk on their balance sheet. And when they get caught red-handed, they only have to blackmail politicians with threats to growth, explaining that if regulatory constraints became too strict, they would have to reduce their lending, thus negatively impacting the economy.

The other specifically European problem is that the Continent's banks and States are locked into a sort of death-dance. As the largest buyers of sovereign debt, banks suffer when the market doubts the States' finan-cial solidity, thereby penalising the value of the government bonds held on their balance sheets. At the same time, banks are totally dependent upon the very same States to bail them out should they befall serious difficulties. The snake is dangerously biting its own tail.

In order to comply with the new Basel Committee ratios, European banks will have to boost their capital by raising 115 billion euros, a difficult goal to achieve in a complicated market environment. If they don't manage this feat, they will have no other choice but to shrink their asset base – in particular their loan books – by 3.2 trillion euros[16], a truly vast amount of money. The knock-on effect would be tragic, most likely provoking a deep and lasting recession in Europe.

The most surprising thing in Europe, however, is that in spite of all the systemic issues, no serious banking reform of any kind has been undertaken when, through the Dodd-Frank law in the US and the Vickers Report in Great Britain, important corrective measures have already been ratified or are under consideration in other countries. The idea of making the ECB responsible for the banking sector across Europe is an important step but sadly the furious lobbying of banks to stop the tide of reform, and Germany's reluctance to take on a bigger role in this area, have thus far prevailed. I remember a discussion with a French senior civil servant from the Treasury early in 2010. He was trying to convince me that Anglo-Saxon reforms simply made no sense for French banks that he considered 'incomparably better managed' than their rivals. This was, of course, before the sovereign debt crisis showed up their extraordinary fragility.

In the US, debt abuse in the banking world was certainly more chronic than in Europe, but from 2008 onwards the Federal Reserve had understood the full gravity of the challenge and taken decisive action. Industry consolidation was quickened and financial institutions forced to recapitalise. In parallel, banks considerably reduced the size of their balance sheets. Debt incurred by American financial institutions had reached a peak of over 8 trillion dollars in 2008; by 2012 this had declined to 6 trillion[17]. Our 'incomparably better managed' European banks still have a long way to go before full financial recovery.

If we really want to save a Western capitalism still very much under the thumb of finance, we will have to radically change our mind-set. However, words and big ideas will not be enough. Tough debate and unavoidably technical measures are required to reform the financial sector. The complexity of the sector means that the debate will often go way over the heads of the people, however, we must avoid the temptation to 'dumb down' the issues or make snap judgements. Banks must once more become the cornerstone of our entrepreneurial capitalism, working for the real economy and not against it. The subject is without doubt difficult, sometimes impenetrable, but the stakes are far too high for us to just give up and take the easy way out.

A rope to hang ourselves or to pull ourselves out of the rut?

As if the pain caused by listless growth, huge deficits, and a fragile banking system wasn't enough, the West also chose to borrow heavily from its main competitors. We are now at the mercy of nations who consider it high time for them to finally take up a geopolitical role in line with their newfound economic power.

A few figures are all it takes to show how the balance of power has changed in recent years. In 2000, when American national debt tipped over the trillion-dollar mark, the country's main creditor was Japan which held 31 per cent of the country's debt exposure totalling 317 billion dollars. Western countries as a whole still featured amongst America's leading lenders, while China had taken on only 60 billion dollars or 6 per cent of the total debt burden. As for Brazil, Russia, and India, they had hardly lent anything at all to the US. In 2010, just a decade later on, it was a whole new ballgame. By then, American debt had more than quadrupled, reaching 4.4 trillion dollars and their top creditor, by far, had become China with 1.16 trillion dollars, or more than 26 per cent of the total. Japan had fallen back into second place with less than 20 per cent, while Brazil and Russia – accounting for 4.2 per cent and 3.4 per cent of the total respectively – were mounting a challenge to the front running lenders[18]. As we move forward, these trends will be reinforced and we will see the BRICs reinvesting their trade surpluses in sovereign debt while Western powers carry on regardless, further consolidating their financial dependency.

And yet the leaders amongst the lending nations have no reason to be complacent, no reason to take pride in their new roles – quite the opposite. They may have become the Great Paymasters of the world, but they now find themselves in the unenviable position of being directly dependent on the solvency of the Western economies and the corresponding whims of the rating agencies. On the other hand, these major money-lenders, particularly China, now know that they can speak on an equal footing with Washington. China has taken advantage of the situation, strengthening its negotiating position on international trade issues within the WTO and blocking or gutting any protocols on environmental protection. Little by little, the great geopolitical equilibrium established after the Second World War is being taken apart.

It is almost tempting to console oneself with the idea that there is a good side to being in debt. After all, it would be very bad news for China if the American government were to default on their trillion-dollar loan. That would amount to almost one third of its total currency reserves. It would therefore be in China's best interests to continue to feed the American ogre, even if that means reaching a state of indigestion. The reality today is that the interdependence of creditors and debtors is rapidly becoming a new form of mutually assured destruction. If China wishes to get paid back one day, the country has no other choice but to keep on lending to the US, thus allowing millions of Americans to keep on buying products *Made in China*.

However, the financial conquest does not stop there. The emerging countries, headed up by China, want to shift from being lenders to owners. Western governments have thus far denied them this change in status, particularly in 'sensitive' industries. Sovereign funds have become the Trojan horses of this policy. The best-known Chinese sovereign fund, the China Investment Corporation (CIC) had over 482 billion dollars at its disposal at the end of 2011[19]. It has acquired considerable holdings in Chinese banks (CITIC) as well as American financial institutions (Blackstone, Morgan Stanley, Visa, Blackrock) but it has more importantly made many strategic investments in mining and energy (KazMunaiGas, Nobel Oil, PT Bumi Resources, Iron Mining International amongst many others). While in 2008, almost 88 per cent of CIC resources were still invested in liquidities with only 3 per cent invested in stocks and shares, in 2010 stocks, both quoted and non-quoted, accounted for more than half of its invested resources[20].

CIC takes its orders directly from the Chinese State's highest executive body, the State Council, and there is no ambiguity in the fact that investments are made with both economic and political considerations in mind. There is a clear strategic shift in the CIC's priorities. Initial investments were almost exclusively made in Western financial institutions with the fund generally happy not to have a representative on their boards. By contrast, more recent investments have focused on the eminently more strategic sectors of energy and natural resources. Nowadays, the fund insists on having the right to appoint a representative to sit on the board of all the companies held in their portfolio.

Just a few years ago, the American Congress worried about Chinese initiatives to buy up American companies or assets operating in sectors deemed to be 'strategic' or 'sensitive'. In 2005, Congress managed to block a bid of over 18 billion dollars made by the Chinese oil company CNOOC on their American rival Unocal, which was being courted in turn by another American oil producer Chevron. In 2007, Congress passed the *Foreign Investment and National Security Act*, which extended the investigative powers of an intergovernmental committee to include investments made by foreign powers in the US[21]. This body is commissioned to analyse transactions that may constitute a threat to national security and submit their conclusions to Congress. This type of political interference would be much more difficult today.

Beyond the central role the Chinese play in financing the US debt burden, they are also the ones who have saved some of the most iconic American financial companies since 2008. Without their help, Morgan Stanley would most probably have had to file for bankruptcy, which, in turn, would have set off a chain reaction with even more serious consequences than the aftermath of the Lehman Brothers' collapse. The American authorities are grateful to them and will not forget the favour. The Chinese shopping spree has only just begun.

Three out of the top 10 sovereign funds in the world are Chinese. CIC, SAFE Investment Company, and the National Social Security Fund have more than 1.1 trillion dollars at their disposal. Among the top players, just one hails from the West: the Norwegian Government Pension Fund. The majority of the others were set up several decades ago by oil and gas producers eager to intelligently reinvest part of their huge surpluses, following in the footsteps of the Kuwait Investment Authority.

Western nations just don't know how to react to this irresistible rise of the sovereign funds and are torn between pragmatism and protectionism. Pragmatism tells them to treat the funds as ordinary institutional investors able to inject significant amounts of cash into companies that desperately need it. Protectionism tells them to be wary of these funds' aims, and to give preference to domestic alternatives.

The dominant Asian, Russian, and Middle-Eastern sovereign funds are the tip of the iceberg. Most of the foreign investments emanating from these countries are made by private groups who have managed to reshape entire sectors of manufacturing and service industries in the West through their financial clout, their swift decision-making abilities, and their operational nous. As we will see in the second part of this book, these companies are often headed by entrepreneurial families who have shown themselves capable of restructuring ageing industries with new ideas. Their ingenuity, much more than their capital, is what is sadly lacking amongst the business leaders and boards of our large organisations.

Investments made in the West by public or private organisations originating from emerging countries have continued to rise inexorably over the last 20 years. These investments have been both organic (through the launch of new production capacities or sales channels) and external (through acquisitions). This pursuit of external growth has soared, as between 2003 and 2010 it amounted to 17 per cent of the world's cross-border transactions compared to just 4 per cent over the previous seven years[22]. Leading up the list are companies based in China, in the Middle East and the Gulf, Singapore, Brazil, India, and Russia.

The overall situation is clearly rather alarming for the West. Having already lost our way on the road to growth, we are now at the mercy of creditors who also happen to be our main competitors. They are taking advantage of the situation to become the prime buyers of Western assets and companies. But there is worse still. Our chronic inability to generate growth has ended up shattering the social models upon which we have built our nations. And our conundrum today is that if we are no longer able to grow, it will become increasingly difficult to convince everyone that wealth redistribution remains both fair and effective at maintaining social peace.

---

1 Source: International Iron and Steel Institute

2 The French term *"monnaie de singe"*, literally "monkey's currency" (Monopoly money) has clear racist overtones.

3 Source: Annual GDP 1980/2011, World Bank Data

4 Calculated according to the purchasing power parity method ("PPP"). This method enables the elimination of price and standard of living differentials between countries at different stages of development. In general, prices of most goods and services are lower in emerging countries than in advanced countries, thus the use of these GDP figures helps reduce the impact of these revenue differentials.

5 PWC 2011 report, "The World in 2050"

6 US Commerce Department Figures

7 Source: World Bank

8 Source: World Bank

9 Source: HM Treasury

10 Source: Eurostat

11 Source: Federal Reserve Economic Data

12 IMF World Economic Outlook, April 2013

13 Source: Trading Economics

14 Eurostat Release, 22 July 2013

15 The Tier 1 capital ratio is the ratio of a bank's core equity capital to its total risk-weighted assets (RWA). Risk-weighted assets are the total of all assets held by the bank weighted by credit risk according to a formula determined by the regulator (usually the country's central bank).

16 Source : RBS

17 McKinsey Global Institute, "Debt and Deleveraging: Uneven Progress to Growth", 2012

18 Source: Department of the Treasury, Federal Reserve Board

19 Source: CIC 2011 Annual Report

20 Source: CIC Annual Reports

21 Committee on Foreign Investments in the United States ("CFIUS")

22 Source: World Bank

Chapter 2

The impossible gamble of redistribution without growth

The implosion of Western social models

With the rise of mass unemployment, and social inequality rampant on both sides of the Atlantic, the foundations of the West's two main social models are being challenged. Both the European and the American models share the need for growth as a prerequisite for making them work. Growth figures of just 1 to 2 per cent in 'good' years are simply not enough to maintain the socio-economic equilibrium.

The European model is entirely built around the idea, as naive as it is praiseworthy, that capitalism with a human dimension demands that market forces be counter-balanced by the State-as-ultimate-arbiter, ensuring wealth redistribution and fair treatment for all. Though the specific tendencies may vary across the European Union, this general consensus applies. Much to our dismay, we have to admit that this protective sea wall has caved in under market pressure, and that well before the debt crisis even began, the State was becoming incapable of playing its redistributive role. Throughout Europe, governments have too often worsened the situation by trying to make up for weaknesses in their economy by stepping in for the economy. This has spawned pernicious behaviour.

In the US, society has never claimed to want to reduce the inequality gap, but rather to ensure that everyone can have a shot at success. As long as every American believes that he or she can become the next Donald Trump, the real estate king and star of *The Apprentice* television show, the system continues to tick over smoothly.

The tragedy in America today, is that the cornerstone of this model, is slowly fading away, especially for the middle classes. At the top of the hierarchy, the percentile of the population with the largest salaries accounts for 20 per cent of pre-tax income in the country, a figure that has doubled over the last 30 years. During this period, this privileged category has enjoyed a 275 per cent increase in after tax income while the 60 per cent of the population positioned around the median salary experienced only a disappointing 40 per cent increase over the same period[1]. The social ladder seems to be broken, leaving the rich at the top and the middle classes, traditionally the drivers of the American dream, pushed down towards the bottom. This trend is highly visible in urban developments across the country. In 1970, when almost two thirds of the American population lived in middle-class neighbourhoods, 15 per cent lived in areas corresponding to the two extremes of the scale, either in very poor, or very rich, neighbourhoods. Today the spread has completely changed. The two thirds of the families who lived in the middle-class areas now account for only 44 per cent of the total, while those living in the very poor or very rich areas now make up more than 31 per cent of the total[2].

If we take the OECD countries as a whole, the results give little more hope for good cheer. The average salary of the 10 per cent most wealthy individuals is almost nine times that of the poorest[3]. This ratio is 15:1 in the US and 18:1 in Great Britain, the country that holds the unenviable OECD record for the fastest growth in inequalities over the last three decades. Since 1978, the bottom 20 per cent of British salaries have experienced a decrease of 43 per cent compared to the rest of the population[4]. France comes off somewhat better when applying the same criteria: the ratio of the highest salaries to the lowest is 7:1, below the OECD average, and has remained relatively stable over this period.

But the disparity in salaries amongst the advanced economies hides other even greater gaps, as we mustn't forget that in order to earn one's pay, one first has to have a job. And yet in most Western countries, having a job, let alone a secure one, is these days considered something of a privilege. By mid-2013, there were an estimated 26.6 million jobseekers in the European Union, an unemployment rate of roughly 11 per cent[5]. Many of these are long-term unemployed who have little hope of ever finding work again, especially beyond the age of 50. The human tragedy is even more acute for young people under the age of 25. In 2013, across Europe, the youth unemployment rate is over 2.5

times greater than the rate for the general population[6]. These Europe-wide averages, as appalling as they may seem, conceal even more dramatic domestic realities, such as Spain and Greece, where in mid-2013 youth unemployment had soared to around 56 per cent and 65 per cent respectively.[7]

Even in the US where high unemployment is more unusual than in Europe, 7.6 per cent of the American population were still unemployed in the summer of 2013, down from a post-war peak of nearly 10 per cent in late 2009 and early 2010. In spite of the improvements chalked up over the last few quarters, one third of American jobseekers are long-term unemployed, a record since the Great Depression. Even more disturbing is the fact that youth unemployment has topped 18 per cent in general and 31 per cent amongst African-Americans. Having that many young people out of work is particularly harmful as it leaves long-term scars on society. British and American studies have shown that, all else being equal, a young person who has been unemployed for a year or more before the age of 25 will earn less, even 20 years later, than an individual who had not suffered the same fate. The salary gap is 23 per cent after ten years on the job market. At the age of 42, the same individual will still earn 15 per cent less than his counterpart who was lucky enough to find work earlier in life than him[8].

Young people are far from being the only ones left high and dry by Western civilisation. Their elders who have worked their entire lives will be lucky to collect their pensions upon retirement. In Europe, increased life expectancy will end up bringing down the extremely generous state medical and pension schemes which hail back to the 1950s. Before 2050, more than one billion people will be over 65 years old. That is more than double the current figure. The additional public expenditure, particularly in medical care, required to support this population will shoot up exponentially, far faster than the revenues from the already hard-hit working population. According to a study carried out by The Center for Strategic and International Studies (CSIS), this spending will amount to more than a quarter of GDP in the main euro zone countries by 2040[9]. Figures in the Anglo-Saxon world are less extreme but remain alarmingly high. In Great Britain, for example, the level of expenditure will be 18.2 per cent.

Attempts throughout Europe to push retirement ages back by just a few years have fallen way short of the mark. And yet States no longer have the leeway to raise taxes and if radical and timely measures are not taken deficits will continue to build up and ultimately lead to disaster. European governments claim to be treating deficit reduction as a priority and yet take measures that lead to a worsening of the situation. For example, in France the government refuses to tackle the sacred cow of social entitlements while considerably raising fiscal pressure despite its recession-provoking effects. And yet how can we hope to reduce deficits without growth?

How should we judge societies who leave the new generation by the wayside while condemning its elders to economic insecurity? The dramatic rise in youth unemployment and the looming bankruptcy of state pension schemes throughout the Western world have set off social decay. The resulting situation is triply dangerous, creating conflict between different social categories, between generations, and also between different communities, as minorities are proportionally far more impacted than the rest of the population.

At the same time, the distribution of the wealth created by businesses over the last few decades has been heavily skewed towards capital at the expense of labour. Since the early 1980s , the profits of Western corporations as a percent of GDP have more than trebled, whilst the share of salaries has shrunk[10]. Market dynamics and the growing strength of institutional investors have probably made these changes unavoidable but it would nevertheless be dangerous to believe that this gap can continue to grow without leading to serious social tensions.

We shouldn't be surprised that protest movements like Occupy Wall Street became so popular in the US and in other countries. Let there be no mistake about it, even if they were not fought under the same banner, the protests that took place in Spain, Greece, and other European countries caught up in the euro zone turmoil all shared the same logic. It is all about millions of people expressing their utter helplessness in the face of what they regard as a breach in the social contract. The guilty parties, however, remain hard to identify. Where on earth should one begin? Bankers and capitalism in general are easy targets but the root causes run deeper and the responsibilities are shared. We should be pointing our accusatory fingers at ourselves and our inability to generate economic growth. But who can generate growth and how should they go about it? Everyone seems to have forgotten.

These protests embody, rightly or wrongly, the economic failures of our modern societies in a globalised world. The very legitimacy of public authorities is at stake. The Western myth that democratic regimes are best placed to create wealth and ensure prosperity has clearly been dispelled. It is, of course, out of the question here to challenge the merits of our democratic liberal convictions. However, for too long we have remained complacent that any other political system simply could not succeed, thus underestimating the abilities of countries such as China to set out on the path to economic hegemony.

Powerless governments: too fast for the economy, too slow for the markets

Western governments have been either unwilling or unable to prepare their populations for the disruptions brought on by the new economic world order. Instead of encouraging the private sector – both large corporations and SMEs – to adapt their business models and stay competitive on the international stage, most governments have chosen instead to further expand the role of the public sector in the economy.

In Europe especially, the pressure of the ballot box has pushed one government after another to make three fundamental errors. First they considered it wise to replace lost private sector jobs with employment directly or indirectly linked to the public sector, thereby further deepening public deficits. In countries such as Great Britain almost one-fifth[11] of the working population is now employed in the civil service – in the broadest sense of the term – with jobs for life, making any meaningful reform close to impossible.

Secondly, public authorities reduced working hours in the hope that more jobs would be created. But, of course, they only succeeded in producing the opposite effect. The additional cost for businesses only made matters worse especially when faced with competitors from emerging countries who were already producing the same goods and services for far less.

And finally, their third mistake: Western governments took the decision to toughen labour laws to make layoffs more difficult or more costly for the employer. Once again, the measures had the opposite effect to the expected result as they only encouraged businesses to avoid taking on new staff for fear of never being able to reduce headcount in the event of a downturn.

With these measures, all many countries achieved was more unemployment and a higher tax burden. In Great Britain, tax revenues were projected to account for 37.5 per cent of GDP in 2012-13.[12] This huge levy on the national resources drawn by the government is much higher than the average in OECD countries where taxation accounts for just under 34 per cent of GDP or in the US where it is only 24.8 per cent[13]. This is how, year after year, a large part of our nations' wealth has shifted from the real economy to an over-inflated public sector, although the private sector is the cornerstone of our economic survival.

This headlong rush towards a fiscal abyss reflects a situation which can no longer be ignored. Throughout the West, political and economic cycles are no longer in synch. In politics, electoral deadlines no longer allow the necessary time for structural reform. In the US, even when the President has a majority in Congress, as rare as this may be, the Executive has barely two years to implement the programme they were elected to carry out. By mid-term, eyes turn to the campaign for re-election and ambitious projects are set aside. Political deadlock morphs rapidly into economic stagnation. The same malaise affects British politics where five-year terms of office and political infighting more often than not render meaningful structural reform unrealistic. The only hope of reform comes during the first two years when governments can get away with measures that require the 'blood, sweat and tears' of their citizens. After this cut-off point, authorities revert to sound bites and photo opportunities staged to capture the *Zeitgeist*.

When it comes to economic policy, the contrast between the time horizons of the major emerging powers is striking. China's success today is too often taken for granted in that we forget the colossal and painful restructuring the country went through during the 1990s. The government acted with patience and determination over almost a decade to open the Chinese economy up to foreign investment, while shutting down inefficient State-owned enterprises, rationalising the banking system, and reforming taxation. The new government is now determined to shrink the dangerously bloated shadow banking sector, knowing full well that it will have to be done over time if it is to avoid unduly penalising the economy.

In Brazil it took 10 years to get to grips with hyperinflation, free up the economy, and reinvent the country as a world leader in renewable energies. The Brazilian government is now facing the challenge of improving infrastructures and reducing the country's dependence on commodities and trade with China. In both countries, a lot has been achieved over the past decade and much remains to be done but public authorities realise that major reform requires endurance and takes precedent over political considerations. This is a lesson that we seem to have forgotten in the West today, even though reforms have become vital.

The pace of politics is also out of kilter with the demands of the financial markets. The markets expect ultra-fast decision-making from political leaders and don't hesitate to pass judgement immediately. We have seen how slow decision-making in Europe accentuated rises in sovereign bond interest rates at the peak of the crisis, thus making it harder still for us to get a grip on the situation. Successive European summits were called in emergency mode, solutions that may have worked weeks earlier were tabled but became obsolete even before the press releases went out. In a market where the State's credibility is all, this is a dangerous situation. That is what Mr Draghi understood when he took the helm of the European Central Bank but his successes will be short-lived if European governments do not become more pragmatic and nimble when faced with the scepticism of the markets.

European deconstruction

The public authorities' crazy gamble of redistribution without growth has done even more damage than just breaking up Western social models. The European dream has also fallen by the wayside.

When Jean Monnet imagined post-war Europe he envisioned an economic union that would bring peace and prosperity. Walking in his footsteps, Jacques Delors began the process that would lead to the creation of the single European currency, a key step that would enable the Continent's poorest countries to aim high and thrive. Failing to foresee that a common currency could not exist without a shared, consistent economic policy, the entire European construction has instead been dragged down into a slump. In the absence of growth, the 'original sin' of European monetary union was exposed: one way or another, rich countries were being forced to subsidise their poorer neighbours.

Initially this system was implicit, allowing countries such as Greece and Portugal to borrow at rates scarcely higher than Germany, pushing them into the trap of over-indebtedness and creating dangerous speculative bubbles. These subsidies became explicit when the market finally grasped the absurdity of the situation, and the Sovereign debt crisis was born. Then everyone was required to dip into their pockets, including already ailing countries like France.

Over 10 years ago, and before the official launch of the euro, I publicly expressed my doubts about the logic of a single currency not backed by a proper system of economic governance. In my 2001 article in the *International Herald Tribune* entitled 'Not much Clout for the Euro without European Sovereignty'[14], I argued that given the European Central Bank's restrictive mandate and the lack of a European finance minister working hand in hand with the ECB's leader to coordinate economic policy across the continent, Europe would be left to walk blindfolded. Those of us who saw a euro devoid of governance as the seed of disaster were few and far between, lost within a fanfare of praise where everyone seemed struck dumb with the political and ideological importance of the monetary union.

Now European governments find themselves in an untenable situation. For those who are better off, the government has to explain to voters that they must support others financially, while their own country remains extremely vulnerable. For those who are already staring into the abyss, political leaders must impose unpopular budget and wage cuts, while remaining unable to promise any light at the end of the tunnel. With this backdrop demogogues of all stripes, particularly from the far right are bound to make significant headways in the months and years to come.

Attempts to create a common economic policy framework for 17 member States are, of course, welcome, but they come too late in the day and sorely lack credibility. Too late because the public finances of eurozone members are in such a shambles that although borrowing rates have fallen somewhat, interest payments remain staggeringly high. Furthermore, austerity measures initiated at the worst possible time have only aggravated the recession and pushed back further still any real chance of reducing the debt burden.

Common economic policy lacks credibility because it relies on the same principles as the stability pact signed in Maastricht 20 years ago and which were never observed. The only real breakthrough compared with the previous framework is the potential threat of sanctions as requested by the Germans, although how this addition to the system could help is unclear. What could possibly be the merit of a penalty charge imposed upon a country that can no longer respect its financial commitments, precisely because it is on the verge of bankruptcy?

Ill-conceived as it was, the euro has taken European nations down a risky path. In so far as the common rules are respected, and this in itself is doubtful, how can we imagine that these same budgetary and fiscal considerations could apply in a 17-strong euro zone including countries as disparate as Germany on one hand and Cyprus, Estonia, or Slovakia on the other? Is it really realistic to think that Cyprus could one day respect the famous 3 per cent GDP deficit cap when Germany itself couldn't manage it? In Cyprus, the monetary union is already a fiction. The capital controls imposed in the aftermath of the banking crisis of the spring 2013 have created a de facto multi-speed Europe. Who is next?

Unless European peoples are prepared to pool their resources and accept huge transfers of wealth between member countries, rather like West Germany's integration of the former DDR, the eurozone will either break up or end up splitting into two groups, membership of which would be according to their economic development. A two-speed Europe would enable both the 'strong' and the 'weak' eurozones, to develop a budgetary and fiscal policy respectively calibrated to the specific needs of its members. The central banks of each zone would finally be able to act as lenders of last resort, like the Federal Reserve, working for both price stability and job creation.

During his final press conference[15] as President of the European Central Bank, Jean-Claude Trichet exclaimed, 'We have delivered price stability over the first 12 years of the euro impeccably, impeccably!', before adding, 'I would like very much to hear congratulations for an institution which has delivered price stability in Germany at a level which is better than that which has ever been obtained in this country over the last 50 years'. It was an unusually emotional appeal for a man so used to conversing in the cold, meticulous language of the central banker. Surprisingly, Trichet's message was one of 'mission accomplished' while Europe was up in flames and he neither seemed to be willing nor able to use the extinguisher of 'Quantitative Easing' (QE) at his disposal[16].

While the US has pumped over two trillions dollars of cash into its economy since 2008 and Great Britain has in turn printed more than 375 billion pounds of new money, Europe has so far rejected the QE which would have given its economies the oxygen they so badly need. Having kept the markets guessing over when it would begin winding up its QE programme, the US Federal Reserve seems set to begin tapering the injections of cash and potentially withdrawing from the economy entirely by 2015. With signs of the US economic recovery becoming increasingly strong, Europe could do worse than look to the US as an example.

The massive programme of loans to European banks[17] initiated by Mario Draghi at the end of 2011 was certainly useful. Without this initiative, the European banking system would almost certainly have collapsed. It also had the effect of lowering interest rates in the peripheral countries. But this programme cannot by itself be a solution as, ultimately, it does not reduce the overall European debt burden nor does it create the conditions for economic recovery. Through his latest programme, the *Outright Monetary Transaction* (OMT), Draghi is doing his best to fracture the German dogma that opposes sovereign debt buybacks. However, his hands are tied. Under pressure from the head of the Bundesbank, Jens Weidmann, the ECB committed to 'sterilising' its operations by systematically removing from the economy amounts equivalent to those deployed to buy sovereign debt. Weidmann's aim is to avoid swelling the money supply, whereas, in reality this would *help* Europe by weakening its currency, avoiding deflation, and ultimately restarting the economy.

The road to recovery in the sovereign debt crisis will be long and require difficult political decisions to be made. But we mustn't forget that the inherent design faults of the euro notwithstanding, we wouldn't be in the desperate situation we are in if growth rates had remained higher. Whatever the structural solutions, no monetary union can operate if it means uniting in misery. The crux of the matter in Europe, as in everywhere else in the West, is the question of how to reinvent our growth models and encourage our businesses to embrace the role they need to play.

The crumbling city on the hill

It is not only in Europe that social models are being challenged. The American ideal of a country driven by an industrious and thriving middle class was already fighting for survival in the run-up to 2008. The global recession all but killed it off. Once the 'platonic form' of middle-class democracy, American society has been battered by domestic and global trends which have gradually worn away the country's middle class.

By the mid-2000s, America's economy had become powered by a wealthy few; the consumer spending power of the '99 per cent' was flattening, while the '1 per cent' seemed set to be the future drivers of the economy[18]. The soul-searching that followed the financial crisis seemed briefly to herald an acknowledgement that the extreme social polarisation created by the boom years was not desirable in any society. Was it right that the Walton family, founders of the Walmart chain, had amassed a net worth as large as the *combined* wealth of the bottom 48 million American families[19]? Had the untrammelled pursuit of individual success created a society where winners won too big and losers lost too hard?

However, this soul searching came to nothing. For the 1% the post-crisis years have steadily seen a return to business as usual. As the economy slowly and painfully recovers, those who had the most wealth before the crisis, seem set to carry on regardless, while the American middle class vanishes from existence, trapped between shrinking median wages, the spiralling costs of living, and servicing debt burdens that had been amassed during the pre-crisis years. The peak of US median income was in 1999, when it reached 54,932 dollars. By 2011, that had slid to 50,054 dollars, close to a 9 per cent decline[20]. With easy credit no longer available, the true extent of America's middle-class crisis is becoming clear. America seems to have lost the ability to create well-paying, middle-class jobs and is suffering for it.

Extreme social polarisation is certainly the main and most damaging consequence of the country's inability to create enough wealth to keep the American dream afloat but it is not the only one. The US is now increasingly organised around political and ideological fault lines. In the 'Big Sort'[21], a book they published in 2008, Bill Bishop and Robert Cushing note that Americans now tend to live in cities or communities where they are surrounded by fellow citizens who think and vote like them. For instance, across the country, the proportion of counties where the gap between between democrats and republicans exceeds 20 per cent has doubled since 1976. One American in two now lives in an electoral district where the candidate of the minority party has abso-lutely no chance of ever being elected. The repercussions in Washington DC are clear. Veterans of American politics routinely admit that the atmosphere in the capital has rarely been as fractious as it is now and that bi-partisan initiatives are almost always doomed. Debt ceiling negotiations between Democrats and Republicans, the resulting goverment shutdown and threat of default, are constant reminders of how dysfunctional American politics have become.

Nor is American society 'sorted' by politics alone. Although it is home to the majority of the world's top universities, a few facts about America's public education system illustrate some of the problems facing the country. According to the Centre for American Progress, half of America's children receive no early childhood education and the country does not yet have a nationally agreed strategy to tackle this[22]. America's students enter the education system with vastly different prospects depending on their economic status. Figures from the US Department of Health and Human Services indicate that economically disadvantaged students potentially enter kindergarten with a vocabulary 50 per cent smaller than their middle-class peers[23]. These disadvantages multiply as students move through the system. With over 20 per cent of children under the age of 18 living in poverty, it is no wonder that 60 per cent of public school teachers say that they have children in their classes who regularly come to school hungry and unable to concentrate[24]. The achievement gaps fuelled by this poverty have worrisome implications for America's ability to create a globally competitive workforce.

America also remains a country where racial tensions are never far from bubbling to the surface. In July 2013, the trial of George Zimmerman, a Florida security guard accused of murdering Trayvon Martin, an African-American teenager prompted a national debate on whether the US had truly stepped out of the long shadow cast by slavery. The not guilty verdict issued by a Florida court prompted outrage and riots across the country. The Zimmerman case highlighted what demographers have known for years: despite improvements since the 1980s, America's cities are starkly divided along racial lines. Census data shows that typical white Americans now live in neighbourhoods that are 75 per cent white[25].

Bridging the gap between these two Americas is an almost impossible task but nothing should even be attempted as long as the country's growth and redistribution model remains broken. There is only one societal value in the US on which everyone can still agree and that is the crucial role of individual initiative and business creation. But with the rise of financial capitalism over the last two decades, this was forgotten. Putting the entrepreneur back at the centre of the American edifice should go a long way towards returning the country to a more sustainable growth path and mending its social fabric.

---

1 US Congressional Budget Office, 'Trends in the Distribution of Household Income'

2 Source: US Census Bureau and American Community Survey

3 The 10 per cent of households with the lowest salaries. Source: OECD, December 2011, "Divided we stand".

4 "All in this together?" TUC, January 2012

5 Source: Eurostat, August 2013

6 Source: Eurostat

7 Eurostat and the Hellenic Statistical Authority, 8 August 2013

8 Studies on the "wage scar", Economic & Social Research Council

9 23.5 per cent in France, 24.7 per cent in Italy, 26.5 per cent in Spain, 21.7 per cent in Germany

10 Salaries went from representing approximately 39 per cent of GDP to less than 33 per cent. Source Datastream, Vantage.

11 Source: ONS Public Sector Employment Release, April 2013

12 Institute for Fiscal Studies: "A Survey of the UK Tax System" October 2012

13 Source: Heritage Foundation 2013 Index of Economic Freedom

14 "Not Much Clout for the Euro Without European Sovereignty", International Herald Tribune, 19 December 2001

15 Press conference, 8 September 2011

16 Method enabling a central bank to generate liquidities then use them to buy back various assets, mainly government bonds, mortgage bonds,or commercial paper. The impact of these unconventional methods is to reinject liquidities into the system while keeping interest rates low so as to restart the economy.

17 Long Term Refinancing Operation Programme ("LTRO")

18 "Can The Middle Class Be Saved", The Atlantic, 24 July 2011

19 "Inequality, Exhibit A: Walmart and the wealth of American Families", Economic Policy Institute, 17 July 2012

20 US Census Bureau

21 "The Big Sort" by Bill Bishop and Robert Cushing, Houghton Mifflin, 2008

22 "The Competition that Really Matters: Comparing U.S, Chinese and Indian Investments in the Next-Generation Workforce", Centre for American Progress, 2012

23 "America's Early Childhood Literacy Gap", Jumpstart, 2009

24 "Hunger in Our Schools" No Kid Hungry Teachers Report 2012

25 "The Persistence of Segregation in the Metropolis: New Findings from the 2010 Census", Logan and Stults, US2012 Project

Chapter 3

From empire-builders to administrators: chronicle of a death foretold

The end of the empire-builder, the root of the West's demise

The debt crisis is often depicted as the root cause of the collapse of Western capitalism. In reality, it is only a symptom. We have seen that the debt spiral to which States, citizens, and banks alike have fallen prey is largely due to the inability of the West to generate growth. The question we must therefore answer at this stage is how and why the West managed to lose the 'user manual' for growth? What has changed in the structures and organisation of our capitalism that could explain the sorry state we find ourselves in today?

The biggest upheaval of the last three decades has been, without doubt, the steady stifling of our entrepreneurial capitalism. This type of capitalism is dominated by 'owner-managers' who, through creativity, determination, and sheer drive, built companies which often became global leaders in their respective industries. Of course, many of these companies still exist to this day, featuring prominently in stock markets on both sides of the Altlantic.

However, a silent revolution is underway, progressively removing these owner-managers and their families from their own company's capital and day-to-day management. Ephemeral shareholders now dominate the capital. Having no emotional bond with the company, these shareholders sell their stakes and leave at the first opportunity as soon as they have pocketed sufficient capital gains. As for management, professionals with no skin in the game are paid in stock options and share awards, almost never risking their own money in the companies they are supposed to be running. Surrounded by armies of legal advisors and investor-relations specialists, these executives are more suited to managing their quarterly results and their stock price than taking the necessary strategic decisions to ensure the long-term prosperity of their businesses. The era of the Sainsburys, Agnellis, Halleys, and Wallenbergs is long gone[1].

And all this is blessed by corporate boards who zealously abide by the accepted standards of good governance. Unfortunately, board members have become so 'independent' that they rarely grasp even the most basic knowledge of the industry in which the company they supervise operates. Back in 2008, how many directors on the boards of the largest Western banks were able to explain what a CDO[2] was? How many of the directors of the main information technology firms today really understand the new challenges related to Cloud Computing? Whatever the abilities of independent directors, it is highly unfortunate that they are so rarely shareholders of the companies whose boards they sit on, if only by receiving their fees in shares instead of cash, for example. The cult of independence has gone too far. Independence has served to sanitise the decision-making process and tip the balance in favour of inertia and the lowest common denominator.

So why should we worry? Because this extreme focus on short-term results has driven our big corporations to reduce their research and development efforts and to hold back their investments in building or improving production capacity[3]. Scaled up across the entire system, it is this attitude that has finally got the better of our growth. The 100 biggest listed companies in Britain (FTSE 100) have 130 billion dollars of cash at their disposal[4]. In the US, the 500 biggest quoted groups (S&P 500) have more than two trillion dollars of liquidities sitting idle on their balance sheets and yielding next to nothing[5]. And what are these companies doing with this amazing war chest? Working to improve their competiveness? Investing in developing their lines of business? Neither. In fact, most choose simply to buy back their own stock or increase dividends, much to the satisfaction of the same investors who wouldn't hesitate to jump ship should things turn sour for the company.

Worse still, American and European companies are betting on the status quo being maintained even though they operate in highly competitive industries where their positions are being threatened every day by emerging country rivals who have remained masters of their own destinies. Being, on the whole, run by their owners, Indian or Brazilian companies invest in their future and are able to take courageous decisions to achieve their ends. We have seen how Ratan Tata acquired one of the jewels in British industry's crown when he bought Jaguar and, more than that, succeeded in turning the business around spectacularly where Ford had failed. Big Chinese companies and their hybrid model of State and family-led capitalism also never lose sight of the long-term perspective. Benefitting from a stable and ambitious shareholder base, these companies have carved out major stakes in many industries, pushing aside their long-established, but none too bold, Western competitors.

It is not surprising that the West's leading exporters are those who have kept a dominant family shareholder base. Germany is a case in point. Even during the throes of the crisis and despite an overpriced euro, the bigger, internationally present SMEs known as the *Mittelstand*, were able to maintain and often consolidate their market positions.

Of the 50 largest European listed companies who form the Eurostoxx 50 index, only seven have kept a substantial family shareholder base, and in only four of these companies does the family have a controlling stake. In the US, the decline in the proportion of founder-shareholders is even more startling. Out of the 30 companies that make up the Dow Jones index, only three still have a significant family shareholder base and not one of these is still controlled by its founding shareholder.

When one considers the 1,000 largest companies in each of the four biggest European economies, listed or not, it is in Great Britain that the decline in family ownership is the most noteworthy. There, families control only 10.9 per cent of the largest companies compared with 35.9 per cent in Germany[6].

Putting to one side the exceptional case of Germany, unique in the West for its high proportion of family-owned groups, a comparison with emerging countries is enlightening. Fifty per cent of listed companies in Asia are controlled by families[7], where the South boasts up to 65 per cent and the North just 37 per cent. India holds the record with 67 per cent of its listed companies controlled by family owners.

These figures are essential to understanding the decline of Western capitalism as many studies have shown that in companies where the founders and/or their families are still involved in governance structures, performance tends to be better than in companies without such an entrepreneurial or family presence. A vast study published in the prestigious *Journal of Corporate Finance*[8] analysed more than 1,600 non-financial companies in 13 different European countries. The study's authors concluded that the family-run companies boasted a 16 per cent[9] higher profitability than companies without a family-owned controlling stake. All other factors being equal, these family-owned companies were worth 7 per cent more than the others. According to this study, family ownership and profitability are even more strongly correlated when the founder is still directly involved in the day-to-day running of the business. Another recent study[10] has shown that European family-owned businesses have out-performed the market by 60 per cent over the last 10 years[11].

This reality is as noticeable in the West as it is in emerging economies. In Asia during the 2000/2010 decade, listed companies controlled by entrepreneurs and their families out-performed local indices in seven out of 10 of the major stock exchanges in the region. These companies had generated a 261 per cent compound return and an annual growth rate of 13.7 per cent over the period[12].

How can we explain this advantage? Entrepreneurial or family shareholders are neither smarter, nor do they manage better than other professionals. And yet, since they have invested both their capital and their life's work in a company that more often than not bears their name, these owner-managers have allied their fates with those of their companies. The importance of this emotional factor should not be underestimated if we wish to comprehend the specificities of family-owned groups compared to their competitors. The decisive factor is not so much the fact of having a controlling stake in the business, as it is now established that entrepreneurial groups tend to out-perform their competitors, even when the founder or their family are minority shareholders. What matters is that the individuals who play a key role in the management of the business also invest a significant part of their personal wealth in it. This combination of ownership and management gives business leaders a greater sense of responsibility and reduces the age-old problem of 'agency'[13], naturally aligning shareholder and executive interests.

The other competitive advantage family-owned groups have, is the prevailing sense of continuity they provide for staff, customers, and suppliers alike. When economic cycles get more brutal, jobs are often the unavoidable adjustment factor. Once you have cut all other costs and optimised productivity, businesses often have no other choice but to cut jobs. Yet experience shows that family-owned groups are far more reluctant to resort to lay-offs than their non family-owned competitors, an attitude that can be explained in part by their relative freedom to accept reduced margins when times are hard. This is what happened in Germany during the crisis of 2008 when unemployment didn't rise above 8 per cent[14]. Family-based shareholders who still wield considerable power in the country's economic structures preferred to soften the social blow by accepting temporarily diminished margins and dividends. In return they got greater staff loyalty and higher worker productivity.

The German machine tool manufacturer Alfred H. Schütte, based in Cologne, is a case in point. Early in 2009 at the worst point in the recession, the company that employed more than 700 people suffered a drop of 90 per cent in orders. Instead of choosing to lay off highly qualified staff, Carl Welcker, the founder's great grandson and company boss, dared to break a taboo and knocked on the door of his bank, asking for a loan; the first ever in over 130 years of the company's existence. Less than two years later, company revenues had shot up by 200 per cent, the loan repaid in full and the staff won over to his cause for ever. Hundreds of family-owned companies like Schütte contribute to making Germany the industrial powerhouse of Europe with near full employment when the rest of Europe is teetering on the brink of disaster[15].

Customers and suppliers are also sympathetic to the idea of the stockholder and managerial continuity found in family-owned groups. Relationships built up over decades result in a veritable ecosystem being woven around such groups, allowing them to ride economic cycles with greater flexibility, and thus relative equanimity.

The final advantage enjoyed by these family groups, and perhaps the most significant one, is to do with their entrepreneurial culture and their ability to take calculated risks. A study of more than 200 family-owned groups showed that they were more prone to invest in innovative technologies, and more likely to launch new products or to attack new markets than the competition[16]. Some, like the Auchan family which controls one of the world's largest distribution companies (with revenues of 46 billion euros in 2012[17]), have turned their entrepreneurial tradition into a system. Six hundred family members have joined forces in the Mulliez Association, putting their heads together to come up with new ideas that could help further develop the family business. This approach has enabled the group to expand beyond the original Auchan supermarket chain to take in stores such as Decathlon (sporting goods), Kiabi (clothing), or Saint-Maclou (carpeting and flooring), all of which have since become leaders in their respective domains.

Another example is EBM Papst, a global leader in fans and energy-saving motors, based in Baden Württemberg. Gerhard Sturm, the company's founder, still enjoys explaining how he managed to pass on the entrepreneurial virus to his employees. Suggestion boxes are disseminated all over the plant and the highest performing staff are pushed to create their own start-ups just kilometres away from EBM Papst. This policy allows the group to nurture callings and careers as well as strengthening their own ecosystem through a network of friendly business owners and their complementary activities.

Finally, we can't overlook the example of the Spaniard Amancio Ortega, the brilliant entrepreneur who founded the hugely successful Inditex (Zara). As his own country slips further into recession, Ortega and his company have taken the number one slot in fashion from H&M. Nothing predisposed this son of a railwayman, who opened his first clothes shop in La Coruña, to build an empire of almost 110,000 staff and worth 68 billion euros on the stock market. Although listed, the group is still controlled by its founder who has no time for the market analysts, knowing that his success is down to his ability to break the rules and create at the speed of his customers' desires, not the market.

The aim here is not to paint an idealised picture of the family-owned business. In numerous cases, no sooner had the founder left the helm, than many of these groups lost their way and were unable to exploit their best managerial talent, remaining stuck in the past. The success of family groups compared to their competitors does not stem from their dynastic dimension, far from it. Rather it is from their ability to develop the new generation of entrepreneurs, be they from within the family or without. We have seen how the Fisher family, founders of the Gap retail empire successfully managed to retreat from the day to day management of the business, while at the same time attracting hugely talented CEOs such as Mickey Drexler[18] who sparked the group's rapid expansion. One of the founder's sons Bill Fisher, who still sits on the board, has often reminded me that although GAP has become one of the largest listed companies in the US, its strength has always been its ability to maintain its entrepreneurial and family-centred culture.

Hierarchies are flat, decision-making processes fast, while risk-taking is both welcomed and generously rewarded. Our biggest listed corporations have forgotten these principles, losing market share to their competitors from emerging countries who are themselves often family-owned. This is also the reason why they have become incapable of reinventing themselves when faced with start-ups and their disruptive technologies that shake up entire industries. Who would have thought that companies like Google, Facebook, Ebay, or Amazon would change the face of the IT and distribution sectors in such a short space of time? How many former leaders of these industries were able to anticipate these changes and adapt accordingly? This paralysis has not happened through any lack of brains, but rather because of shareholder structures and governance models that encourage inertia and end up dragging down our overall economic growth.

The return of entrepreneurial capitalism would be one of the most important economic developments of the 21st century. The paradigm of the all-powerful professional manager that has dominated Western capitalism since the 1980s would at last face a strong challenger. Either we choose to give the entrepreneur back his rightful place in our businesses in the West and thus give ourselves a chance to get back on track for growth, or we remain on our current trajectory and watch our capitalism slowly but surely fossilise.

Can we still make elephants dance?

In September 2010, when Léo Apotheker took the call telling him he had got the top job at Hewlett Packard (HP), the slightest of smiles lit up his face. In just a few weeks this European polyglot, as well known in the industry for his straight-talk as for his visionary leadership of the German software firm SAP, was to take the helm of one of the world's tech greats[19]. Quite a career for the man who began his working life in the 1970s as a humble management controller at the University of Jerusalem. With a staff of 350,000 and annual revenues of more than 127 billion dollars when he took over, HP was a veritable elder statesman of Silicon Valley, the California-based heart of global tech innovation. Countless inventions have sprung from the firm since the 1930s from the first oscilloscopes to computers, or printers and semi-conductors.

And yet, the assignment HP's board had in mind for Léo Apotheker was no walk in the park: as iconic as it was, the company had quite simply lost its way. At a time when the information technology industry was undergoing fundamental upheaval, HP was still making most of its money on low-margin, mature products. PCs still accounted for almost one third of revenues in 2010 although margins struggled to reach 4 per cent. Software on the other hand generated margins of 17.6 per cent but only made up 3 per cent of revenues.

The company had made several major acquisitions over the previous few years in an attempt to diversify revenue streams in higher value-add segments (EDS in 2008, 3Com in 2009, Palm in 2010) but the market was finding it hard to grasp the underpinning logic of this spending spree. The purchase of Compaq in 2002 for more than 25 billion dollars had grounded the group in the realm of hardware at the exact same time the Chinese, amongst other low-cost Asian manufacturers, were about to declare a price war. HP had become, for better, but above all for worse, worldwide leader in a commodity market. Every attempt to miti-gate this fact was bound to fail.

Léo Apotheker's recruitment at last marked the clear choice of radical transformation on the part of HP's board. During his 20 years with SAP, this unusual character had climbed every step on the corporate ladder, transforming the company as he went to become leader of the

American-dominated ERP market. HP's choice was one of a software expert recognised across the globe, and it was in this sector that the board saw their salvation. HP's choice was also a breakthrough thinker with strong views who would not be afraid to go against his staff and shareholders should he think they were getting off track. An action-oriented manager with strong beliefs, Apotheker was anything but politically minded and HP's board were soon to find this out.

His first move upon arrival at the Palo Alto headquarters in September 2010 was to go about understanding the business. Apotheker took three months without making the slightest of declarations and met with major clients as well as the business line and subsidiary executives across the world. Three key takeaways came from these few months of total immersion. The first was that the company needed to adopt a totally new strategy before it was too late. PCs and printers were clearly shrinking businesses but still benefitted from a considerable customer base of which synergy-seeking buyers could take advantage. HP could focus on developing new core businesses around software and services for enterprise customers within the open architecture of Cloud Computing and multiple-support connectivity. In a nutshell, Apotheker suggested that HP stop selling boxes and start selling 'intelligence' taking advantage of its extraordinary customer base and distribution.

The second of Apotheker's key observations was that HP had ceased to be proactive, preferring to attack new markets with 'me too' products that only imitated more innovative competitors. Such was the fate of HP's TouchPad tablet, launched to combat Apple's extraordinary iPad as well as the discount Asian manufacturers' copycat versions. Apotheker quickly put an end to the TouchPad.

The third of his conclusions, and probably the most embarrassing, was one that doubtless explained the first two: HP's board members didn't possess sufficient IT industry knowledge to prepare the company to take on the extraordinary, relentless challenges of the tech revolution. The group suffered from the syndrome of the super tanker that takes more than 20 minutes to change course by just 45 degrees; in the IT business, such strategic inertia is often fatal.

HP announced the appointment of five new board members in January 2011. Once his new strategy had been approved by the newly extended committee, Apotheker knew he had no time to lose. During the San Francisco AGM of March 2011, he made his new strategy public and immediately set about implementing it. Over the following quarter he began talks with Autonomy, the British infrastructure enterprise software leader. He announced Autonomy's acquisition for 12 billion dollars in August of the same year. In parallel, Apotheker came out publicly in favour of selling off HP's PC business, widely considered a sacred cow – both by the market as well as by certain board members. True to his reputation, Apotheker was steering the super tanker like a speedboat and this was inevitably not to everyone's liking.

First the markets panicked. In a nervy period for stock markets reeling from the sovereign debt crisis and the US credit rating downgrade, 2011's institutional investors were selling off their technology portfolios, choosing the safety of less cyclical stock. Apotheker's moves further deepened shareholder anxiety. Some took fright at the thought of dumping 30 per cent of revenues without a handle on what HP's future would be built on. Apotheker spent long days in vain explaining himself at roadshows but nothing could stop the company losing almost half its market value in just a few months.

That is when the board itself got scared. How could they continue to support Apotheker's strategy when the all-knowing markets had rejected it? It didn't seem to matter to the board that it had okayed his course of action many times, it was time to appease the wrath of the Gods, sacrificing the CEO by way of atonement. Apotheker, one of the rare Europeans running a major American group, ended up having to go in September 2011.

Why this sacrifice? In 2001 when the group absorbed Compaq, the family of founder William Hewlett who still owned 5 per cent of the capital, voted against the acquisition, deeming it a grave financial and strategic error for their group. In their opinion, and in the opinion of many other analysts at the time, why would a group that gained world renown through its creativity and countless patents suddenly want to become the world's biggest box maker? There can be no doubt that the banks advising on the takeover made a big deal of the fantastic synergies between the two groups and the increased market value they would bring. But what is the point of short-term synergies when the underlying trend is one of hugely dwindling margins?

In 2004, just three years after HP's buying Compaq, IBM did the exact opposite, off-loading its entire PC division to the Chinese group Lenovo, even though the business generated almost 20 billion dollars in revenues. Like Apotheker, IBM's President and CEO Samuel Palmisano met with tough opposition, with an important difference: IBM's board did not buckle under market pressure, instead allowing him the time to prove his strategy's relevance. And this is how Palmisano was able to refocus IBM on the high-margin businesses of software and services, achieving one of the finest industrial turnarounds of the decade. Today IBM's market capitalisation is over 200 billion dollars, more than four times HP's, even though its revenues are considerably lower. In November 2011, Warren Buffet, a man who rarely backs the wrong horse, shelled out 10 billion dollars for a 5 per cent stake in the corporation. As for Lenovo, the company's profits soared and by mid-2013, with a market share of 16.7 per cent, it had managed to capture HP's crown in the PC market.

The problem with Western capitalism is that for every one IBM-type success story, there are 10 HP-type tales of woe. Most of the large listed groups are accountable to financial shareholders and their short-term objectives. This short-term pressure prevents them from taking bold initiatives whose outcomes are by no means certain, and yet whose success would mean the profits of tomorrow. This is what Michael Dell realised when he decided that the only way to reconstruct the business he founded was to take it private. All over the Western world, boards tend to bless indecision as they consider making elephants dance far too dangerous an endeavour. What they don't seem to realise is that as a result of their fear-fuelled inertia, the elephants will soon be extinct.

The rise of the nomadic investor

Institutional investors – pension funds, insurance companies, and investment funds – are steadily replacing existing family shareholders and the acceleration of this movement goes some way toward explaining the metamorphosis of Western capitalism. Between 1995 and 2009, assets held by institutional investors within the OECD countries went up from 25 to 65 trillion dollars[20]. In the US, based on shareholder analysis of the top 1,000 listed companies, institutional investors have raised their ownership of public companies from 46 per cent in 1987 to more than 73 per cent at the end of 2009[21]. The percentage is even higher in Europe where institutional investors possess 86 per cent of all listed companies' capital. This spectacular rise of the institutional investor has been accompanied by two distinct but complementary trends that brought about a sharp fall in the average holding period of listed stocks.

The first trend is the internationalisation of company capital. The paradigm of the French or Dutch insurance company who remained the undemanding stockholders of their national champions through thick and thin is simply no more. These days, the Dutch pension fund with a line of Royal Dutch Shell stock in its portfolio will sell in a split-second, replacing them with Exxon shares if these are deemed more promising. Today, on average 37 per cent of listed European companies' capital is held by foreign shareholders. This figure reaches 70 per cent and 62 per cent respectively in countries such as the Netherlands or Finland. In France the share is 41 per cent while in Germany it is as low as 21 per cent[22].

The second trend in the institutional world was the meteoric rise of investment funds compared to pension funds and insurance companies. These funds manage today over 25 trillion dollars of assets, almost three times the level reached in the early 1990s[23]. Investment funds were the smallest players in the industry just 20 years ago but they have now taken centre stage. This is a highly disparate group, comprised of all sorts of mutual and hedge funds with as many different investment strategies. The one thing they all have in common, however, is a much shorter time horizon than pension funds or insurance companies.

While pension funds invest the savings of future pensioners who contribute throughout their working lives and insurance companies invest their own cash surpluses, investment funds act as mere intermediaries. These investment funds' capital flows are therefore far less predictable than those of the other funds mentioned. Performance is published on a daily or monthly basis[24] and should it disappoint, the sanction falls immediately: investors simply redeem their shares and reinvest their money elsewhere. As fund managers' remuneration depends on the size of the asset pool they manage, underperforming the market, even for a short period, is a terrifying prospect for them as such a lapse would lead to investor exodus and a dramatic fall in their income. This fear drives them to a trading frenzy, which is ultimately counter-productive for everyone: themselves, their investors, and, even more importantly, for the companies they invest in.

Up until the 1980s when investment funds really took off, the average holding period of listed stock in the US was around five years. Today, this figure has fallen to just five months[25] and we see the same picture throughout the OECD countries.

The advent of High Frequency Trading (HFT) funds only makes matters worse. HFT funds are based on supposedly sophisticated quantitative models and 'managed' by software programs that buy and sell securities across the globe with holding periods measured in microseconds. Today, these funds account for more than 70 per cent of volumes traded on American markets and around 40 per cent in Europe. In 2012, high frequency traders were responsible for moving 1.6 billion shares a day[26]. We saw how dangerous this system can get during the 'flash crash' in May 2010, when the Dow Jones index lost 9 per cent of its value in seconds because algorithms had driven the computers mad. The same thing happened again in July 2012 when the trading programmes of Knight Capital caused prices of 148 stocks to fluctuate wildly, some plummeting by more than 60 per cent and others rocketing by 150 per cent in just hours. These errors were to cost Knight Capital some 440 million dollars, their company motto 'the science of trading, the standard of trust' ringing ingloriously in our ears when such mistakes can cost naive investors billions and hundreds of honest workers their jobs.

And even if we were ready to accept living with the inherent dangers of trading programmes flying the financial system on autopilot, we would have to accept a corresponding and exponential increase in market volatility. The economist Robert Schiller carried out a study in the US comparing stock price volatility and intrinsic company value over the last century[27]. He noticed that up to the 1960s, stock price volatility was approximately twice that of the true company value. Since the 1990s, stock prices have become six to 10 times more volatile.

This short-term mindset is worrisome first and foremost for those who trust these funds with their savings. Experience shows that the most successful investors, from Warren Buffet to Sir John Templeton, are capable of adopting a longer-term view. Berkshire Hathaway, Warren Buffett's listed holding company, holds on to its stakes for an average duration of 20 years. Here, we couldn't be further from those *high frequency* traders. . . When we dare to quiz the wise man of Omaha about his favourite time horizon to hold stock for, the answer is inevitably 'forever'.

The other disturbing aspect for investors is the exorbitant cost of these funds. Most hedge funds charge their clients management fees amounting to 2 per cent of their overall investment as well as performance fees that usually come to 20 per cent of the annual gains, even if they are latent. Investors often fail to grasp how this siphoning off of their funds destroys the overall return on their investments.

To illustrate this point, the example of Warren Buffet is once again enlightening. An investor who handed over 1,000 dollars to Mr Buffet in 1965, the year he founded Berkshire Hathaway, would now have an investment worth 4.3 million dollars[28]. Now, if Warren Buffet had been a hedge fund manager, charging 2 per cent of the total investment annually and 20 per cent of the profits, our investor would no longer have 4.3 million in his pocket, but just 300,000 dollars. . .and this is a best-case scenario given that not all hedge fund managers have Warren Buffet's talent!

Probably the most worrying thing of all, beyond the consequences for the savers or the pension funds trusting such fund managers with their money, is the impact of the nomadic investor on the management of our big corporations. Corporate executives are faced with two highly polarised investor-types: the silent and the restless. The former never attempt to influence their chosen company's course of action, simply making sure that quarterly results are in line with analysts' expectations and that the company adheres to rules of good governance. They will chop and change after just months, preferably reaping some profits in the process. The latter adopt a more active slant and are willing to retain their stake somewhat longer to achieve their ends, maybe one or two years. Obviously, there is nothing intrinsically wrong with being an involved shareholder, except when the sole focus is on ultra-short-term value creation. Many of these 'activist' funds look to maximise company liquidities with the aim of forcing them to distribute rather than reinvest the cash in forward-looking projects.

The other banner call of such activist funds, is to narrow the scope of the activities pursued by their portfolio companies. Their creed is that diversification calls should be made by the investor rather than the company's management team. This black and white attitude prevents them from seeing that a group's main asset is not necessarily sector expertise but rather its human capital, the business acumen that enables it to take the initiative and go after new markets in innovative ways. In groups such as General Electric who have managed to achieve leading positions in seven or eight business segments, synergies are first and foremost managerial and cultural, that is to say, based on good sector-specific intelligence, rather than basic considerations of profit and loss. This is exactly the lesson learned by Indian and Chinese groups which, although conglomerates, have managed to remain at the cutting edge in a great number of business areas.

Western business leaders are stuck in a double bind: they try to placate both their silent and restless investors and ultimately build their strategy around the lowest common denominator. They soothe the limited concerns of the former, mitigating risk wherever possible. They avoid the wrath of the latter, boasting their pursuit of 'shareholder value' through stock buybacks and inflated dividend payouts. The only one losing out is the company itself. What the business leaders really need is a third category of investor that is few and far between in the West: the long-term activist.

From financial myopia to the erosion of our competitiveness

Shareholder short-sightedness has brought about a fundamental shift in the way decisions are taken at board-level in our largest corporations. Consciously or not, business leaders draw up budgets and prioritise projects while constantly asking themselves how the markets will react. Investor relations managers and PR agencies are systematically involved upfront in any internal discussions pertaining to serious projects. And, of course, legal advisors and other consultants are never far away.

In this type of working environment, how can vision and initiative play anything other than supporting roles? Research and development (R&D) spending remains high in the West, but competitors from emerging countries are catching up fast and making each dollar they spend much more relevant in meeting customers' expectations. Investment in creating or developing production facilities is also in relative decline in the West. Decisions on new factory locations or research facilities are too often taken exclusively on static cost-based analysis when the German model shows that other criteria such as workforce qualifications and productivity play vital roles in long-term competitiveness.

R&D: the head start of companies with a stable capital base

Countries such as the US, Japan, Germany, France, and Great Britain are still, unquestionably, major global players in the field of R&D. As a percentage of GDP they spend far more than most emerging countries (2.77 per cent for the US compared to 1.84 per cent for China[29]) but these figures hide a disturbing underlying trend. With the exception of Germany, which has seen its R&D spending rise from 2.4 per cent to 2.8 per cent of GDP over the last 10 years, investments in all the above countries have stagnated, Great Britain bringing up the rear with spending of just 1.77 per cent of GDP[30]. China, by contrast, has increased R&D spending exponentially in both relative and absolute terms. Between 2000 and 2010, R&D investments went up from 0.9 per cent of GDP to 1.6 per cent, while GDP was rising at 10 per cent per annum. This enormous effort has already paid off when we consider that China has increased its hi-tech exports 12-fold, amassing a trade surplus of 129 billion dollars on this segment alone. The US managed a trade deficit of nearly 200 billion dollars[31] over the same period, and in an industry where American superiority had been hitherto considered indisputable.

In Brazil, R&D expenditure remained at around 1.1 per cent of GDP over the last decade but here again, given the strong growth the country experienced until recently, investments have increased dramatically in absolute terms.

The gap has widened during the recent financial crisis. While the big Western corporations slashed their R&D budgets, emerging countries continued on their merry way. In 2009, US businesses cut their R&D

budgets by 4 per cent while Chinese and Indian companies ramped theirs up by 40 per cent. In 2010, when the global economy was beginning to show signs of recovery, American and European firms increased their R&D spending, up on the previous year by 10.5 per cent and 5.8 per cent respectively, while their Chinese and Indian counterparts continued on the same path with another consecutive increase of 40 per cent on the previous year[32].

During the crisis, Western business leaders of listed companies did the only thing they thought themselves capable of in the circumstances: they cut costs, even those that bolstered their company's competitiveness. This cost-cutting enabled them to generate considerable liquidities, but at what price? That, we will never know.

Throughout periods of crisis, those companies who are lucky enough to have a more stable shareholder base than their competitors will inevitably be under less pressure to abruptly slash their costs. We saw this recently in emerging countries but we have also witnessed the phenomenon in more mature economies. Great Britain, although boasting one of the West's most open economies, makes for a fascinating case study. If we take the 1,000 biggest businesses in Britain, the listed companies invest on average only 1.4 per cent of their revenues in R&D, the non-listed companies 2.1 per cent, and those with a majority stake held by foreign capital, often from the emerging countries, invest 2.6 per cent of their revenues[33]. In 2009, pressured by the crisis, private enterprises were the only ones who chose to raise their R&D investments (+5.2 per cent) while the listed companies reduced their own (-1 per cent). They were, in turn, also the only ones to experience an increase in revenues (+9.8 per cent) while the listed companies' revenues fell (-6.7 per cent)[34].

However, in terms of R&D, what really matters is not only the amount one spends in absolute terms, it is also, and above all, about how one spends it. Apple, one of the most innovative firms of all time only invests 2.7 per cent of its revenues on R&D compared to 14 per cent for Microsoft and 12.8% for Google[35]. Yet its revenues and margin growth have considerably out-stripped their main rivals. And the reason is clear: to quote the consulting firm Booz & Co, Apple is one of 'the Need Seekers', a category of companies that use their R&D facilities as a means to wowing customer wants and needs. They are less concerned with fundamental research than with creating a product that will sell. Such companies are driven by a love of innovation but applied, pragmatic, marketing-centric innovation. Entrepreneurial or family-owned businesses are usually more comfortable with this type of approach than big groups who do not have a reference shareholder. Consequently, even when they spend less on R&D than their listed rivals, they still manage to achieve more tangible results. We can observe this phenomenon in German companies where R&D, customer service, and marketing departments tend to work hand in hand. This tight-knit collaboration has enabled firms of the *Mittelstand* to become world leaders in their sectors even when they are often considerably smaller than their competitors.

Deindustrialisation: torn between pragmatism and the easy way out

The stagnation in Western R&D investments is a revealing manifestation of the new balance of power between the financial shareholders of our largest corporations and their top management. Deindustrialisation is yet another sign, this time even harder to ignore, of this new redistribution of power.

Over the last two decades, the share of Western countries in the world's manufactured goods has been steadily falling. China has become the second biggest manufacturer globally, just behind the US and will undoubtedly take the top slot in the very near future. Between 2001, when China first joined the WTO, and 2009, the country's progress had proven spectacular in almost every sector of the economy. For instance, in the apparel sector, China's share of exports went up from 17.4 per cent to 32.1 per cent; in the furniture sector from 7.5 per cent to 25.9 per cent; in telecom equipment, up from 6.5 per cent to 27.8 per cent; and from 4.9 per cent up to 32.6 per cent in computer hardware. Over that same period the US lost more than six million jobs in manufacturing[36].

Throughout the OECD countries, 70 per cent of GDP is now generated in service industries[37]. Even in the industrial sector, 35 per cent of staff are employed in service jobs. The reasons for this deindustrialisation are obvious. In markets where competition is global, companies try as best they can to cut back their manufacturing costs to the strict minimum. They have thus resorted massively to off-shoring production facilities and closed thousands of factories in countries where the labour force was considered too expensive.

In sectors producing low value-add products, this move probably made the difference between life and death. However, in most other sectors, under the pretence of pragmatism, large companies chose to take the easy way out and ended up putting their long-term competitiveness at risk. What seemed like a straightforward choice turned out to be over simplistic.

In recent years, Chinese workers' wages have gone up much faster than their productivity. In 2000, the average hourly wage of a Chinese worker was just 52 cents compared with 16.61 dollars in the US; by 2015, hourly wages will hit 4.41 dollars in China and 26.06 dollars in the US[38]. Throughout China, wages are rising steadily by 15 per cent to 20 per cent per annum.

If we consider that American workers still have a considerable lead in productivity and that the yuan will continue to strengthen, the Chinese worker will soon cost just 30 per cent less than his American counter-part. And, as labour costs account for only 20 per cent to 30 per cent of a product's total manufacturing cost, the competitive advantage of the Chinese seems to be fading fast.

Other manufacturing costs have rocketed in Asia. Transport costs have gone up by 71 per cent over the last four years in line with the rise in oil prices[39]. Electricity prices have almost doubled in China since 2001.

But beyond escalating costs, quality control and a supply chain as unre-liable as it is inflexible have pushed a growing number of firms to repat-riate their production facilities back home. Caterpillar, the world's leading producer of excavation and construction vehicles announced that it was to build a 60,000 square metre factory in Texas. NCR Corp announced that the company was to reshore its ATM production in Georgia. The major American furniture manufacturer Sauder is to do the same.

All of these firms had closed their factories and laid off skilled workers at great expense in the 2000s. They are now faced with the challenge of rehiring and retraining employees that are currently thin on the ground. They also have to shell out huge amounts of money to build new facto-ries. This round trip is most probably a good thing for Western econo-mies, benefitting from the reshoring movement, but this begs the ques-tion of their companies' top management teams and the quality of their decision-making. When they presented their boards with plans to close their company's historic plants, thereby calling into question supplier relations built up over decades, were they just being realistic or were they caving in too easily to market pressure?

Divergent interests as a system

Across the Western world, those in charge of the economy seem to lack enthusiasm and imagination in equal measures. They lead their companies more with caution than daring. The market requires them to produce results exactly in line with analysts' expectations while boards bless strategies driven exclusively by the desire to seek consensus and continuity at all cost. The Western sailboat goes with the flow of a long, trouble-free river, while competitors from emerging countries set out to conquer the oceans every single day.

When a senior executive takes office, is he ever asked to prove his faith in the company by investing any of his own money in its capital? The answer, of course, is never. He more often than not is guaranteed a 'golden hello', a welcome bonus that amounts to millions of dollars before he has even begun to do the job. And to prevent him worrying too much about his future should things turn sour, he is also assured a 'golden parachute', an indemnity that can be worth millions of dollars paid out to him should he get fired. After all, why shouldn't poor performance be compensated?

Once he is reassured about his financial prospects, our captain of industry can at last get down to business. The burden of his responsibilities is so great that it is considered normal in the US that his annual pay amounts, on average, to more than 325 times that of the average employee. This ratio was just 35 to 1 in the 1970s. Not only have these inflationist tendencies in executive pay reached historic highs in the US, they have also affected all other major Western economies. In Great Britain, senior executives' median salary in the top 100 listed companies has topped-out at 52 times the mean salary[40], compared with an 11-fold difference in the 1980s. Continental Europe has followed the same path.

This talent war and subsequent pay escalation began in the 1990s when management boards of the big listed groups took the decision to link executive pay more directly to company performance. This 'pay for performance' philosophy brought about considerable creativity in the way pay was structured. In addition to the basic salary would come an annual or deferred bonus paid in cash and/or stock, provided certain performance targets were hit, stock options, share awards, and top-up pension schemes ensuring these executives a life-long pay cheque.

All of this is blessed by HR consultancies who submit lengthy studies to the boards hiring the CEOs in order to justify these decisions based on 'benchmarking': a detailed comparison of executive compensation in companies of comparable size and sector. What is set up as totally objective is neither expressed in absolute terms nor a comparison of the CEO's compensation with that of his senior executives. All that counts is what the competition is doing, even if what they are doing is wrong. Board members are increasingly behaving like football team managers. You want to recruit a star player and hold on to him? Then you must pay for the transfer at market price, whatever it is. Should such decisions arouse shareholder indignation, board members can always brandish external consultants' benchmarks and thus shirk responsibility.

This spectacular rise in the executive compensation of listed company bosses wouldn't be so reprehensible if it had only brought about at least a proportional increase in the value or the results of those companies they managed. Sadly, this was not the case. A report commissioned by the British government on the correlation between wages and performance in the top 100 listed companies showed that although executive pay had risen by 111 per cent between 2000 and 2010, the market capitalisation of these companies had only gone up by 3.8 per cent on average[41]. The pre-tax profit had risen by just 50.5 per cent. In practice, paying for performance has become synonymous with paying staggering amounts regardless. Some recent research has even suggested that overconfidence generated by excess pay causes losses for shareholders as CEOs undertake value-destroying transactions which may boost stock prices in the short term but have disastrous consequences in the long run[42].

If we take a look at executive compensation for both FTSE100 CEOs and for all board members of the 350 largest listed British companies, the disconnect between pay and results is identical.

This perversion of the initial objectives in performance-related pay was made possible by two key weaknesses in the compensation structure offered to top executives. Firstly, the supposedly performance-based part is calculated over periods of time that are too short to be meaningful. One to three years is the norm. Should there be a stock price, profit, or revenue increase over that period, substantial payouts are made. Were these indicators to turn south, we would never imagine asking the executive to pay back his bonus even if the shareholder were worse off than before the executive's arrival.

Secondly, the complacency of board members who, as if it were not enough to assess CEOs on periods that are far too short to be relevant, also set objectives that are far too easy to achieve. Put another way, they set the bar too close and too low.

Senior executives get the message loud and clear: all they have to do is meet their objectives over a two or three year period and they will be free from financial worries for the rest of their lives. By stark contrast, should they ever make the wrong strategic decisions, and as long as their company doesn't take a hit too quickly, their personal finances will be wholly unaffected. Shareholders could always lodge a complaint but would have little chance of achieving anything.

This misalignment of the interests of the key stakeholders is, of course, very different from the situation in entrepreneurial groups, especially in emerging countries. There, the only concern the owner-manager has in mind is the long-term impact of today's decision-making. Yet another weakness of the approach to executive pay in the West is that even when the CEO in question is deserving, having contributed to his group's results, his pay is structured as if he were entirely and exclusively the only one to thank. Another British study carried out in over 400 listed companies[43] showed that there is almost no link between a firm's success and its middle-management's compensation. The correlation between their pay and company performance is five times weaker than that of top executives.

This near deification of the leaders of the biggest listed companies has resulted in the construction of a compensation system that is as dysfunctional as it is dangerous. Instead of tightly linking executive and shareholder fates, the system allows the former to get rich quick whatever happens to the latter. Instead of encouraging the boss and his staff to stand by each other, it allows the former to reap the rewards of collective efforts, while the latter turn into corporate mandarins. But it is precisely because these rewards are generated by collective effort, that we must look to behavioural incentives, rather than punitive measures to encourage the sort of long-term thinking our system has lost. The British Parliamentary Commission on Banking Standards caused a stir in June 2013 by recommending that a new category of criminal offence be created[44]. Those found guilty of 'reckless misconduct in the management of a bank' could be jailed. The Commission's report acknowledged the need for deferred remuneration and for better accountability, but to criminalise the behaviours at the top is a step too far. Our banking system's problems stem from collective behaviours at CEO, board and employee level and collective incentives are required to correct it, not personalised punishments.

Corporate governance: when the tree hides the forest

In the West, corporate governance has been on the front pages of the economic press and at the heart of shareholder debates for years now. Following the scandals of Enron, Tyco or WorldCom in the US in the 1990s, the main concern has been to ensure the independence of corporate boards and to establish a system of checks and balances to mitigate the risks associated with an all-powerful CEO. Each country adopted its own governance charters reflecting its history and the specifics of its own corporate culture. The most widespread practice includes the separation of the chairman and CEO roles, the appointment of a majority of directors who are not company employees, the creation of committees dealing with such subjects as audits or remuneration, and the appointment of an 'Independent Senior Director'.

Nevertheless, after more than 20 years of 'good' governance, we have to face up to the fact that these measures have not had a positive impact on company performance and that they have not improved either the quality or relevance of the decision-making process.

Through the example of executive pay we have seen how board members have created a decision-making environment and incentive system entirely geared towards the short term. They seem happy to copy models used by their competitors without really wondering about their effects on the company they are supposed to oversee.

However, the board's woes do not end here. Another of their flaws is that their independent directors rarely possess the necessary skills and sector knowledge to enable them to understand the industry dynamics and risks inherent in their own business. If we consider complex sectors such as banking or insurance, how can we expect a director from, say the retail or energy sectors to understand, and *a fortiori* control their institution's derivative risk exposure? And yet they are requested to sit on audit or risk committees when even the senior management team has trouble ensuring wringing reliable management information from the outer reaches of their often sprawling groups. One dishonest trader left to his own devices and just a few weeks is all it takes to bring down a group employing tens of thousands of people. Reports presented at these independent directors' committees are often prepared by the finance or risk departments whose best interests are not always to reveal the extent of their worries. And when they finally choose to come clean, it is often too late. The independent director has become the rubber stamp of a clear conscience whose benediction may be held up to the markets, although he has neither the time, the expertise, nor the tools to carry out his mission.

Let's look at another example, this time from the IT and mobile telecom equipment sectors. Year on year, the market supremacy of the sector's established corporations is challenged by new, aggressive, and innovative players who shake up everything from the rules of the game to the very business models of the incumbents. Who would have thought that the powerhouse Microsoft could be pushed aside by Google, a company that didn't even exist 20 years ago? Who would have dreamed that Nokia, the uncontested market leader of the early 2000s would be washed away by the tidal wave of iPhones and end up in Microsoft's shopping basket? Or that Samsung, the South Korean conglomerate would in turn manage to threaten Apple on its own turf?

What these groups need in their fight for survival is not independent directors overwhelmed by the speed of technological change, but visionary and courageous leaders who are willing and able to gamble on a revolutionary new development for the future of their company. And in a world of litigation, board directors are simply not willing to take this kind of risk. They have become an opposition force countering the entrepreneur, tying his hands and ensuring the status quo.

When Steve Jobs was hounded out of Apple in 1985 and replaced by a more traditional boss, Pepsi Cola's John Sculley, the board's thinking was to make Apple into a 'normal' company. Jobs' character, as temperamental as it was brilliant, scared them to death. In less than 10 years the independent directors of Apple managed to kill off the firm's magic and brought it to the brink of bankruptcy. When Jobs returned to Apple's helm having created NeXT and Pixar in the meantime, he had to fight to give the company back its soul and restore its taste for innovation and risk-taking. As we now know, he won the battle and enabled Apple to become the most profitable company in the sector with a market capitalisation today of over 400 billion dollars.

Naturally, not all the CEOs of listed companies are made of the same stuff as Steve Jobs, and not all independent company directors are out to kill off business initiative. And it is not that these directors do not have a role to play in our big corporations. Nonetheless, it is important to pinpoint how the system has gone astray.

When the Sarbanes-Oxley Act was voted in in the US in 2002, intentions, it seemed, were praiseworthy. According to the bill's sponsors, it was a matter of 'protecting investors by improving the reliability of the information provided by firms'. In order to achieve this, corporations' CEOs and CFOs were invited to be personally accountable for certifying their company's accounts themselves. It was also required that the majority of board members be independent, that they preside over audit committees and thus take direct responsibility in the communication of financial data. Any breach thus became a criminal offence, punishable by up to 20 years in jail and could result in directors losing their entire personal fortunes.

And what was the predictable outcome of these measures on American companies? First and foremost, the huge cost companies bear just to handle the process. According to a study on the impact of the Act, each listed company in the US would spend on average between six million dollars annually for the smallest ones, and 39 million dollars for the largest, in direct and indirect costs due to Sarbanes-Oxley. When scaled up to the entire economy, that would mean an annual spend of between 19 and 75 billion dollars[45].

This bill reduced the US share of IPOs, leaving the lion's share to other financial centres such as London and Hong Kong. While in 2002, 67 per cent of companies going public chose Venue USA to launch their IPOs, by 2011 this figure had fallen to just 16 per cent.

But by far the biggest cost incurred as a result of this legislation was the arrival of independent directors on corporate boards, which in turn meant a huge growth in risk-aversion. Several American studies have established that, all else being equal, those corporations with the highest numbers of independent directors are the ones who tend to invest the least in research and development[46]. Another study on the impact of the Sarbanes-Oxley bill[47] compared corporate behaviour pre- and post-legislation rollout, and observed not only a noteworthy drop in R&D expenditure, but also a slowdown in investments in general. This loss of interest in risk-taking has hit particularly hard companies active in innovation intensive sectors and is giving their main competitors a dangerous head start over them.

The Sarbanes-Oxley mindset has crossed the Atlantic and impacted corporations' governance policies throughout the Western world. Indeed, in globalised industries the same institutional investors expect all the companies they have in their portfolio, whether located in the UK or France for example, to apply the same rules of governance as those in force in the US. It would be unthinkable for corporations such as Axa or Danone to put themselves at odds with investors like CALPERS, America's biggest pension fund managing over 250 billion dollars for the employees of the State of California[48]. These institutional investors have driven a standardisation of governance procedures throughout the world by choosing, naturally, the highest of standards at their disposal.

While the management of our biggest corporations wear themselves out trying to comply with these guidelines, and while independent directors consider it their duty to avoid getting into projects they consider too adventurous, competitors from emerging countries drive on with courage and determination. Whether owned by families or States, these companies have understood that in a world that is in perpetual motion, it is vital to have a small number of decision-makers that are able to decide fast. These companies understand that for a 15-strong board, consensus seeking usually results in always choosing the least disruptive course of action when often the opposite is required. It is about time we woke up to the fact in the West that the tree of 'good' governance has ended up hiding the forest of managerial effectiveness.

Litigation culture and risk-aversion

The litigation culture rife in the US has steadily spread across the entire Western world and considerably changed the way our companies operate. In addition to the staggering costs of these lawsuits, Western companies innovate less than in the past, preferring to cancel or postpone new product launches for fear of being taken to court by an unhappy customer.

A survey conducted amongst 500 American business leaders revealed that court cases, more often than not groundless, had prompted 36 per cent of companies to stop production of certain products, 15 per cent to lay off workers and 8 per cent to close factories[49]. In another survey carried out by Gallup, 26 per cent of American SME bosses admitted to having pulled new products or services because of the threat of legal action. The direct cost of court cases in the US has been estimated at 250 billion dollars per annum, roughly 1.6 per cent of GDP and more than twice the levels found in Great Britain or Japan[50]. These costs include legal fees and cash payouts in the form of out of court settlements. However, if we add the indirect costs, for example, the shortfall in innovation in the manufacturing or medical industries, the total cost would be in the order of 600 to 900 billion dollars a year, or between 4.3 per cent and 6.5 per cent of GDP.

If Americans hold the unenviable record for litigation, not one of the big Western economies can consider itself safe. Companies exporting to the US or those who are listed on American stock markets, for example, are all subject to the same regime. A report drafted by Zurich Financial stressed that insurance premiums covering management or boards of directors of European companies listed in the US had gone up by 300 per cent in just a few years while the level of cover accepted by insurers has gone down.

Individual legal action is just one part of the story, as group efforts are becoming more and more commonplace. With the advent of class action lawsuits, specialised lawyers have become rich and companies have been plunged into relentless and ruinous legal trench warfare. According to a recent survey, 36 per cent of responding companies with a market capitalisation above 10 billion dollars have had to resort to their insurance policies to protect their directors from the financial consequences of these attacks[51].

The collateral damages of litigation culture are awesome. Preferred targets of such legal action, business leaders tend to avoid taking the slightest risk because even though they are covered by their insurance policies, they know they will have to devote an enormous amount of time to their defence should they be taken to court. And what becomes of capitalism if those who are supposed to be taking the risks find themselves holed up behind barricades of lawyers, taking every precaution before ever opening their mouths?

Requiem for an entrepreneur

So it seems that our big corporations and their leaders have irreparably lost their love of adventure and their will to conquer. Then can we count on our entrepreneurs to pick up the baton? Unfortunately, the news here is less than encouraging. In most of the Western countries, micro-enterprises and SMEs are caught in the crossfire from the State, big businesses, and banks.

By increasing the fiscal burden, social security contributions, and administrative red tape, the State has made life impossible for the entrepreneur. In addition to the direct costs from taxes and payroll levies, the stifling labour laws in many European countries have finished off companies who no longer have the means to adapt to changes in the economic cycles. Costs related to redundancies have become so high that some companies consider it less costly to put their companies into receivership rather than attempting to restructure. In the global competitiveness rankings compiled by the World Economic Forum, the UK was ranked 33rd out of 144 countries for its hiring and firing practices; France finished 141st.[52]

But the problem goes way beyond the cumbersome nature of the labour market. In a study carried out amongst more than 4,800 SMEs[53] in Great Britain, administration costs incurred through legislative red tape was put at over 16.8 billion pounds sterling per annum. Nearly one quarter of the respondents said they were less competitive because of the energy required by management to deal with these issues.

The surviving SMEs must however face up to the merciless competition from big corporations who use their sales and financial strength to crush them. This phenomenon is particularly prevalent in the retail sector as well as in many industrial activities. While the West's major companies resorted massively to offshoring their production to reduce cost, SMEs found it hard to follow suit and consequently lost considerable market share.

The last hurdle the SME has to jump, and by no means the least, is the attitude of Western banks who have considerably reduced their exposure to the sector since 2008. Getting a loan or renewing a line of credit has become an uphill struggle. Thousands of small firms have had to refuse orders simply because they were unable to scrape together the cash flow required to fund their product's manufacturing process. In a survey by the European Central Bank[54], 15 per cent of SMEs quote lack of financing as their main concern. As European banks will have to reduce their debt exposure significantly over the next two years, we can expect a huge increase in the number of small business failures. A recent study by credit insurer Euler-Hermes revealed that the number of bankruptcies among French companies with over 15 million euros of revenues had jumped by 15.7 per cent in the first five months of 2013. Even more worryingly, those with more than 200 employees had seen bankruptcy filings jump by 33 per cent.

Even in the US, still deemed the Promised Land by business creators, the spirit of initiative is on the wane. By way of example, out of all the

OECD countries, the US is second to last for the number of individual enterprises as a proportion of the working population (7.2 per cent compared to 9 per cent in France and 13.8 per cent in Great Britain)[55]. The US is still the country were the number of young companies[56] as a proportion of the total adult population is the highest of the G7 countries, although this figure is in freefall, plummeting from 12 per cent in 2005 to just 7.6 per cent in 2010. In Great Britain and France, the figures are 6.5 per cent and 5.8 per cent respectively and rank slightly above the G7 average.

Entrepreneurs can only thrive in a favourable culture, and to a certain extent, in a culture where they are admired. This is very much the case in many emerging countries but it is much less true in the West, especially in Europe. In a study published in 2011[57], 1,000 entrepreneurs in each G20 country were questioned on the criteria that had a significant impact on their ability to set up and develop their own businesses. When asked the question, 'Do you think that the culture in your country encourages entrepreneurship?', Great Britain arrived in 14th position, with only 30 per cent fully agreeing with the statement.

In addition to the barriers facing business creators in Europe, many quote the stigma associated with failure as a curb on entrepreneurial spirit. The most dynamic countries are those who have a higher tolerance for business failure and where the entrepreneur shares the belief that you learn from your mistakes and can thus bounce back more easily. Following in the footsteps of the American model, British capitalism has adopted this philosophy. On the continent, however, bankruptcy casts a permanent shadow on any career. Let us bear in mind that until recently the boss of a bankrupt company in several European countries was liable to prosecution.

The contrast in attitude of countries such as India or China who head up the rankings, is all the more remarkable. Ninety-eight pre cent of Indian SMEs consider their country's culture as favourable to free enterprise and 47 per cent see failure as a learning opportunity. Furthermore, whereas our SMEs have been abandoned by the banks, 80 per cent of Indian entrepreneurs declare having observed a notable improvement in their access to funding. This additional capital they have at their disposal comes both from Indian banks and from venture capitalists. Between 2005 and 2010 venture capitalists increased their investments in Indian companies by 523 per cent, reaching six billion dollars, market flotations increasing by 21 per cent over the same period. [58]

Of course, China is not to be outdone here either. Ninety-two per cent of small business leaders in China believe that their country encourages entrepreneurship and that the State plays an important role in business. Fifty-eight per cent don't see failure as an inhibitor but rather as an opportunity to start afresh. At the State's instigation, Chinese banks play an increasingly important role in small business financing, although a big part of it is still covered by unauthorised lenders charging exceptionally high rates. The government's attempt to clamp down on this practice could have far reaching repercussions, but so far, Chinese SMEs have found ways of funding their working capital needs. Chinese entrepreneurs have also benefitted from an influx of private equity funds; 5.6 billion dollars were invested in 2010, a gain of some 223 per cent compared to 2005. In 2010 the number of IPOs amongst Chinese SMEs had grown 13-fold since 2005.

As if it weren't punishment enough to watch their credit lines from their banks dry up, European entrepreneurs have also suffered a spectacular drop in their venture capital funding. Between 2005 and 2010, the drop was almost 50 per cent and the number of IPOs had bottomed out[59]. Most European stock exchanges set up to enable SMEs to raise money more easily are no longer playing their part. Institutional investors seem to have lost all appetite for smaller companies as transaction volumes on stock exchanges have plummeted and stock liquidity reduced. Even AIM, formerly known as the Alternative Investment Market and the London-based historically most dynamic market for innovation-driven companies, has taken a hit during the downturn. Around 1,200 companies are still listed there today when there were almost 1,700 in 2007. Among the survivors, almost 500 have a market capitalisation below the 10 million pound mark and will potentially no longer be able to take advantage of their listing to raise any more money. In an effort to boost small and high-growth companies, the UK Governments 2013 Budget included a pledge to abolish stamp duty on AIM-listed shares from April 2014 onward. Whether this will achieve the desired surge in investment or not, remains to be seen.

The outlook for Western SMEs is not at all promising. There is too great a gap between the go-getting political stance and the day-to-day reality faced by these small businesses. A lot is at stake here. If we can no longer count on business creators today to become our captains of industry tomorrow, then the entire edifice of Western capitalism is in jeopardy.

The end of the partnership and the triumph of the Banker-King: 'Heads I win, tails you lose'

The crisis of 2008 might have been avoided if Wall Street and the City had stayed in the hands of partnerships rather than listed financial behemoths. Within these partnerships, where the firm's capital made up most of the partners' net worth, risk was seen in a totally different light. Each important decision would be weighed up according to how it would impact clients, and it was out of the question to 'sell' risky deals for the simple reason that they would bring in big profits for the bank. The banker in such a partnership would be doubly concerned with limiting the risk for his firm's capital, that is, his own capital, and with building up long-term relationships with his clients. This is, indeed, the reason why Anglo-Saxon investment banks traditionally concentrated more on client advisory work or pure intermediation, activities which were, by definition, less risky: mergers and acquisitions, security offerings (stocks, bonds, commercial paper), and brokering. The capital of the firm was utilised as an enabler and not as an end in itself. Of course, some of the capital was also utilised in trading operations for the bank's own account but the amounts concerned were strictly limited.

Even in an advisory role, generally remunerated by success fees, the bank's main worry was developing client loyalty. I remember a discussion with Sir Derek Higgs, a City legend and Managing Director of SG Warburg where I was learning the trade 20 years ago. He explained to me that he was almost prouder of the deals he hadn't done, because he had advised his clients against them, rather than the deals he had done and which had nevertheless secured his fame and fortune. Today we are light years from this mindset.

It was in the 1980s that the world of finance changed dramatically on both sides of the Atlantic. Bankers figured out that instead of simply 'passing the plates' on to their clients, they might share them or even eat them up on their own. It was at this time that many institutions decided to shift from being simple intermediaries to becoming themselves principals. And they made a move on capital-intensive activities that brought far greater risk but also far greater profit. It was also the period when the magic of debt became irresistible. Wall Street banks took the decision to increase their firepower by raising more capital and getting into debt. In the space of a few years, all the partnerships were to become public limited companies listed on the stock market.

Merrill Lynch showed the way in 1971, then all the other majors followed suit: Bear Stearns in 1985, Morgan Stanley in 1986, Lehman Brothers in 1994, and Goldman Sachs in 1999. Even the noble Lazard couldn't resist the market sirens and was one of the last great partnerships to abandon this type of legal structure and succumb to the lure of an IPO in 2005.

This fundamental shift inevitably had a profound impact on the City post Big Bang. All the old houses found themselves in a sort of no man's land, too small to compete with aggressive, better-funded American banks, and yet too big to limit themselves to just client advisory work. The result was not long coming. One by one, these several hundred-year-old institutions were bought out by the biggest banks in Europe and America.

This metamorphosis of Wall Street and the City completely transformed bankers' behaviour and their attitude to risk. The banker, who once a upon a time was the shareholder of his own business, proud to know every one of his partners and clients and deeply concerned about limiting risks taken with his own capital, suddenly became an employee. He became a pawn in a sprawling multinational, utilising the capital of faceless third parties to engage in ever-riskier and unpredictable activities. Instead of a dividend he would now receive an annual bonus that he would look to maximise by conducting as many transactions as possible, for better or for worse. The equation was getting dangerously too easy to solve. If the best-case scenario came about, his pay would amount to tens of millions without having taken the slightest personal risk. And yet in the worst case, any loss incurred would be for someone else: the client, the shareholder, or, whenever necessary, the taxpayer. This is when the banker-entrepreneur, up until then the owner-manager *par excellence* suddenly became just another apparatchik empowered by their institution to take insane risks, which as we were to find out to our cost, could impact the whole economic system.

This mindset 'heads I win, tails you lose' explains to a large extent how the financial bubble, built up over nearly two decades, blew up in two steps: in 2000 when the tech-sector crisis spread across all sectors of the markets and then later, in 2008, with the debt crisis hitting both private and sovereign borrowers. In both cases, the major institutions of the world of finance had peddled paradigm shifts that turned out to be illusions. The first comprised fantastical valuations of companies floated at the end of the 1990s despite booking losses that matched their revenues. The second, in the 2000s, saw logic-defying debt ratios that we weren't to worry about because, as the saying goes, 'the market is always right'. So what if a German bank was stupid enough to buy mortgages taken out by jobless families in Arizona living below the bread line? Where is the problem? Our banker will have been the rational middleman in a deal that brings the American dream to the latter and higher profitability to the former. If the beautiful country that is Greece needed to hide the extent of its debt exposure, where was the evil in setting up swaps that would enable the country to keep borrowing at a rate close to Germany's? In so doing, the prestigious Anglo-Saxon bank that drew up the deal pocketed more than 600 million dollars[60]. Not so crazy after all if the market was willing to swallow it.

Here, we are not going to fall into the trap of making the banks the scapegoat of all the evils of capitalism (as temping as it may be!). We have seen now the roles that many have played in our Western melodrama, including, above all, our governments as well as the executives and board members of our large corporations. We must remember, however, that the banker is not a benign economic agent. A vital channel between capital and the real economy, he is far more than just a middleman; the banker is the system's true arbiter. All stakeholders turn to him to size up risk, price that risk and allocate the capital accordingly. If he chooses to absolve himself from this task as he has done in recent years, with the excuse that the market is clever enough to do it for him, then everything and anything is possible, including the nonsensical.

Should we rely solely on the integrity or the intelligence of the banker to play this role? I don't believe so, as like any other economic agent, he is fallible and has the right to make mistakes. What is wholly unacceptable, however, is that because he is allowed to remain disconnected from the long-term consequences of his acts, the banker may directly or indirectly take advantage of his own errors. No one else enjoys such a privilege. Moreover, it would be reasonable to expect him to cease laying claim to his arbiter role when he is himself party to a deal. He should be asked to choose more clearly – and to disclose – whether he is acting as an advisor, a principal, or a salesman.

Giving up on the owner-manager model in the banking industry had serious consequences, but doesn't by itself explain how we have managed to drift so far off course these last few years. The industry's other silent revolution took place in the 2000s when banks surreptitiously shifted their centres of gravity from activities primarily focused on serving corporations to activities centred around capital providers. While the absolute top priority for investment banks had always been to serve big business, suddenly they realised that there was far more money to be made around the major investors, be they private equity funds, hedge funds, sovereign funds, or other large institutions. Where companies might make only one acquisition or undertake one share-issue every few years, private equity funds renew such operations constantly. Each transaction generates advisory fees but also, and more importantly, interest and placement fees on the debt secured for its funding. And when these funds seek to realise their investments, they often do so through IPOs which will generate commissions that are higher still than the initial advisory fees. Hedge fund activity constitutes a veritable Godsend for banks. Through their prime brokerage activities, banks work with these funds on a daily basis in areas such as trading or securities lending where the volume of business has ballooned over time. Banks have been able to derive significant profits from these activities. As a sign of the times, most of the executives who head up the big American banks now come from the trading floor rather than from client advisory roles. Until recently, the exact opposite was true.

So why worry about this development? Because we now live in a world where, first and foremost, finance serves finance. The system feeds itself in a near-incestuous atmosphere where fund managers, themselves former employees of the big banks, are keen to maintain a privileged working relationship with them.

In London, just a few months before the 2008 crisis, I was paid a visit by one of the stars of the hedge fund world, a sort of Mick Jagger of finance. His two billion dollar fund had chalked up annual returns of around 40 per cent over the previous few years and investors fought – literally – for the privilege of giving him their savings. My curiosity was all the greater, having read in one of the many tabloids that covered this colourful figure's lifestyle, that in 2007 his compensation had exceeded 100 million dollars, and that in order to avoid wasting even a few moments of his trading genius, his firm had set up mini trading rooms in each of his many residences.

And my colleagues and I were not to be disappointed. This character, never seen without a 'marketing assistant' who could easily have made the cover of Vogue, finally turned up a good half hour late. He bore the look of those who have recently made it in the City or Wall Street, who regard their talent as an art form and that no one would dream of asking an artist to wear a suit, let alone a tie. With his shoulder-length hair, designer stubble and jeans, carrying a BlackBerry in each hand that he proceeded to check every 10 seconds to keep track of the markets, 'Mick' as we shall call him clearly didn't have the time for futile presentations.

He opened with, 'So what can I do for you?' no sooner than he had sat down. 'You know, my fund is practically closed to new investors,' he added with all the eloquence of a Bloomberg screen.

Sensing my discomfort, the Chief Investment Officer of Stanhope Capital attempted to give the meeting a more habitual turn and explained that we were always on the lookout for experienced fund managers and were curious to understand his strategy and investment focus areas. Mick had not come to the meeting brandishing the proverbial PowerPoint presentation; he wouldn't have had the time for something so patently beneath him.

'Listen up, my strategy is to make money for my investors', he declared before adding, 'I take the opportunities as and when I find them, from emerging country sovereign debt to shares, commodities, or currencies'.

'Yes, but what are you targeting at the moment?' asked my partner in turn.

A text message and a few seconds later, Mick raised his head from his BlackBerry and looked at us as if about to put us out of our misery with a killer argument and get back to the office as quickly as possible to set about doing what he did best: conducting his trading symphony.

'I really don't understand your question. You mean what am I focusing on now? This afternoon? This evening?' He continued theatrically: 'Listen, I turn over my portfolio on average nine times a day. Do the maths. That's several billion dollars a day on all markets and all time zones, and do you know what that means?' Suspenseful silence, then the answer to his rhetorical question, 'That means that I pay more brokerage commissions to City banks than most. All that can be known and is worth knowing, I know it.' He could have added that banks also expressed their gratitude by lending him mind-boggling amounts of money to hugely increase his gains – or his losses as he would find out later on – over the course of his fabulous career.

Seeing the dismayed look on our faces, he realised he hadn't scored a bullseye this time. Our hedge fund hero took his leave and we called it a day. Just a few months after our encounter, the financial crisis had got the better of his fund, which had accumulated positions that were now completely illiquid and unsellable. His investors were to lose more than half their equity, but this didn't stop Mick starting afresh and taking up once more his frenetic activity in greener pastures with other investors who in turn would get caught in the headlights of his charm.

Such insular finance is, of course, bad news for the real economy for at least two reasons. The first is that banks, especially in Europe, can only comply with the new Basel ratios by making tough choices on how they allocate their capital. Money allocated to the type of trading activities described above will not be available to satisfy funding requests from businesses. The second reason is that even when these banks are mandated by companies, they cannot absolve themselves of the temptation, conscious or unconscious, to take into account the interests of their other big customers, the financial investors. In an ideal world, the interests of businesses and financial shareholders should converge, however as we know, this doesn't happen in reality.

The CEO of an American listed company recently shared with me the story of a surreal meeting he had with one of his major investors. His company had just announced solid profits, which were below analysts' expectations and he had taken the decision to tour the country explaining the situation to as many shareholders as he could. One of them was a 'deep value' fund specialised in acquiring stakes in companies trading at a steep discount to the value of their underlying assets. This particular meeting lasted just 10 minutes. No sooner had he entered the conference room, than the investor had dismissed the CEO's presentation. He had only one question: 'Why not liquidate the company?' Before the bafflement of the CEO, the investor explained that according to his calculations the company was worth more dead than alive. The solution was straightforward enough: the CEO had to sell the group's real estate, auction off their two or three profitable activities, and distribute the company's cash to investors. When our business leader replied that there was no way he would consider doing such a thing, the investor didn't even try to argue. He simply got up and left.

And this was no ordinary investor. Similar to our friend 'Mick', star of the City, this fund manager is a Wall Street hero, literally adored by bankers who never fail to present potential investment targets to him in the hope of financing his acquisitions. Yet just 20 years ago, this financier was completely unknown; the centre of attention then was the captain of industry, today abandoned in a conference room. The roles have been reversed.

For decades the world of finance represented a major competitive advantage for the West, when it has now become its Achilles' heel. Instead of being an enabler for businesses, the financial sector has set itself up at the heart of the economic system and pushed companies to the outer reaches. And now it is the tail that is wagging the dog. However, I am convinced that this trend is not irreversible. By taking the entire economic system to the brink, finance has effectively shot itself in the foot and now has no choice but to reform itself. Faced with the anger of politicians, regulators, and society in general, the banker will be forced to reinvent himself and return to the basics of his profession. This change will be as beneficial for him as it will be for the entire system.

But let us make no mistake; putting finance back in its rightful place is no silver bullet. The demands of global competition are such today that we must go much deeper. If the capital of our largest corporations remains in the hands of nomadic shareholders, if their executives lose their appetite for risk-taking, and if our entrepreneurs are left by public authorities and banks to fend for themselves, then Western capitalism will end up getting sidelined. It is not only about jostling for supremacy with the emerging powers and their spectacular progression. What is at stake today is our capacity to preserve the prosperity of future generations.

---

1 CEOs of Sainsbury's Fiat, Carrefour, and Bouygues respectively.

2 Collateralized Debt Obligation, a financial instrument known for its complexity and opacity, whose very existence became symptomatic of the excesses leading to the banking disaster of 2008

3 See chapter III, section 5

4 Source: Thomson Reuters Datastream

5 Source: JP Morgan Chase

6 "The life cycle of family ownership: a comparative study of France, Germany, Italy and the UK" by Julian Franks, Colin Mayer, Paolo Volpin, and Hannes Wagner, April 2009

7 Study carried out by Crédit Suisse, September 2011, sample containing 3,568 listed companies in 10 different Asian countries.

8 "Family ownership and firm performance: empirical evidence from Western European corporations", Benjamin Maury, *Journal of Corporate Finance* 12 (2006)

9 Based on asset profitability ("return on assets")

10 Analysis prepared by Eric Bendahan, Banque Syz, September 2012

11 Overperformance of European family-owned companies relative to the Eurostoxx 600 index from 27 April 2002 to 27 April 2012

12 Source: Crédit Suisse

13 Agency Theory drafted and extensively developed by professors Fama and Jensen (1983)

14 Source: Eurostat

15 "The Family Secret Behind the Economic Boom", *The Local*, German Edition, 18 May 2011

16 Zahara, S, "Entrepreneurial risk taking in family firms" *Family Business Review*, 2005

17 Source: Company accounts

18 Mickey Drexler left GAP in 2002 and subsequently took the reins at J.Crew

19 Industry leader by revenues

20 OECD Journal, Financial Market Trends 2011

21 The Conference Board, 2010 Institutional Investment Report

22 Share ownership structure in Europe, Federation of European Securities Exchanges, December 2008

23 "Promoting longer-term investment by institutional investors: selected issues and policies", OECD, 2011

24 Hedge fund performance is often published quarterly

25 Source: OECD, World Federation of Exchanges

26 "How the Robots Lost: High-Frequency Tradings's Rise and Fall", *BusinesWeek*, 6 June, 2013

27 Intrinsic value calculated according to the cash-flow actualisation method

28 Source: Terry Smith, CEO of Tullet Prebon, 2010

29 Science and Technology Indicators, OECD, May 2013 and the Chinese National Bureau of Statistics

30 Science and Technology Indicators, OECD, May 2013

31 Science and Engineering Indicators, 2010

32 The Global Innovation 1000, Booz & Co

33 The 2010 R&D Scoreboard, Department for Business Innovation & Skills, UK

34 The 2010 R&D Scoreboard, Department for Business Innovation & Skills, UK

35 Source: Bloomberg

36 "Made in America (Again), BCG, August 2011

37 Science and Technology Industry Scoreboard, OECD, 2011

38 "Made in America (Again)", BCG, August 2011

39 Source: IHS Global Insight

40 "Firm Performance and Wages: Evidence from Across the Corporate Hierarchy", Brian Bell and John Van Reenen, Center for Economic Performance, London School of Economics, November 2011

41 "What are we paying for? Exploring executive pay and performance", The High Pay Commission, 2011

42 "Performance for Pay? The Relation Between CEO Incentive Compensation and Future Stock Price Performance", Cooper, Gulen, Rau, 2013 Working Paper

43 "Firm Performance and Wages: Evidence from Across the Corporate Hierarchy", Brian Bell and John Van Reenen, Center for Economic Performance, London School of Economics, 2010

44 Parliamentary Commission on Banking Standards, "Changing Banking for Good", June 2013

45 "How costly is the Sarbanes Oxley Act? Evidence on the effects of the act on corporate profitability", A. Ahmed, M. McAnally, S. Rasmussen, C. Weaver, September 2009

46 Coles, Daniel and Naveen. Lehn, Patro and Zhao, 2008

47 "Sarbanes Oxley and Corporate Risk Taking", L. Bargeron, K. Lehn, C. Zutter, March 2008

48 Source: CALPERs, June 2013

49 "US Senate Commerce Committee Report on Product Liability Reform Act of 1997"

50 Theodore Frank, American Enterprise Institute, statement presented to the Senate Republican Conference, March 2009

51 Towers Watson, Directors & Officers' Liability Survey 2012

52 The Global Competitiveness Report 2012/2013, World Economic Forum

53 "Beyond the banks", NESTA, September 2011

54 "Survey on the access to finance of small and medium sized enterprises in the euro area", European Central Bank, 2011

55 "An international comparison of small business employment", Center for Economic and Policy Research, Jonathan Schmitt and Nathan Lane, August 2009

56 Total Early Stage Entrepreneurial Activity ("TEA"), enterprises in existence for less than 3.5 years. Source: Global Entrepreneurship Monitor, M. Hart, J. Levie 2010

57 "Entrepreneurs speak out", Ernst & Young, 2011

58 "Entrepreneurs Speak Out: A Call to Action for G20 Governments", Ernst and Young 2011

59 Rise of 2.7 per cent in IPOs in Europe between 2005 and 2010

60 Greek officials revealed that the transaction allowed them to swap Greek debt stated in dollars for yen and euros using a fictional exchange rate and thus reducing their total debt exposure by around 2 per cent.

Part Two

Their conquests, our recipes: how emerging powers made our entrepreneurial capitalism their own

Chapter 1

Emerging powers: how the war was (almost) won

Two winning models, one horizon

There is something ironic about the *Schadenfreude* of many Western economists and market pundits when they report on the slower growth rates experienced by emerging powers over the last two years. China's new normal of a 7 per cent annual growth rate is depicted as a source of grave concern for the country and the world when, at the same time, Europe is struggling to turn out a positive number and the US's 2.5 per cent figure is cause for celebration.

In truth, whilst emerging countries continue their inexorable march towards economic supremacy, albeit with a few wobbles on the way, we in the West seem to be sleepwalking towards the edge of a cliff. Our politicians belatedly demand blood, sweat, and tears from people who would rather hear about a brighter future. Our business leaders act as mere gatekeepers to businesses under siege. And our financiers pursue their aimless hustle and bustle. In contrast to our 'spontaneous' capitalism, which hopes that the invisible hand will bring prosperity to us all in the end, the emerging economies practice a 'premeditated' capitalism that leaves almost nothing to chance. Whereas spontaneous capitalism expects instant gratification, premeditated capitalism plans for the future and remains in the hands of economic players that can afford to take the substantial financial risks required to meet their ends.

Two distinct models are at the heart of the emerging powers' success today: 'Statentrepreneurial' capitalism and family-centric capitalism. The former, built around close collaboration between the State, cornerstone of the system, and both public and private enterprise, has enabled China and Russia to become growth engines of the global economy and essential powers on the world stage. These two countries have each adopted their own versions of this Statentrepreneurial model, with varying amounts of State in the mix. China chose to open up to capitalism progressively, with the Communist Party keeping control of State-owned companies in virtually every sector while also supporting the emergence of privately funded national champions. The transition was considerably less controlled in Russia. Having lived through the untrammelled capitalism of Yeltsin, the country performed a U-turn in policy. Under Putin, the Kremlin regained control of the biggest companies, either directly or indirectly, in the strategic sectors of energy, mining, defence, and banking. Despite noteworthy differences in the way their respective brands of capitalism came about and in the way they operate, China and Russia share the belief that it is this hybrid economic system that has boosted both their own development as well as their conquest of foreign markets. And, for the moment, history seems to be on their side.

The second model, built up around the great entrepreneurial families acting as both owners and managers of their groups, took India and Brazil to the top in a broad array of manufacturing and service industries. In these countries, private enterprise also cooperates with the still economically powerful public authorities, but in contrast to the former model, the initiative remains by and large in the hands of the private sector. In India, family-owned groups tend to be multi-generational conglomerates that have been around for decades. On the other hand, Brazilian family groups are generally rather less widely diversified and compete for business with listed companies in which the State is often a minority shareholder through its BNDES development bank. This family-led capitalism, more entrepreneurial than dynastic, is also at the heart of the remarkable success of economies such as Mexico and Turkey. Over the next two decades, these two countries will account for a bigger share of global GDP than most European countries.

For those of us who have lived most of our lives in the free-market system begotten by Reagan and Thatcher, the staggering rise of these two models has taken us by surprise, both practically and ideologically. We take the very existence of such Statentrepreneurial capitalism as veritably anachronistic. Following the fall of the Berlin Wall, it seemed to all that the State and business would remain unlikely bedfellows and that it was vital to allow market forces to play their role without inter-ference from public authorities.

Our surprise at China's economic breakthrough is two-fold. First of all, the very fact that mostly State-owned businesses can compete on a global scale shakes up our prejudices. In 2012, 73 Chinese (including Hong Kong and Taiwan) companies featured amongst the Fortune 500 largest corporations in the world, putting China in second place behind the US and ahead of Japan[1]. The majority of these companies are State-owned. At the start of 2013, the Industrial and Commercial Bank of China unseated Exxon Mobil as the world's largest company, while the Chinese Construction Bank moved into the number two spot[2]. The Agricultural Bank of China has also entered the world's top 10 largest companies, with PetroChina and Bank of China lurking just behind. China's largest companies have annual revenues of hundreds of billions of dollars and size up to Western giants such as Walmart, BP, or Nestlé. Even their margins match those of their main competitors in their respective sectors.

The other surprise is that a strong public sector and private enterprise can happily live side by side, and even work together closely. If we include fully State-owned companies as well as businesses in which the State is a reference but non-majority shareholder, the public sector accounts for 40 to 50 per cent of China's GDP compared with over 70 per cent at the end of the 1990s. The private sector has thus made spec-tacular progress, but not, as we imagine in the West, in spite of the State, but rather because of it.

The success of family capitalism throughout the world has further challenged our preconceptions. For almost 20 years now we have grown accustomed to seeing family shareholders retreat to make way for insti-tutional investors, a shift we came to consider as natural and almost inevitable. Over the years, the idea of family capitalism has been dismissed as terribly old-fashioned. Management gurus in our finest universities tirelessly explain that family control can only by definition constitute a transition phase in the life of a business, as company growth requires access to external financing and the public markets. Succession planning is also quoted as an insurmountable issue as it is supposedly impossible to replicate the founder's genius with each new generation. The conventional wisdom is that the younger generations are not hungry for success and are generally more interested in their art collections or charitable foundations than in the balance sheets of the companies they have inherited.

We are also led to believe that conglomerates are relics of the past and by definition value-destructive. With the exception of the American group GE that continues to command our respect, Western managerial dogma considers that a company cannot achieve excellence with, and develop synergies between, activities that are too dissimilar.

The experience of major Indian, Brazilian, Mexican, or Turkish companies clearly invalidates this hypothesis, both in their domestic markets and abroad. Indian groups such as Tata or the Ambani family's Reliance Industries have never failed to find the capital required to fund the development of their historic businesses. In fact the opposite is true. These groups haven't thought twice about investing several billion dollars in launching new businesses where professional managers of American or European listed companies might have considered such diversification inappropriate or overly risky. Moreover, even if the question of succession is never far from their minds, these groups have often managed to juggle family presence and a managerial meritocracy in a culture of excellence.

When trying to understand the increasingly prominent position of Statentrepreneurial and family capitalism in world business affairs, we must realise that the great strength of these two forms of capitalism is their ability to rely on a stable shareholder base, which in turn allows their companies to build for the long term. By contrast, Western business leaders live under the dictatorship of the next analysts' meeting and are required, implicitly or explicitly, to make decisions for tomorrow, not the day after. The State or family shareholder thinks in a very different way.

The second difference is to be found in the perceived relationship between profit and risk. In the Western mindset, the primary mission of senior management is to identify and implement projects generating the best risk-adjusted returns, i.e. offering the best possible returns for a given level of risk. In this way, projects capable of generating solid but below target returns will be systematically rejected. The underlying philosophy is that capital is thin on the ground and that if it is allocated to a sub-optimal project, then the company will be unable to fund those investments that are really worthwhile. While this thinking would seem logical at first sight, it simply doesn't hold up in practice. Western businesses have certainly cut back on their investments, but at the same time stockpiled huge amounts of liquidities that generate almost no return whatsoever. They prefer to buy back their own shares or pay out an exceptional dividend rather than commit capital to projects that don't look like they will generate, within a relatively short period of time, a return on capital employed of at least 15 per cent; a kind of magical threshold that most boards have mysteriously set themselves. This approach condemns Western groups to watching countless projects that fall short of the self-inflicted 15 per cent barrier slip through their fingers. In addition to being wholly unfounded, this profitability threshold prevents these companies from pursuing opportunities that may well have been highly profitable in the long term.

This phenomenon has not gone unnoticed amongst the competition in emerging countries who have stormed through the door left open for them. They have shown a completely different attitude regarding both the perception of risk and the expectations of returns. As they are used to navigating in an unstable political and economic environment, such companies are generally less risk-averse than their Western competitors. And even if their business environments are objectively rife with risk, they don't see it that way. As far as return expectations are concerned, these companies and their shareholders, whether public or private, worry less about opportunity cost than their Western counterparts. Experience has shown that in China and Russia, the strategic shareholder, that is the State, is willing to sacrifice a few years of profitability to pursue and reach its long-term goals. Leading family shareholders in India and Brazil, amongst others, tend to leave most of their personal equity in their businesses, so much so that the question of an alternative use for such capital or of a share buyback is rarely raised, even when the company is listed. If banks' interest rates on deposits are at 5 per cent and the entrepreneur feels that a new project has the potential of greater returns, then he will most probably go for the new project. No arbitrary thresholds, no pseudoscientific calculations to assess the probability of success. The entrepreneur will simply do what he has always done best: utilise his know-how but also his networks and instinct to better his odds of success.

As different as they might be, what Statentrepreneurial and family-led capitalism have in common is a long-term time horizon which has allowed them to gain significant ground over the last few decades. However, as GDP growth in China, India, or Brazil is weakening, it is becoming increasingly common these days to call into question the sustainability of these models. Western commentators tend to perceive these setbacks as the long awaited proof of the inherent fragility of these emerging powers and as early signs of a possible return to the old world order. They are deluding themselves. Without belittling the scale of the reforms still required in many of these countries, their recent woes are mere air pockets on their journey towards economic success. The West's consolation prize, as paltry as it may seem, is that the huge advantages the emerging powers have so far enjoyed are first and foremost the reflection of our own weaknesses. Provided we show a willingness to retrieve the essence of our brand of entrepreneurial capitalism, it is still possible to avoid being pushed to the sidelines and to remain relevant in the global competitive landscape.

The secrets of Statentrepreneurial capitalism

The new Middle Kingdom

Since the 1990s, the Chinese communist regime has set up a hitherto unprecedented economic system that has shattered all the paradigms we had taken for granted for so long. Favouring a gradual, rather than brutal, shift to a free-market economy, the communist State positioned itself at the heart of the system while fostering the emergence of highly effective State-Owned Entreprises (SOEs), often listed on the stock market, and leaders in their respective industries. The regime managed simultaneously to support the creation and development of thousands of private firms in which they play no direct role but which do business in perfect symbiosis with the public sector. While in 1978 the capitalistic entrepreneur was deemed the 'class enemy', by 2001 these same entrepreneurs had earned the right to become full-blown Communist Party members. Some have even become leading party figures since.

It is impossible to understand the success of China today without first understanding the way the titanic, immensely complex, but remarkably effective, public sector functions. China's public sector enables the orderly governing of a nation of 1.3 billion inhabitants and an economy which, before the recent hiccups, had historically grown at close to 10 per cent per annum.

The Chinese public sector still accounts for around half of the country's GDP today and is structured around tens of thousands of SOEs spread out across the breadth of the nation, and taking orders from centralised, regional, or local public authorities. In 2003, The State Council of the National People's Congress ratified the creation of SASACs (State-owned Assets Supervision and Administration Commission of the State Council), which act as holding companies, controlling stakes in State companies that were formerly held directly by the State itself.

The 117 biggest State companies are under the direct supervision of the central SASAC while the others are under the supervision of regional or local SASACs[3]. The central SASAC and the communist party retain control over the entire system through their authority to appoint, promote, or transfer managers and directors to the main State-owned companies. Alongside the SASACs, The Central Organisation Department of the CCP (Chinese Communist Party) acts as a vast human resources department, overseeing the career paths of the main leaders as much within the constellation of State enterprises as within the party itself. However, the most surprising element in a system so dominated by the Communist Party, is that its leaders are promoted and financially compensated according to the profitability they generate for their companies. With an average salary of 88,000[4] dollars per year, these business leaders responsible for revenues of tens of billions of dollars earn less than a junior financial analyst at an Anglo-Saxon investment bank. This has not stopped them becoming formidable managers over the years. Should they succeed, they can look forward to furthering their public sector career, or take one of the many bridges connecting them to private enterprise. Those taking this second route can of course aspire to amassing veritable fortunes.

The effectiveness of the Chinese public economy comes down to its exceptional underlying 'capillary action'. Central State enterprises have all spawned national business groups officially registered as such and including certain key components. At the heart of the group is, of course, the State enterprise itself under the direct authority of the SASAC. The enterprise often holds a majority stake in one or more listed companies in China or abroad. These publicly listed companies comprise the public face of the group however it is easy to forget that they are subsidiaries; the central State enterprise is never listed itself, as the government wishes to remain the sole master of its national champions. Even the listed subsidiaries openly admit that minority shareholders are not their main worry and that their mission is first and foremost to serve their parent company. This is how China Telecom Corp. Limited, listed on the New York Stock Exchange despite 71 per cent of its capital still being held by its parent China Telecom Group, makes no bones about writing in their regulatory documentation for the stock market authorities[5]: 'We will continue to be controlled by China Telecom Group, which could cause us to take actions that may conflict with the best interests of our other shareholders'. It would be difficult to make the message clearer. From CNOOC to Sinopec or the Aluminium Corporation of China, almost all the listed subsidiaries of Chinese State enterprises have made the same type of declaration, showing it is these companies that are exploiting the financial system and not the other way around.

In addition to their listed subsidiaries, the State enterprises at the heart of these 'business groups' acquire holdings, both minority and majority, in a huge number of non-listed companies that can be either other State enterprises or private companies. This has given rise to powerful networks that are used as much to commercial ends, including customers, and suppliers for example, as to financial ends. In this case, the State enterprise plays the role of a veritable venture capital firm.

These 'business groups' always include two additional important components: a banking subsidiary providing the group's companies access to financing at preferential terms and conditions, and a research and development subsidiary. This R&D facility gives group members the chance to pool their research efforts and thus generate considerable economies of scale. These research centres work closely with local universities who are encouraged to harness their top scientific talent to work on applied research projects.

Internal cooperation within these 'business groups' is not the only priority. The SASACs and the party also encourage cross-fertilisation between 'business groups', with the aim of increasing their competitiveness on external markets. In this way, joint ventures have been created in the steel industry, for example, between Baosteel, Wuhan, and Anshan in order to cooperate with the shipbuilding or car industries.

Even though private enterprise is not under the thumb of State bodies, both formal and informal ties with the public sphere are very real. First of all, as we have seen earlier, State enterprises often hold stakes in private companies with whom they have developed working relationships. But beyond these relatively widespread cases, a certain number of medium-sized State enterprises have been floated on the stock market and privatised, the State accepting to hand over control to the management and to other private shareholders. These Chinese-style management buyouts have usually taken place on the sly and have helped former State enterprise and party leaders to build fortunes beyond their wildest dreams. The China Ping An Insurance Company is a case in point. Founded as a State enterprise in 1988 and floated first on the Hong Kong stock market in 2004, then in Shanghai, the biggest shareholders today are the company's executives and staff along with certain Western financial institutions. It is easy to see why this new breed of capitalist – to be found throughout China – has good reason to remain faithful to its former masters.

Then there are private enterprises operating in industries where they are entirely dependent on the goodwill of the authorities to obtain permits. This is particularly so in sectors such as real estate, construction, or mining. In these industries, companies are predominantly in the hands of entrepreneurs, although the local authorities naturally expect their pound of flesh. For instance, a government body owns a 7 per cent stake in China Vanke, the biggest residential real estate company in China founded by Shi Wang. Present in over 20 municipalities[6], the company has become Shenzhen's biggest market capitalisation.

Lastly, the Chinese economy is also made up of millions of genuine entrepreneurs who have set up their own companies and in certain cases built them up into national champions and global leaders in their industries. Lenovo is a perfect illustration. A 1984 start-up christened Legend Computer, and initially funded by the Academy of Science, today Lenovo has become the biggest PC manufacturer in the world. Gome Electrical Appliances is another example, a chain of 800 electrical goods stores founded by Huang Guangyu, the rags to riches story of a peasant's son turned billionaire. The car manufacturer Geely, who bought out Volvo in 2010 and is establishing itself as a major player in the industry, is another example. Thousands of other companies in retail, electronics, or software operate independently of the public realm, secure in the knowledge that should they need to attack new markets, the State will be there to help out.

The official private sector has an unofficial counterpart, operating with the tacit consent of the State who now understands the damage. This underground economy is comprised of thousands of companies, mostly urban SMEs who are not registered and yet employ illegally a vast population of migrant workers prepared to accept extremely low wages. Like millions of other Chinese, these companies have access to financing sourced from a huge underground banking industry. These institutions issue loans in minutes, inevitably lending at prohibitive rates, but they at least provide an alternative to the State banks who often prefer to direct their resources towards other public institutions. These 'shadow banks' also offer individuals investment schemes boasting a much higher return than the high-street banks.

Although statistics are sadly lacking to enable us to grasp the full magnitude of this underground industry, all the observers agree that its importance is considerable throughout the Chinese economy. With household debt having tripled over the last five years, the State has become increasingly aggressive vis à vis unauthorised lenders. Average debt represented 50 per cent of disposable household income at the end of 2011, against 30 per cent in 2008[7]. The level of corporate debt is also a worry having shot up from 90 per cent of GDP in 2007 to 124 per cent at the end of 2012[8]. Official banks were told to slow down their lending, particularly in sectors suffering from overcapacity, but shadow banks were prompt to fill the void. The State is now in a difficult position. It is aware that if it wishes to maintain social peace and avoid threatening economic growth, deflating the credit bubble will be a tough balancing act.

In spite of the complex linkage between public and private sectors, as well as the growing importance of entrepreneurs in the economy, we mustn't forget the pivotal role the public authorities continue to play in the system. As strange as it may seem, it is not because the private sector gains ground that the State weakens its grip. It all begins with a five-year planning process, which strikes us in the West as totally obsolete, and yet forms an authentic roadmap that is painstakingly followed by every single stakeholder of the economy.

The eleventh five-year plan covering the period 2006/2010 had set the consolidation of production facilities in certain traditional industries and quality improvement, particularly through the acquisition of new technologies, as the country's top priorities. The main goal was to further improve China's competitiveness in industries where national champions were in head-to-head competition with Western firms. The plan was, needless to say, a huge success.

The twelfth five-year plan that covers the current period shifts the focus towards rebalancing the economy by making domestic consumption a counterweight to exports. The other featured priority is to speed up the creation of national champions in emerging industries such as biotech and clean energies.

Once these five-year plans are released, the chain of command is clear. Directives are drafted and finalised at regional and industry level while local authorities, SASAC directors and the State enterprises are there to ensure that all the necessary means have been implemented to achieve these objectives.

The fifth plenary session of the fifteenth central committee of the year 2000 gave rise to the governmental directives that have had the most direct and lasting impact upon us Westerners. This is when China's globalisation strategy was first formulated (the policy of *zouchuqu*) and when the largest State enterprises and sovereign funds (principally the China Investment Corporation) officially became the weapons of their overseas conquests. The top priority was, unsurprisingly, the rush for natural resources, followed closely by expansion in finance, transportation, agriculture, and technology. Chosen hunting grounds were, ranked in order of importance: Australia (coal, gas, aluminium), the US (finance), Brazil and Argentina (agricultural raw materials, farmland),

and, of course, Sub-Saharan Africa (energy and mineral ores), a continent where Chinese companies reign supreme. Europe was also in the line of fire, especially in tech-intensive industries.

Over 400 billion dollars have been invested abroad by Chinese companies, and this is the only the beginning[9]. In 2012, Chinese investment in Europe rose by 21 per cent from the year before to 12.6 billion dollars[10]. The latest five-year plan has authorised State enterprises more flexibility in their foreign acquisitions by raising the thresholds above which formal government approval is required. The main instigators of this policy of *zouchuqu* are groups like the financial giant CITIC or COSCO (China Ocean Shipping Group), one of the world's largest shipping companies. According to a recent study[11], four entities alone account for almost half of Chinese overseas investment since 2005. The oil companies CNPC and Sinopec, the metals colossus Chinalco, and the sovereign fund CIC make up this powerful quartet.

The crisis of 2008 was taken as an extraordinary opportunity, and one not to be missed, to step up State enterprise expansion plans. Prime Minister Wen Jiabao made no effort to hide the fact when in July 2009 he addressed an audience of Chinese diplomats and declared: 'We must accelerate the implementation of our globalisation strategy by combining the use of our currency reserves and the expansion plans of our companies'. This sentence packs quite a punch when we consider that today China has over three trillion dollars in reserves at its disposal.

Is this capitalism versus capitalism? Maybe, but comparisons with the situation in the West certainly raise concerns. While our major corporations cut back on investments and prefer to simply hand back their vast cash resources to shareholders, Chinese companies have never invested as much as in recent years and their shareholder is both willing and able to put a few trillion dollars more on the table. Our companies do not lack the financial means, but rather the will to utilise them in projects that won't necessarily show an immediate return. And it is not brains that are lacking either; yet our governments and enterprises don't have the will to plan. In the age of Twitter, the very concept of a plan can inspire mockery. Instant access to information gives us the false impression that a manager's or politician's skill consists in changing tack as fast as is humanly possible upon hearing the latest news. This is an unfortunate and costly mistake, particularly when the main competitors in your business environment know how to stay on course. It is precisely because history is accelerating that we must learn once again how to manage a multi-year planning process. The plan is not necessarily a straitjacket, but rather a tool to help us think collectively about our future priorities, as well as a sort of contract in which parties commit to deploying the human and financial resources necessary to make it happen.

The Chinese example should also encourage us to reconsider the way the State and the private sector interact in the West. Up until the 2008 crisis, the 'small government' way of thinking seemed to have become received wisdom, not only in the Anglo-Saxon world but also across Europe. We expected the State to redistribute wealth as discretely as possible and to avoid interfering with private enterprise at all costs. The financial crisis made us change our attitude here, brutally reminding us that the State is also ultimate arbiter of the system when all other defences have caved in. What we also continue to forget is that somewhere between the redistributive State and the saviour State there is also the *partner* State. Not a partner looking to dominate or dictate its will to private enterprise, but a proactive ally who is ready to help out businesses in need. We in the West have almost completely abandoned the concept of industrial policy, although the State has an important role to play in this area. Industrial policy is not about sending a minister to empathise with picket line strikers in time for the evening news, as we often see on TV, or about nonsensically putting pressure on a struggling company's boss not to close a factory. Genuine industrial policy involves identifying the key industries in which the State is willing to dedicate resources over the long term and stimulating the private sector to better coordinate its efforts. In industries such as energy or the environment for example, close-knit collaboration between the public and private sectors is absolutely essential.

Do we really wish to emulate the Chinese model? Of course we don't. Being more clear-sighted on the strengths of this Statentrepreurial capitalism does not mean neglecting its weaknesses, even less than it means ignoring the brilliance of our free-market capitalism. However, the threat for us in the West is to remain stuck in a post-Thatcherite ideological time warp and fail to step up to the challenges from economic powers where State and private enterprise working together has become a powerful weapon in international competition.

Kremlin Inc.

The other Statentrepreneurial power at the forefront of the economic and geopolitical scene today is Putin's Russia. Unlike China, where a progressive and planned opening up to capitalism took place, Yeltsin's Russia chose unfettered capitalism and dived in headfirst. A huge number of privatisations in a short space of time allowed a small group of individuals to take ownership of the country's resources and build up extraordinary personal fortunes under what could generously be described as dubious circumstances. Some of these oligarchs committed the fatal error of trying to use their wealth to extend their political influence, thus giving the Kremlin the perfect excuse to tighten its grip on the system once more. After the period of post-Soviet chaos, and under Putin's leadership, came a phase of systematic reorganisation of the State apparatus, and the economy as a whole. The highly symbolic arrest of Khodorkovsky for tax evasion, his detention, and the dismembering of his group signalled the start of the Kremlin's campaign to systematically take back control of the country's corporate giants. The message sent out to the other oligarchs could not have been clearer: either accept sharing their power and wealth with the Kremlin and their lives of luxury in London, St Tropez, and Gstaad could continue unhindered; or refuse and end up in a prison cell with 200 other inmates in a penitentiary lost somewhere in the snowy plains of Karelia. The oligarchs were quick to make up their minds.

The State now has direct control over companies in the strategic industries of energy (Gazprom, Rosneft), banking (Sberbank, VT Bank), and defence (Sukhoi). Some of the most important government ministers sit on the boards of these groups which have often been renationalised. In May 2012, Igor Sechin, formerly Deputy Prime Minister of the Russian Federation, one of the most influential characters in the Kremlin, became President of Rosneft, the company that inherited most of the assets of Yukos. Rosneft is now one of the top oil and gas groups in the world after acquiring TNK-BP, the joint venture between AAR, a consortium owned by three oligarchs, and BP.

The economic power of the State is also, and above all, indirect or 'mixed'. A dozen oligarchs who have managed to hold on to assets the

State has not taken over have become vassals of the Kremlin and no longer make any decisions of importance before first referring to the highest authorities. From this perspective, the 2008 crisis represents a turning point as a certain number of these oligarchs had got themselves heavily into debt with Western financial institutions, having put up their own shares as collateral. They were discretely rescued from bankruptcy by the State authorities. The Kremlin released almost 100 billion dollars of which half was deposited in public banks who in turn used a good deal of this money to refinance the debt of those oligarchs closest to power. The other half was used to bolster the capital of national champions such as Gazprom or Rosneft, as well as other companies in industries as diverse as metals, electricity, or automotive. One of the main public institutions used to channel these funds was Vneshekonombank (VEB). VEB made a loan of 4.5 billion dollars to Oleg Deripaska's Rusal, so that he could refinance his foreign bank debt exposure that was guaranteed by 25 per cent of Norilsk Nickel shares, the world's leading producer of the metal. Officially, the government demanded nothing specific in return, but nevertheless imposed its representatives on the board.

In such an environment where credit is used by the State as a tool to exercise influence if not as a blatant means of control, the power of the State-owned banks should not be underestimated. During a trip to Moscow in October 2008, when the credit crunch hit Russian businesses hardest, I had the opportunity to dine with an oligarch who had made his fortune after the first wave of privatisations and was thus less politically exposed than his peers. Having ordered a 5,000-dollar bottle of Romanée Conti and made a special request to the chef for a pizza with truffle topping – a rare find indeed – this character told me how times were tough. He had found himself with his back to the wall, having to pay back two 100 million dollar loans at the same time, one taken out with a State-owned bank, and the other with a privately owned Russian bank. What was he to do? 'I will tell the private bank that I am defaulting on the loan, and I will pay back the State bank their 100 million', he told me with a certain nonchalance. 'But why not pay back half of what you owe to each bank and negotiate a restructuring of your outstanding debt?' I suggested somewhat naively. Our friend gave me a condescending look. 'No, no, you don't understand. You don't fool around with the State banks.' That is when I understood that Russia has a two-speed financial system.

Another company that is symptomatic of this new and opaque mixed economy is Russian Technologies, run by Sergei Chemezov, a former KGB official known as part of Putin's inner circle. Having begun his business career in the automotive and metals industries he succeeded in convincing the Kremlin to turn Russian Technologies into a holding company comprising over 480 State-owned businesses in industries as varied as automotive, aerospace, or defence. Even though it is officially a State-owned company, linkage to the private sector is prevalent at every level allowing group executives and Kremlin senior officials to wield immense power.

By placing their *siloviki* – an informal network of ex-State security personnel – in key positions of the administration and enterprises, the Kremlin's hardliners seem to have taken over from the liberal faction embodied by Dimitri Medvedev. To Putin's credit, the Kremlin's takeover of the main levers of economic power has undeniably maintained a degree of stability in a country whose history has been marked by periods of chaos and even bloody upheavals. From this point of view, he has succeeded where many of his predecessors had failed. At the same time, an unprecedented concentration of power has opened the door to excesses largely covered by the Anglo-Saxon press[12]. The fortunes amassed in just a few years by Gennady Timchenko and Arkady Rotenberg, both close to those in power, are starting to raise eyebrows. In 2003, Gennady Timchenko's Netherlands-based Gunvor was but a small player in the oil business. It is now one of the largest oil trading companies in the world with estimated revenues of 93 billion dollars[13]. Its biggest supplier is the State company Rosneft. Recently things got even more controversial when Novatek, a company in which Timchenko holds a 20 per cent stake, took control of the project Yamal LNG, a vast natural gas field, in which Total is also involved. As for Rotenberg, he made his multi-billion-dollar fortune selling metallic pipes to Gazprom, yet another State company.

In this context of a return of the State's presence in the Russian economy, the 2011 announcement of a series of privatisations worth more than 60 billion dollars came as something of a surprise. However the reality of this wave of sell-offs will change nothing in the Kremlin's ever-tighter hold over the country's main companies. By way of example, we need look no further than the banking industry. The State first encouraged the two largest public banks Sberbank and VTB to buy out many of their smaller competitors, then announced its intent to reduce its stake in these institutions by selling off shares in the marketplace. However whichever way we look at it, the State remains firmly in control. The State raised 3.3 billion dollars by offloading 10 per cent of VTB's capital via a London listing, thus reducing its stake to 75.5 per cent. A new tranche of shares may be sold over the next two years but the State has already announced its intention to retain at least 50 per cent of the capital. It is the same story for Sberbank, the country's biggest bank with balance sheet assets of nearly 500 billion dollars[14] and one of the best run. The State currently holds 57.6 per cent of the capital but aims to put up slightly more than 7 per cent for sale before year end 2013. Control will thus be maintained.

With candidates such as Aeroflot (airline), Sovcomflot (freight), or Sheremetyevo (Moscow airport), FSK (electricity provider), Rosselkhozbank (farming bank), or the national railway company, the privatisation programme certainly doesn't seem to lack ambition. But let us make no mistake; this is in no way a turning point in the Kremlin's politics. The administration has already regained control of these companies over the last few years and is now just raising some cash and throwing a few signs of goodwill and transparency to the West.

Blessed with extraordinary reserves of natural resources, Russia will further strengthen its status of major world power, both economically and geopolitically, over the coming years but its handicaps remain considerable. First of all, the country's demographics seem overwhelmingly problematic. Today the country boasts 142 million inhabitants but loses 700,000 people a year through an extremely low birth rate and a mortality rate that is twice the level of the West's. At this rate the country will count just 100 million inhabitants by 2050. Russia's other disadvantages are well known: a legal system operating under heavy political influence and most of all, widespread corruption at all echelons of society that ends up sapping the country's creative energy. Some think-tanks have estimated that bribery and payoffs amount to 300 billion dollars a year in Russia, or nearly 20 per cent of the country's GDP[15].

The example of Russia should be a warning to the West, as although private and public sector cooperation is certainly less smooth than in China, it still functions with daunting effectiveness. The Chinese have nurtured their national champions in almost every industry whereas Russia has focused on just a few key sectors. But in these sectors the State has wielded all of its financial might and political influence to support its chosen, official and less official, champions. Russian energy or mining concerns don't just make do with exploiting the country's natural resources. They enter into joint ventures with Western groups, make important acquisitions, and have no qualms about going public on the stock markets of the world. If only they would involve their own public authorities in a more up front way, Western companies would be far more effective vis-à-vis their Russian competitors and partners. Bringing in heads of State for the photo-call when a big energy deal has been signed is certainly a good thing, but it is not enough. The political stakes and corresponding financial risks are so high that such contracts require a much greater collaboration, even if it remains informal, between our private and public sectors. Up against these Statentrepreurial powers, we will never be able to win the economic battle if we remain under the illusion that market forces alone will let our corporate giants prevail.

The comeback of family capitalism

Family-led capitalism is the second model prevalent in the emerging world with India and Brazil as its two chief flag-bearers, two countries which, in spite of their recent difficulties, are expected to feature in second and fourth places respectively in the global GDP tables of 2050. Several other countries, such as Mexico and Turkey, also subscribe to this model and will play an increasingly important role, but for the time being we shall focus on the dynamic that has already enabled India and Brazil to take centre stage both economically and politically.

India: the Raj of entrepreneurs

With India's economic growth falling to its lowest level in 10 years[16], it is tempting to put in doubt the country's ability to bounce back and retrieve the momentum which, until recently, had made it one of the most exciting emerging markets globally. Although a number of structural reforms are required to unleash India's full potential, the pessimists gravely underestimate two of the country's greatest competitive advantages. Firstly, the resilience and dynamism of its entrepreneurs and major family groups who, in spite of the numerous hurdles put in their way, have managed to achieve world leading positions in a number of sectors. These family groups have literally carried the country on their shoulders and can largely be credited for the 4 to 8 per cent annual growth rates experienced over the last ten years[17]. Secondly, unlike China, whose economic growth is still fundamentally export-driven, the Indian economy is fortunate enough to benefit from a domestic consumption amounting to around 57 per cent of its GDP[18]. In a country of 1.2 billion inhabitants, this can be a very powerful weapon to regain the upper hand domestically and on the world scene.

What surprises most about India are its contrasts. First and foremost, the contrast between the extraordinary wealth of these industrial dynasties and the extreme poverty of the vast majority of the population. While the country had only five dollar-billionaires just 10 years ago, India now has over 50[19] and yet 42 per cent of the its people still live below the breadline. But also, the contrast between a majority of inhabitants earning a living as traditional subsistence farmers and a state-of-the-art high-tech industry.

Symbolising India's technological prowess are cities like Bangalore, a sort of Asian Silicon Valley, or companies like Infosys, a start-up founded in 1981 that has become one of the world's leading providers of IT services and software employing 145,000 people in 29 countries. The third and final contrast is to be found between a thriving private sector and a still inefficient public sector that nonetheless still makes up a meaningful part of the economy, especially in energy and infrastructure. Although the public sector share is shrinking steadily, the State remains a stakeholder to be reckoned with.

This continuing, paradoxical presence of the State in a country better known these days for its private companies is the product of its history. India has experienced three phases in its economic development. Up until 1991, the year in which India began to deregulate, the economy was dominated by nationalised groups and family-owned groups whose entrepreneurial spirit was strong, but whose presence remained discrete. Family groups tried as best they could to do business in an excessively bureaucratic and over-regulated environment. This was the period known as the 'Licence Raj' where the slightest initiative required a permit, obtainable principally through acquaintances within the Congress Party.

During the second phase that spanned the years 1991 to 2003, the lifting of price controls and the freeing-up of exchange rates sent a shockwave through the system. This liberalising force brutally restructured the economy and forced the hands of many private companies who had no choice but to consolidate or disappear. Competition got even fiercer locally. Several large textile groups that reigned supreme in India for generations collapsed, and those who managed to keep their heads above water like the Mafatlals group became shadows of their former selves.

As difficult as this period of restructuring must have been, it sharpened the efficiency of the Indian economy and its big conglomerates, making way for the spectacular economic boom the country has experienced since 2003. Growth rates had hitherto hovered between 2 and 4 per cent per annum, but suddenly rocketed to 6.8 per cent in 2003 and remained roughly at this level until a couple of years ago. It is during this third phase that the traditional, family-led groups achieved their most spectacular growth. They have been able to increase their market share in industries where they already had a foothold, buying smaller competitors, diversifying into new activities in India, and expanding massively abroad. Over the last decade, Indian groups have spent 129 billion dollars in acquisitions abroad[20].

Tata Group, the most important and iconic in the country, is a perfect illustration. Founded back in 1868 and now run by the remarkable Ratan Tata, a fifth-generation member of the founding family, the group comprises today over 100 operational companies. Thirty-one entities within the group are listed, each one managed independently with its own board of directors and a distinct shareholder base. Tata employs 455,000 people and has consolidated revenues of more than 100 billion dollars, of which 58 per cent is generated overseas[21]. As many other Indian groups, Tata made a significant number of acquisitions abroad, particularly during the 2000s. During the period 1995 to 2003 the group carried out just one acquisition a year whereas during the fiscal year 2005/2006 alone no fewer than 20 companies were successfully acquired. Tata has invested over 20 billion dollars acquiring businesses beyond its own borders, with Great Britain featuring as the prime hunting ground. The first important purchase was Tetley Group, the well-known brand of tea, for 450 million dollars. From then on, transactions became increasingly ambitious. In 2007 Tata Steel bought out Corus, Europe's second largest steelmaker for 12.1 billion dollars and shortly afterwards Tata Motors laid their hands on Jaguar Land Rover (JLR) for 2.3 billion dollars, as well as Daewoo Trucks, the Korean's truck division. Acquiring Jaguar made Tata the biggest private sector employer in Great Britain.

The companies and brands bought by the group are so iconic that some accuse Ratan Tata of embarking on a big game hunt for the industrial crown jewels of the former colonial power. At least for the moment, history would seem to be proving the critics wrong. While Jaguar had turned itself into a financial bottomless pit for its previous owner Ford, Tata pulled off one of the greatest industrial turnarounds in British history. After two years of industrial rationalisation and brand repositioning, Jaguar chalked up profits of more than 1.1 billion pounds sterling for fiscal year 2011/12, compared with barely 15 million the previous year. The next year, Jaguar's pre-tax profits rose again to 1.67 billion pounds sterling. As the curse of deindustrialisation hit Great Britain hard, as it did most of the old Western powers, an Indian shareholder took the markets by surprise announcing his intention to increase headcount by an additional 1,000 employees, taking his total British-based production site staff to 17,000. China has since become Jaguar's top market, and for the first time in the company's history a foreign market has overtaken the British domestic market. Moreover, expansion into other emerging markets will not stop there as Tata now has Russia, India, and Brazil in its sights.

The group's success stories go well beyond Tata Motors. Having acquired Corus, Tata Steel went on to buy Thai Millennium Steel and integrated its various subsidiaries across the globe. Tata Steel is now suffering from the global downturn affecting most players in the steel industry but its situation would have been much worse if it had not been able to derive substantial economies of scale through acquisitions.

Following in the footsteps of GE, and going against the grain of Western management doctrine, Tata believes that business excellence is not necessarily about specialisation, not artificially limiting activities to specific industries. The group clearly doesn't have a problem balancing heavy industry, services, telecoms, food and drink, and chemicals. In each of these industries, as dissimilar as they are, the group has managed to work its way up to the worldwide or regional top slots. First, IT services with Tata Consulting Services, one of the world leaders in software, recently overtaking their world-renowned local competitors Infosys and Wipro. Hotel services too with Taj running one of the biggest luxury hotel networks in India. Telecoms where Tata Communications is one of the leading providers of wholesale voice transport, particularly in emerging countries. Chemicals, where Tata Chemicals is the world's second largest sodium carbonate producer. And finally in the food and drinks industry where Tata Global Beverages has moved up to second place in the tea business, just behind the corporate giant Unilever.

Indian groups' extraordinary ability to diversify both vertically (from manufacturing to sales) and horizontally (between industries that would appear to have nothing whatsoever in common) is a complete mystery to our Western eyes. It can be explained in part as a product of India's own history where State inefficiency, hindering bureaucracy, and inadequate infrastructure forced companies to do themselves what they would normally have subcontracted out to third parties in a more stable environment. This is the 'soft state' theory as put forward by Krishna Palepu, one of my former professors at Harvard Business School. The other explanation is that the country was subjected to tight control of capital flow for so long that Indian families, prevented from reinvesting their dividends abroad, had no other choice but to opportunistically and eclectically set up new businesses in India.

Although these factors are certainly part of the story, they are probably somewhat simplistic. We tend to forget that above and beyond their specific circumstances, Indian entrepreneurs have simply managed to retain a taste for industrial initiative and a respect for their family heritage. Unlike their Western counterparts, they have been lucky enough to avoid the iron hand of the public markets and the correspondingly rigid and somewhat artificial governance standards. No shareholders demanding the sale of 'non-strategic' activities or imposing their dogmatic vision of 'shareholder value'. No boards dominated by independent directors emotionally and intellectually disconnected from both the history and the destiny of their companies. In fact, a business environment not at all dissimilar to that of Great Britain, France, or even the US of just a few decades ago, before financial capitalism booted out entrepreneurial capitalism. We should give these Indian families the credit they deserve. They have continued to run their businesses far from the noise of the markets, driven by the will to ensure the long-term future of their groups. Of course these families are interested in making money, but how could we hold this against them? However, their ambition is, above all, to build over time.

As well as Tata, the same qualities are to be found amongst countless other Indian families who head up similarly sprawling conglomerates and who have also actively pursued their expansion abroad. Amongst the oldest families are the Aditya Birlas, now in their fourth generation, leaders in mobile telecoms, cement, textiles, and metals. One of their biggest acquisitions was Novelis, the American aluminium producer for 6.2 billion dollars in 2007. In 2011 they bought Columbian Chemicals, another American company for 875 million dollars. Mahindra is another example, the family's third generation, operating in finance, hotels, and the automotive industries. In 2010, the Mahindra group bought the Korean car manufacturer Ssangyong which was then in receivership, and is now in the throes of restructuring. Amongst the more recent dynasties, the Ambani brothers, with their endless squabbles and immense fortune, have earned themselves a special place in the hall of fame of the country's most powerful families. First of all Mukesh Ambani, fourth richest man in the world with a fortune of 29 billion dollars[22], runs Reliance Industries, an energy and chemicals behemoth. And then there is his younger brother Anil Ambani, 36th on the world's rich list, and who, following the company split in 2005, took control of the telecom, infrastructure, energy, and media activities from within Reliance.

Indian family capitalism is not just dynastic, far from it. Some of the biggest groups find themselves in the hands of self-made entrepreneurs whose sheer boldness has enabled them to build up veritable empires. The Ruia brothers and their Essar group are an interesting case in point. Founded in 1969 by Shashi Ruia and his brother Ravi, the group is involved in energy, electricity, telecommunications (via a joint venture with the British company Vodafone), shipping, and ports, and employs 73,000 staff in 20 countries for annual revenues of around 40 billion dollars[23]. It is a similar story for Sunil Mittal's family, not to be confused with Lakshmi Mittal, who won one of the four mobile phone licences in the government sell off of 1992 and transformed his group into the country's leading mobile phone provider and the world's fifth largest with over 190 million customers in 19 countries. In 2010, the group bought Zain Africa, one of the continent's biggest mobile operators for 10.7 billion dollars. This transaction constituted the second biggest overseas acquisition ever made by an Indian group, proving once more their reluctance to just make do with being leaders in their domestic market. The Bharti group also diversified into television, distribution, and finance.

Amongst these entrepreneurs there are also countless typically Indian success stories, like Azil Premji, the owner and CEO of Wipro who transformed a cooking oil producer into a leading group in the IT outsourcing, software, and medical equipment industries. Headquartered in Bangalore Wipro now employs more than 145,000 people and had revenues in excess of 7 billion dollars in 2012/13[24]. When analysing India and companies like Wipro, we should not waste any time trying to identify possible synergies between the diverse businesses which can be found within the same groups. There are none. More often than not the only tangible synergy turns out to be the founder's boundless sense of entrepreneurship.

We cannot of course complete our picture of the dominant Indian families without mentioning the Mittals and the Hindujas, two families who have built their fortunes predominantly overseas and are thus not considered as part of the inner circle of Indian capitalism. To think so would be a mistake, as both in their business culture and operational methods the Mittals and the Hindujas are perfect examples of the kind of inventiveness and entrepreneurial drive that characterises their country's brand of capitalism. Starting out in the 1970s with just one Indonesian steel mill, Lakshmi Mittal's group is now the world's leading steel producer with annual revenues of over 80 billion dollars in 2012[25]. The next generation is already in place: his son Adit, CFO of Arcelor and a board member, is recognised as a highly talented businessman while his daughter Vanisha is also an active non-executive member of the board. Unlike most other Indian families, the Mittals have stayed focused on their core business and have never attempted to build a conglomerate. Notwithstanding this, the London-based Hinduja brothers are by no means an exception to the rule, their group operating in a great many industries, notably automotive, defence, chemicals, oil, and banking.

The Indian miracle has its limits, however. Despite the country's reputation for technological leadership, research and development spending in more traditional areas remains poor. Where Chinese companies have become highly proactive in R&D, their Indian rivals tend to follow rather than lead. Moreover, backwardness in infrastructure and public sector inefficiencies have become endemic issues which often prevent Indian businesses from providing their customers with service on a par with international standards. The government seems to share concerns to solve these problems but for the time being inertia prevails. Certain measures have been taken to restimulate growth (the opening of multi-brand retailers and civil aviation to foreign companies for example) but progress is still far too slow.

The complexity of these family-owned groups' capital is another source of worry. Indian families have become adept at retaining control of their corporate empires through a cascade of holding companies, some of them listed, with minority investors at every level. They have yet to suffer as a result of these opaque arrangements, although one day, when these groups are required to raise considerable sums of cash and knock on the doors of international investors, they will have no choice but to simplify their structures. Vedanta, the London-listed metals and natural resources concern founded by Anil Agarwal, provides a useful example for the others to follow, having recently announced its intention to merge several Indian subsidiaries and review its organisation and capital structure.

In spite of these obstacles, Indian capitalism has become a global force to be reckoned with, able to rely on its strong domestic market as well as on the ability of its family conglomerates to expand aggressively abroad, both in the East and in the West. We should take the success of these groups as a wake-up call and a challenge. A wake-up call first because for decades we felt entitled to sermonise to them when we would have done better trying to learn from their example.

The rise of these groups is also a challenge as their international expansion brings them increasingly into direct competition with our own corporations. They enter this race run on our home turf with certain handicaps but with one enormous advantage: their decision-making process. The lightning speed and boldness with which these groups take multi-billion dollar investment decisions commands respect. Mittal Steel's 2005 purchase of Arcelor is a perfect example. Where, after months of dithering, Western company directors would doubtless have deemed the opportunity too high-risk, the Mittals, father and son Adit, took just weeks to green-light the 23 billion dollar operation, the biggest ever in the steel industry. Similarly, if Ratan Tata had been in charge of a Western group, we can be sure that his board would have used the usual arguments to prevent him buying out Jaguar. And yet history has shown how successful these two operations were to prove to be. Without a doubt, the Raj of the Indian entrepreneur has only just begun.

Brazil: can the country of *jeitinho* become a great emerging power?

Gone are the days when China's seemingly unquenchable thirst for commodities produced in Brazil propelled the country's external accounts to new heights whilst a strong currency increased the purchasing power of most Brazilians. For the past three years, GDP growth has slowed significantly, the real has lost 25 per cent of its value, and mass protests are casting doubts on Dilma Roussef's ability to convince voters that she has solutions to their problems. Yet, it is easy to forget that Brazil went through much harder times in the past and nevertheless managed to bounce back and create an economy which, until 2010, was one of the most dynamic in the region. Commentators also forget that, like India, Brazil is home to some of the most successful entrepreneurial dynasties in the world, companies which will undoubtedly be at the forefront of the country's fight to retrieve its economic health in the next few years.

Not too long ago, Brazil was cited as one of the prime contenders to increase its contribution to the IMF, a surreal state of affairs when we remember the disastrous state of their public finances in the 1990s. Between 1990 and 1995 inflation averaged 764 per cent per annum while public debt continued to hit record highs. Deregulation of the economy was kicked off in 1990 by Fernando Collor and his government, but it wasn't until 1994 that, under the leadership of Fernando Henrique Cardoso, the Brazilian miracle would come into being. Cardoso succeeded in fighting his country's rampant inflation, introducing a new currency indexed to the dollar. In less than two years, his gamble paid off and the country's economy stabilised to such an extent that by 1999 the government had decided to float the real. The other key element in Cardoso's programme involved putting up a large number of State companies for sale. Between 1990 and 2002 both the local and federal authorities raised more than 87 billion dollars through the privatisation of 165 companies.

This wave of privatisations had a huge impact on the Brazilian economy as a whole, allowing its hitherto poorly managed major groups to restructure, and even in certain cases to achieve global leadership positions in their respective industries. Take the example of Embraer. Founded by the State in 1969, this specialist aviation manufacturer got off to a good start through its joint venture with the Italian firm Alenia and the ensuing AMX range of fighter planes. However, in a highly competitive market, Embraer was unable to hold its position for long and ran into trouble at the beginning of the 1990s. The 1994 privatisation opened up opportunities for the company to reposition, and in just a few years it would become the civil aviation leader for small and medium-sized planes used by regional airlines and business travel. Today exports account for more than 95 per cent of revenues.

Other success stories include the oil giant Petrobras, now the twentieth biggest company in the world[26] and who in 2010 pulled off the largest ever market transaction in history, raising over 70 billion dollars; Vale, a global leader in mining, excelling in the production of iron-ore, nickel and copper amongst other minerals and whose market capitalisation today exceeds 125 billion dollars; CSN, Brazil's largest steel producer, whose pre-privatisation production methods were reminiscent of the industrial revolution and who is now up amongst global industry leaders after having undergone extensive restructuring in just a short space of time.

Throughout this period of deregulation, the State-owned Brazilian National Development Bank (BNDES) played a vital role. BNDES was initially the State's executive arm, supervising the privatisation process and lending large sums of money to both public and private companies. Later, via its BNDESPAR subsidiary, the bank bought minority stakes in many private companies, both listed and non-listed. These holdings of between 15 and 20 per cent[27], didn't grant the Brazilian State a veto, but enabled it to maintain a steady supply of capital to companies that wouldn't necessarily have had access to venture capital or the market financing. Overall, BNDES's portfolio of listed holdings accounts for about 4 per cent of the Brazilian market, or 50 billion dollars.

Despite the historical importance of the role played by the public authorities in the economy and the country's business activities, placing Brazil in the same category of State-led capitalistic models as China or Russia would be a mistake. Brazilian capitalism is above all a capitalism of entrepreneurs who have proven their ambition and considerable adaptability – the famous *jeitinho* or resourcefulness Brazilian style – particularly when the country was going through tough times.

A perfect illustration of the dynamism of Brazilian family capitalism is the conglomerate Odebrecht, founded in 1944 and now managed by the family's third generation. Given its size, diversification, and strong family culture, the group recalls many of the Indian companies described above. Odebrecht boasts a staff of 175,000, and operates in 11 different industries including construction, engineering, petrochemicals, ethanol and, infrastructure. The group has beaten all growth records, ramping up revenues from 4.2 to 41.3 billion dollars[28] in just the last 10 years. Like Ratan Tata, the company's boss Marcelo Odebrecht never tires of explaining that his group's diversification is by no means the result of some masterplan, but rather the embodiment of the family's will to keep up the entrepreneurial spirit from one generation to the next. Devolving decision-making processes is at the heart of the company's philosophy, picking out the best managers for each of the group's businesses, getting them to buy into the company's culture and history and training them to be its future architects. Group founder Norberto Odebrecht coined this culture the "Odebrecht Entrepreneurial Technology" (TEO) and established a set of guidelines which are still the pillars of the group's philosophy today.

Another example of the extraordinary dynamism of Brazilian family groups is Votorantim, a conglomerate with interests in cement, mining (aluminium, zinc, nickel), steel, paper, food, and finance with the country's third largest bank Banco Votorantim. The group described by the *Wall Street Journal* as 'a kind of tropical General Electric' today has revenues of more than 18 billion dollars[29] and employs almost 100,000 people. The founder's grandson Antonio Ermirio de Moraes runs the company along the lines laid out by Marcello Odebrecht: autonomy and accountability for all business line leaders along with the upholding of the family culture as a vector of entrepreneurship.

The champions of Brazilian family capitalism are not only multi-generational companies. Many were set up by brilliant entrepreneurs who grew their companies on a grand scale in spite of years of disastrous economic conditions. The country's two most emblematic entrepreneurs have to be Jorge Paulo Lemann and Eike Batista albeit with very different destinies. Having founded Banco Garantia and built it up into one of the country's premier investment banks, Lemann took control of AmBev who would become the leading brewer in Latin America. In 2004, AmBev merged with the Belgian Interbrew (owner of the Stella Artois brand) and the resulting company InBev went on to grow, organically and externally to become the world's number one brewer.

Eike Batista's career path was no less meteoric. An entirely self-made man, Batista turned his EBX group into one of the major Brazilian conglomerates with five companies listed on the Bovespa in industries as diverse as mining (MMX), oil (OGX), energy (MPX), logistics (LLX), and offshoring (OSX). In 2011, he was listed by Forbes as the 8th richest man in the world with a fortune estimated at 30 billion dollars. Unfortunately for Batista, market reality caught up with him. His flagship oil company OGX revealed that its wells in production had flopped which triggered a 90 per cent drop of its stock price and cast doubts on the entire group. Batista's fortune reportedly melted to one or two billion dollars but the story of this former boat racer is no less symptomatic of the raw entrepreneurial drive which, for better and occasionally for worse, can be found in some of these emerging powers.

There can be no doubt that heavy industry, mining, and energy dominate the country's economic mix, but major entrepreneurial concerns have achieved breakthroughs in sectors that one doesn't usually associate with Brazil. This is the case for Natura Cosmeticos, founded in 1969 by Luiz Seabra, now at the top of the cosmetics and healthcare products industry through an original positioning with an environmentally friendly slant. The company refuses to use models to promote its image, calling instead on women with whom their customers can identify. Natura markets its products directly through an 800,000-strong network of consultants paid on a commission basis, similar to the Tupperware business model. Group revenues have today reached 3.2 billion dollars with 6,000 staff and was floated in 2004. Almost 40 per cent of revenues is achieved through sales of products launched over the last two years.

Like their Indian counterparts, Brazilian groups have expanded globally, particularly in the US and emerging countries. They have taken advantage of their brazenly healthy balance sheets and, from a time, the strength of the real to buy up companies that give them access to new markets. Vale pulled off one of the biggest ever foreign acquisitions when they bought the Canadian group Inco for 18 billion dollars. Family groups have enjoyed a similar fate. In recent years InBev bought the American brewer Anheuser Bush for 52 billion dollars. The food-industry leader Marfrig swallowed its American rival Keystone Foods for 1.25 billion dollars to become one of the biggest meat suppliers for Subway and McDonalds. JBS Friboi, another food-industry family concern acquired the American Pilgrim Pride. Votorantim took major holdings in several leading cement companies such as the Portuguese Cimpor, the Argentinian Avellaneda or the Uruguayan Artigas. Gerdau, run by the eponymous family's third generation, bought out Ameristeel. Examples abound ad infinitum. These companies are gaining the upper hand over Western buyers who have been hibernating since the 2008 crisis. They also have a crucial advantage over the Anglo-Saxon private equity funds who find it more difficult to borrow money from the convalescing Western banks. The window of opportunity for these companies is thus huge.

Brazil isn't just interested in winning over the West, far from it. The country has been increasingly leveraging its vast natural resources to become an unavoidable partner for other major emerging countries such as China. Brazilian ultra-deep offshore oil reserves could soon catapult the country into the fourth slot of the world's oil producers behind Russia, Saudi Arabia, and the US. By 2020 Petrobras will be able to produce four million barrels per day.

As a whole, Brazilian exports to China have soared from 1.1 billion dollars in 2000 to more than 41.2 billion dollars in 2012[30], thus making China Brazil's number one trading partner. The bulk of these exports are made up of commodities from the agricultural, mining, or energy industries. Now Brazil is paying a heavy price for this over-dependence.

Over the years, relations between Brazil and China have become so intertwined that it is hard to tell today which country is more dependent on the other. Brazil has certainly found in China an insatiable importer of its raw materials, but Chinese expectations for compensation in return are considerable. For example in 2009 China took advantage of the stir created by the global financial crisis and lent 10 billion dollars to Petrobras in return for their commitment to supply them with oil for the following ten years. This is how China skilfully brought the entire African continent to heel. However this is not the end of Sino- Brazilian inter-dependence, as China has become one of the most important foreign investors in Brazil. In 2010 the Chinese giant Sinopec spent 7.1 billion dollars for a 40 per cent stake in Respol-YPF, owner of exploration rights on two important oilfields. The China Brazil Business Council (CBBC) considers that Chinese investments in Brazil have reached 12.6 billion dollars, an ever-increasing figure. Between 1990 and 2009, Brazil only made up on average 3.5 per cent of Chinese investment in Latin America, whereas now that share has risen to 43.4 per cent[31]. And there can be no room for doubt regarding the political and strategic nature of these investments, as 99 per cent were made by Chinese State enterprises in close cooperation with the government[32].

Despite the undeniable success of its economy, Brazil still has considerable challenges to face up to. The riots of summer 2013, which saw a quarter of a million Brazilians take to the streets, highlighted the cross-roads that Brazil finds itself at currently. Long periods of growth have seen millions of Brazilians lifted out of poverty, though millions of its citizens remain among the world's cripplingly poor. Expectations of the 2014 World Cup and the 2016 Olympics are high, but so are griev-ances over the billions of dollars earmarked for stadiums that many feel would be better spent on lifting yet more of the population out of poverty. An increasingly better-educated middle class is demanding more from the country's leaders and more, better public services in return for their taxes. The State apparatus remains highly inefficient and is a permanent headache for businesses. The 2013 'Doing Business' World Bank rankings put Brazil in the 156th slot for the criterion 'ease of paying taxes' with SMEs spending on average 2,600 hours a year on such matters. The country managed only 121st position for 'ease of setting up a company'.[33] Excessive red tape is one thing, but social inequality is quite another, with millions of people still living in favelas in squalid conditions. It is foreign companies who have developed cut-price products targeting these populations where the informal econ-omy still rules, when many Brazilian companies seem oblivious to what is happening on their own doorsteps. Another issue is the over-depend-ency of the Brazilian economy on the country's natural resources, and its reluctance to invest more in research and development. The share in exports of natural resources compared to that of manufactured goods is at its highest level for 40 years and the country still refuses to up its R&D spend. If Brazil is serious about building for the future, the coun-try will have to start thinking about how it can rebalance its economy. Guido Mantega, the country's finance minister, is trying to address the issue by launching an ambitious investment drive, including an infra-structure programme to build road and railways through concessions, the privatisation of airports, and the sale of oil blocks. But will he go far enough?

It is nevertheless an absolute certainty that the extraordinary transfor-mation of Brazil into a 192 million-strong major emerging power will go down in history as one of the geopolitical and economic turning points of the century. And this new power is also a great democracy, which can but help put Western minds at rest. It is nonetheless regret-ful that the West should have taken a backseat for so long, watching disbelievingly while both Brazil and India blossomed instead of becoming a strategic trading partner, a role China now monopolises. Once more the same damaging combination of complacency and prejudice – both managerial and maybe even colonial – has biased our better judgment and prevented us from seizing unique opportunities. We were either unwilling or unable to believe that these formerly public sector groups or family-owned conglomerates would ever be a match for our businesses. We were even less ready to accept that some of them would be so bold as to acquire some of our oldest and most prestigious corporations and manage them with much more talent than we had shown at their helm. We must learn from these mistakes and re-examine the managerial dogma which, for too long, has been holding back our companies in a rigid and outmoded vision of value creation.

The domestic victory: the creation of a new middle class

Conquering foreign markets will always be a strategic priority for the major emerging powers, however a new front is opening up, that of their own domestic markets. At stake here is the rise of the new middle classes and the huge potential markets created to fulfil their ever-increasing consumer needs. Of course local groups have a head start, but competition has become global as a few big Western corporations are starting to understand the sheer magnitude of the opportunity and are actively trying to position themselves, sometimes against the odds. There can be no doubt that in the coming decades, the growth of the middle classes within the major emerging countries will be a determining factor in the new world order.

A few figures help illustrate the extent of the changes underway. Ten years from now, the middle classes in Asia (excluding Japan)[34] will outnumber those in the US, the European Union, and Japan put together[35]. China alone will have overtaken the US in 2020 and the European Union in 2027 while India will outstrip the US by 2021 and the European Union by 2026. Perhaps even more surprising is that Indian middle classes will outweigh their Chinese counterparts by 2023.

The absolute numbers are as impressive as the relative trends: while 1.8 billion individuals currently belong to the middle classes globally, they will reach 4.9 billion in 2030, 85 per cent of this growth coming out of Asia. Over this same period, middle-class spending will rocket from 21 trillion dollars a year to more than 56 trillion with over 80 per cent of the growth coming once more from Asia, principally China and India. While just a short time ago these two countries accounted for under 5 per cent of global consumption amongst the middle classes, in just 20 years their contribution will hit 40 per cent. According to analysts at the Nomura bank, retail sales in China will overtake comparable spending in the US from as early as 2014 onwards.

Although they are often linked in the minds of the general public, realities in China and India are in fact very different. In China the main driver of middle-class expansion is government policy as stated clearly in the 12th five-year plan, which aims at rebalancing the country's economy through the stimulation of domestic consumption as opposed to exports. To achieve this goal, the State wants to foster labour-intensive industries such as transport, logistics, and hotels. It has also been supporting pay increases and has broadened access to social security and pension schemes. As their standard of living rises, the Chinese – who still have one of the highest levels of savings in the world – will be induced to spend more.

The Indian economy is already somewhat better balanced, with post-crisis consumption at around 57 per cent of GDP, much higher than China and close to Japan. Growth in the Indian middle classes is therefore more demographics-driven. India has one of the youngest populations in the world with a median age of just 26 (compared to 36 in China[36]). If the Indian economy continues to grow at a rate of 5 to 7 per cent per year over the next 10 years, then household income could almost treble[37] and thus contribute to a dramatic rise in an extremely dynamic middle class. Urbanisation will also be a key factor. Whereas in China 47 per cent of the population live in cities, in India the urban population amounts to just 30 per cent of the total[38]. Growth potential amongst city-dwellers in both countries is therefore very high.

Moreover, as the standard of living of a population improves, the way they spend their money changes dramatically. Whereas traditionally the lion's share of spending went on basic products like food or clothing, the middle classes tend to spend an ever-increasing proportion of their budget on transport, leisure activities, healthcare, or consumer goods. Companies in such industries, be they local or foreign, should do extremely well over the years to come,

Even if China and India are undeniably the region's two main powerhouses, it would be foolish to underestimate the importance of the new middle classes in countries like Indonesia with its 240 million inhabitants or Vietnam and its 85 million population. As the middle classes in these countries expand, Asia is destined to become the centre of gravity of global consumption.

Brazil along with a few other Latin American countries however will not be far behind. A recent study[39] showed that households earning between 1,064 and 4,591 reals a month (587 – 2,535 dollars) accounted for 42 per cent of the population in 2004 but 52 per cent today. The legal minimum wage in Brazil has almost doubled in the last few years whereas the child benefit 'Bolsa Familia' programme has been made available to more than 12 million underprivileged households. Higher up the social scale, the standard of living of the upper middle classes has also improved dramatically in recent years. There are more Tiffany jewellery shops in São Paulo today than in any other city in the world. Louis Vuitton makes its highest margins per square metre in its São Paulo outlet. Potential growth in mass-market product consumption is also considerable. There are more than 165 million mobile phones in circulation in Brazil today. However, consumer goods companies are not the only beneficiaries of this trend. Financial institutions are obviously not far behind. Consumer credit alone has grown by 28 per cent over the last three years and mortgage lending, which still accounts for only 2 per cent of GDP compared to 85 per cent in the US, is bound to become much more common in the next few years.

Drawn by the lure of the enormous market opportunities created by the emergence of these middle classes, countless Western companies have rushed into these new Eldorados with an innocence and eagerness which often ended up costing them dearly. For example, Danone had an unfortunate experience in its joint venture with Wahaha, the leading Chinese non-alcoholic beverage company. The French group was forced to break off this joint venture in 2009, having accused Wahaha and its founder Zong Qinghou of having taken advantage of their agreement to cut highly lucrative parallel deals. Danone's story is perhaps one of the least damaging, as often there is much more at stake than just money. Chinese companies almost always require their partners to provide them with specific technologies that they then freely exploit outside the joint-venture framework. Eager to be the first to capture the enormous potential in high-speed rail transportation in China, the German group Siemens ended up paying a high price. Siemens now competes head to head with Chinese companies who market products worldwide using the very same technologies 'transferred' within the joint venture.

Western companies are aware of such risks. They know full well that it will be near impossible to protect themselves but the business potential is so great that they are nevertheless happy to enter into partnerships which will most likely come back to haunt them. One of the most recent examples concerns the American group GE who set up a joint venture with the State's Aviation Industry Corporation of China (AVIC). According to the terms of this deal, GE is to provide the Chinese with one of the world's most sophisticated onboard electronics systems as used in the Boeing 787 Dreamliner. The first customer of the GE-AVIC joint venture will be Commercial Aircraft Corporation of China, another State company who is developing and building the C919, an aircraft planned for 2016, capable of transporting 200 passengers and targeting directly the Boeing 737's and the Airbus 320's market. For the time being GE seems to be benefitting from these agreements, but who knows what will happen tomorrow.

When these Western companies set out to conquer emerging countries – often so ingenuously – they run risks beyond those associated with technology transfer. They are also relentlessly subjected to political and bureaucratic vagaries. When in 2004 the bank HSBC took a 20 per cent stake in Bank of Communications, a minor Chinese State bank and the only one at the time acquirable by private shareholders, the transaction seemed more than promising. HSBC's spirits were dampened when the Chinese authorities changed their minds having witnessed the tremendous growth of Bank of Communications and suddenly decided to block third-party takeovers. India is not exempt from such problems. The Norwegian and Russian telecom providers Telenor and Sistema learned this lesson to their cost when their mobile network licence was revoked while they had already invested more than 5.8 billion dollars to develop their activities in the country.

Other Western groups such as Procter & Gamble and Unilever have had more luck and are steadily turning emerging countries into the cornerstone of their expansion. These groups use their joint ventures as a tool to become more familiar with local practices and to adapt their products or business models to suit the specific needs of these markets. Should the potential prove worth their while, they don't mind buying up their local partners at premium prices. This is also the path taken by Starbucks and Coca-Cola with a good deal of success.

Furthermore, these groups are ambitious. Emerging countries already account for 55 per cent of Unilever's revenues, a share that the group wishes to take to 70 per cent in the not too distant future. Nestlé is following suit and has already opened up several R&D facilities in the region. These groups are constantly adapting to local tastes, developing specific products at highly competitive prices for the largest possible number. Their marketing strategy consists of providing consumers with an entry point to their product ranges and then expanding the offer as their purchasing power grows.

One of the most determined Western companies when it comes to expanding in emerging countries and probably the best positioned to benefit from the rise of the middle classes is undoubtedly the retail giant Walmart. Having opened its first store in China in 1996, the group now possesses over 390 outlets with plans to open 100 more stores by 2016[40]. The founder Sam Walton has his photo on display in each of the group's immense stores, and Chinese employees seem to treat him with an awe that usually reserved for Chairman Mao. But the parallels don't stop there. The sheer vastness and power of the group that boasts a staff of 2.1 million and revenues worthy of national GDP figures, combined with authoritarian management tendencies makes Walmart an unexpected but near-natural ally of the Chinese regime.

Walmart launched its activities in Brazil at about the same time as in China and now has 562 stores. Such impressive growth was both organic and the result of its policy of targeted acquisitions. Walmart first put its hands on a 118-strong chain of stores when it purchased Bompreço in the Northeast of the country, then 140 additional stores when it bought Sonae in the South. Today the group is cited as a potential buyer of the 236 Brazilian stores owned by French group Carrefour.

In India where the big retail groups were legally prohibited from distributing their goods directly to local consumers, Walmart took a different route, setting up a joint venture with the Bharti group. Held in equal proportions by its two main shareholders, Bharti Walmart is now a chain of 20 stores[41]. From Carrefour to Metro all the major global retail groups have grasped the significance of emerging markets. While sales in the West remain flat or falling, the Indian retail market alone has grown to represent over 500 billion dollars of sales per year, one of the world's most promising. Western retailers are however up against an Indian government who makes no bones about the preference for 'buying Indian'. While the authorities had accepted in principle that Western retailers could take a controlling stake in local retailers, the government changed its mind at the end of 2011, reverting to the rigid and discriminatory position it had held previously.

The protectionist attitude of Indian and Chinese governments, together with their demands in technology transfer or governance in joint-ventures, expose the West to a harsh reality we have long tried to ignore. In this global battle for the new middle classes we are not competing on a level playing field. As paymasters of the Western governments, emerging powers are now able to impose their corporations upon us and our markets. As exporters, as well as buyers of Western companies and assets, the major Chinese, Indian, or Brazilian groups no longer meet with any kind of resistance whatsoever. Is the reverse also true? In return for the ever-wider opening up of our markets have we benefitted from an equally fair treatment on the part of public authorities in the emerging countries? Not in the slightest. Western groups doing business in emerging countries still have to put up with the most arbitrary conduct, both politically and legally. When our heads of State set out for China or India, cap in hand, asking them to come to the euro's rescue, or to sign a contract that might save some of our industrial dinosaurs from extinction, their interlocutors understand just one thing: the US and Europe are at their mercy.

In the West, the high priests of free trade depict the rise of emerging countries' middle classes as the opportunity of the century for our businesses.

They believe that as these populations reach Western standards of living, their governments will be naturally inclined to remove trade barriers and let our groups develop unhindered. For them it is only a matter of time before the International Consumer will sweep aside everything in his wake, leaving our free-market model to dominate the world. This is however a naive and dangerous way of thinking. The emerging powers have already adopted their own models and have no intention whatsoever of changing them. Their models are built on a frighteningly pragmatic vision of the balance of economic power, one which has positioned their local companies to be by far the main beneficiaries of their own middle classes' prosperity in the years to come. The irony of it all is that such models are the very same models that made Western capitalism so hugely successful: a strong State working hand in hand with entrepreneurs who form the cornerstone of the economy. It would seem that some lessons from our rise and subsequent decline have not been lost on everyone.

---

1 Source: Forbes

2 Source: Forbes Global 2000, April 2013

3 See: www.sasac.gov.cn

4 In 2009. Source: *The Economist*, 21 January 2012

5 China Telecom Corporation Limited, Form 20F, 2011

6 Source: CCER Database

7 Source : Peterson Institute for International Economics

8 Source : JP Morgan

9 US-China Economic Review Commission, October 2011 and IMF Stock of ODI

10 "Nice to see you, EU", *The Economist*, 20 April 2013

11 Global Investment Tracker, Derek Scissors, July 2011

12 "Midas Touch in St Petersburg: friends of Putin glow brightly", *New York Times*, 1 March 2012

13 "Gunvor Reports 93 billion dollars in revenues for 2012", *Moscow Times*, 15 May 2013

14 At mid-2013

15 Source: INDEM (Information for Science and Democracy)

16 Five per cent GDP growth for the year ending March 2013. Source: government statistics

17 With the exception of 2008 when the country achieved GDP growth of 3.5 per cent

18 Source: OECD

19 Source: Forbes

20 "Running with the bulls", *The Economist*, 3 May, 2012

21 www.tata.com/htm/Group_Investor_GroupFinancials.htm

22 Source: Forbes

23 Essar Corporate Profile

24 Wipro Corporate Profile

25 Arcelormittal Corporate Information

26 Source: Forbes Global 2000, May 2013

27 "Leviathan as a minority shareholder – a study of equity purchases by the Brazilian National Development Bank (BNDES), 1995-2003", Sergio Lazzarini, Aldo Musacchio, Harvard Business School, 2011

28 Annual Report 2012

29 Year end 2012

30 Source: Brookings Institute and brasil.gov.br

31 Source: Economic Commission for Latin America

32 Ninety-three per cent of Chinese investment in Brazil was carried out by Central State Enterprises, 6 per cent by other State Enterprises and just 1 per cent by private enterprises. Source: Chinese Investments in Brazil, China-Brazil Business Council, 2011

33 "Doing Business 2013: Smarter Regulation For Small and Medium Sized Enterprises", World Bank/ International Bank for Reconstruction and Development

34 The middle class is defined as households with revenues per head of between 10 and 100 dollars per day adjusted for local standards of living

35 "The emerging middle class in developing countries", Homi Kharas, OECD, January 2010

36 CIA World Fact Book 2011

37 "The Bird Of Gold: The rise of India's consumer market", McKinsey Global Institute, 2007

38 CIA World Fact Book

39 Study carried out by Fundaçao Getulio Vargas

40 "Wal Mart Says China Growth is on Target", *Wall Street Journal*, 1 April, 2013 and Walmart corporate reports

41 Walmart Corporate Reports

Chapter 2

How we were robbed of our own capitalism

The Entrepreneur-State-Market triangle: a Western invention

One of the great Western myths of the last couple of decades is that the success of modern capitalism is entirely down to entrepreneurial initiative coupled with the withdrawal of the State. Growth in the US under Reagan or in Great Britain under Thatcher convinced the finest minds that all we had to do for the economy to prosper was to let the invisible hand go about its business unhindered, with help from efficient capital markets to bridge the gap between savings and investments. In spite of the ravages of recent crises, the myth lives on. Yet the reality is very different, something that our competitors from emerging countries have understood only too well. We forget that the West built its success not on unbridled liberalism but on the triangle of the Entrepreneur, the State, and the Market. In this system the entrepreneur of course plays a central role, but the State has a clear mission to foster initiative and support economic activity.

Take the US for example, always presented as the country of free enterprise and laissez-faire *par excellence*. As far back as we can go in the country's economic past, the State has always been an essential partner, even an instigator of individual initiative and innovation. Through the Pacific Railway Act of 1862 it was the President Lincoln who ensured the financing for the construction of the transcontinental railroad along with the two operators Pacific Railroad Company and Union Pacific at a time when private investors were few and far between. Later on in the 1930s it was the US army's research facilities that gave rise to the aircraft industry. Private companies like General Electric, Westinghouse, or Pratt & Whitney received federal funding to develop the very first jet engines and obtained their initial big orders from the air force. In the 1960s, firms like Texas Instruments or Fairchild Semiconductors, inventors of the revolutionary semiconductor, could never have made a mass-market of their technologies if they hadn't found in the air force an enthusiastic customer capable of buying their products in huge quantities.

It is tempting to think that the computer industry first saw the light of day in the garages of a few Californian technology nerds, but once again, the cliché does not tally with reality. In fact the army developed the first supercomputers, whose first civilian usage was in the social security administration. In the 1970s the American government played a vital role in the emergence of the software industry, setting up the Advanced Research Project Agency (ARPA) partnering with universities including Stanford, Carnegie Mellon, and MIT.

ARPA rapidly became a breeding ground for the most brilliant minds in the budding IT industry, minds that would go on to create or expand companies such as Xerox, Microsoft, or Apple. The very concept of the Internet arose in public research institutes as a means of enabling the American army to communicate without interference from the Soviet enemy. The same is true for the GPS satellite navigation system or for the algorithm behind research engines such as Google's all ground-breaking technology that now forms part of our daily lives and that we associate with entrepreneurial genius, ignoring the State's critical role in developing it.

Many other industries have been transformed in depth through the State partnering with the private sector. The US biotech industry would not be what it is today if the federal government had not subsidised it to the tune of billions of dollars. Between 1995 and 2008 the funding increase made available to the National Institute of Health (NIH), up from 11 to 29 billion dollars per year, really began to pay off[1]. Out of the 15 star products (accounting for annual revenues of more than one billion dollars) marketed by American biotech companies, 13 had received financial support from the federal government at some stage in their development. The same goes for the solar energy industry in which 13 of the 14 major technological breakthroughs of the last three decades resulted from largely State-funded research. Wind power met with the same good fortune when NASA and the Ministry of Energy joined forces to provide companies like GE Wind, now the world's second largest turbine manufacturer, with the resources to get their businesses up and running. Overall the State still accounts for 26 per cent of the total R&D spend in the US, compared to 67 per cent for the private sector. However, as far as fundamental research is concerned, Federal spending amounts to 57 per cent of the total[2].

Examples such as these abound but are often overlooked by the general public and the media who prefer to idolise business heroes rather than recognise the vital role played by the State in many of the greatest inventions. Federal interventions may take many forms, but they have a few things in common. First, thanks to the quality of its scientists and the extensive funding they receive, the State can act as a huge research facility developing new technologies in partnership with universities and the private sector. The State has the capacity to invest in the future without worrying too much about the immediate commercial applications of its R&D efforts. In this way, the State acts as a scout, leading the way, when the private sector is reluctant to take big financial risks. The federal government has often played the role of long-term lender, and even that of venture capitalist, ready to invest in start-ups when their technologies have been deemed top priority. Last but not least, the federal government is an enormous customer who, through the sheer size of its orders, can literally create a market from scratch and provide its private sector suppliers with the critical mass necessary to make the product commercially viable.

Recognising the State's vital contribution to the architecture of our modern capitalism does not in any way mean underestimating the importance of the other two corners of the triangle, entrepreneurs and the market, in our collective success. Of course nothing would have been possible without the genius and initiative of entrepreneurs capable of transforming a great idea or promising technology into concrete applications. Similarly, there can be no doubt that finance, as lambasted as it may be today, played midwife and nurse to groups who today employ tens of thousands of people. In the US, venture capitalists relatively unknown to the general public like Sequoia Capital, Draper Fisher, or Sevin Rosen were the ones investing in the first rounds of companies like Apple, Cisco, Oracle, or Google when all they had as assets were their founders' enthusiasm and single-page business plans. The financial markets then took over, allowing these same companies to go public and set out to take over the world.

All of this should be beyond question. And yet ever since the 1990s the zealots of 'less State' are out to destroy the triangle or modify its geometry. In the West, the triangle has been changed into concentric circles with the financial markets at the centre, entrepreneurs in the second circle, and the State pushed as far out from the centre as possible. Except of course in times of crisis when we accept it back at the centre to act as lender of last resort, arbiter of the system when all other protective barriers have caved in. The same great minds that held forth learnedly about the self-regulating magic of the markets bang their fists on the table screaming for quantitative easing from the central banks[3] or asking governments for a reprieve in public deficit reduction so as to stimulate business. We adored the famous invisible hand, until it pushed us to the brink of disaster; now we call out in chorus for the return of the good old, highly visible hand of the State to avoid the worst.

This Western schizophrenia coupled with our inability to return to a more harmonious and balanced relationship between entrepreneurs, States, and markets explains why we are losing out to China, India, and Brazil in international competition. The 'triangular' capitalism that we invented but progressively abandoned is the brand of capitalism the major emerging countries have adopted to extraordinary effect. Naturally, their models remain in many respects unbalanced. The Chinese triangle leaves too large a place for the State even though, as we have seen previously, the State has turned itself into an entrepreneurial force working side by side with a private sector that gets stronger every day. Nor are the Indian and Brazilian triangles perfect. In both cases, the countries' entrepreneurial families have to contend with bureaucratic States which are not always acting in the best interests of business. However, one of the great strengths of these great emerging powers, in stark contrast to the West, is that they have thus far confined their financial markets to a secondary, supporting role. They are there to grease the wheels of trade and raise capital, not to shape the behaviour of the main stakeholders.

In leaving the key decisions in the hands of entrepreneurs and the State rather than the markets, these countries' systems are by no means infallible, far from it, particularly when we are reminded of how corrupt or inefficient the State machinery can get. But they at least have the considerable advantage of allowing a long-term perspective, a strategic vision.

We remain in awe at the ability of an immense country like China to plan centrally and control its economy of 1.3 billion people with such remarkable agility. Sectorial priorities are fixed every five years, human and financial resources dedicated, and those accountable appraised according to their results. What should we possibly find surprising or innovative in this approach? This is in fact the way that Europe and Japan rebuilt themselves after the Second World War, defining national priorities then planning, thus preparing the ground for the spectacular development of the post-war boom. In France, coordinated efforts involving the now defunct Ministry of Planning, the Ministry of Trade and Industry, and the *Banque de France*, made it possible to channel capital and credit to critical industries such as defence and energy, in particular nuclear energy. Even in Great Britain, where the population has little time for the State, the government managed to leverage the public sector to stimulate several key industries. The publicly funded Research Councils supported technologies, which not only advanced scientific knowledge but also created jobs and wealth for the country. By way of illustration, 15 of the 75 best selling drugs in the world were developed in Great Britain using techniques established by the Science and Technology Facilities Research Council[4].

Can we really therefore label the post-war activities of these countries as latent communism? Absolutely not. This was the golden age of the all-conquering Western capitalism we have forgotten today, a period which saw the birth of our biggest companies while the State acted decisively and with the full approval of the private sector. Entrepreneurs who would become some of the most famous captains of industry of the 20th century, founded and nurtured their businesses regardless of the markets, because even if their companies were listed, they remained in control. The investor, be they the small shareholder or the insurance company, was simply invited to take part in the group's growth, not determine its future strategy. Management boards were run very differently from today's standards of good governance. At that time there were almost no independent directors on the board, and chief executives tended to have a paternalistic, even autocratic management style that would be considered far from politically correct today. Were we really worse off as a result? Can we honestly maintain that today's standards of good governance have made our business leaders any more accountable or paved the way for a stronger alignment of their interests with those of their shareholders?

This form of capitalism where the owner-entrepreneur still managed his own company and where the State supported such private initiative made Western capitalism great many years ago, and is the force that is now making the new emerging powers what they are today. But who says that the writing is on the wall? Without necessarily having to turn back the clocks, why shouldn't we be able to recreate the conditions of this triangular capitalism? Admittedly most of our big corporations no longer have entrepreneurial shareholder bases and so it would be pointless to reminisce on times past. Though why couldn't we imagine redesigning our executives' pay structure to make them behave more like business owners? Who says we can't question our companies' rigid governance dogma so that our boards' independence no longer condemns us to inertia? Why couldn't we imagine our governments talking calmly about industrial policy and long term planning without it being interpreted as a fundamental challenge to our free-market economy? The success of the emerging powers and the fierce competition they are waging in the war for business leadership is forcing us to dig deep down into our collective memories to try to understand what brought us our earlier successes. The future will not resemble the past, that is a certainty. However, another certainty is that we will be unable to regain the initiative unless we establish, once more, a better balance between the entrepreneur, the State, and the market. A task we must carry out with an open mind and without ideological taboos.

The architects of yesterday and tomorrow

In the British business world, Lord Bamford, the owner of JCB, is seen as the 'Last of the Mohicans'. Anthony Bamford went against the grain of all the prevalent trends followed by large companies in his native country and transformed the company, founded in 1945 by his father, into a world leader in excavators and other construction equipment, Despite its size, JCB is still controlled by a family, not by financial share-holders; it is active in heavy industry, a sector where, with the exception of Germany, the leaders are no longer Western groups, but Japanese, Chinese, or Korean; lastly, the company has chosen to remain based in the UK, a country which for better and for worse has traded in its indus-trial heritage for the world of services. The decline of industrial know-how in Great Britain is such a cause for concern for Lord Bamford, a die-hard engineer, that he drew up a bold report on the question for Prime Minister David Cameron in 2012.

Bamford's non-conformism certainly paid off as JCB today has reve-nues in excess of 2.75 billion pounds, employs around 7,000 people, and markets its products in over 150 countries. The mechanical beasts bearing the legendary yellow and black logo are manufactured in 18 factories located in Great Britain but also in Germany, the US, Latin America, India, and China.

I recently asked Anthony Bamford the secret of his success in such an extremely cyclical industry demanding enormous investment and where the competition relentlessly copied and discounted heavily. I expected a long digression on JCB's sales and industrial strategy, although his reply came instantly and was just four words long: 'I have stayed private'. Bamford enjoys recollecting that meeting that took place in the City in the 1970s, which set in stone the future of his group and his family. Doubly pressured by the runaway inflation rates and prohibitive taxation that were suffocating British industry at the time, Bamford had set up an appoint-ment with Sir Evelyn de Rothschild to consider a possible flotation of JCB. After just a few minutes Sir Evelyn looked at our CEO and said, 'Listen, if I were you, I would never sell out'. Bamford who was already none too keen at the thought of running a listed company reckoned that if a banker was ready to offer up such an opinion, thereby giving up his commission, then his advice could only be but wisdom itself.

Like so many other great entrepreneurs, what Bamford values above all in JCB's remaining private, is his freedom. Freedom to expand his production facilities throughout the world without having to justify the huge investments required; freedom to battle through a difficult patch without having external pressure from shareholders who panic and force asset offloading or factory closure that would be sorely regretted at the first green shoot of recovery. For example, JCB saw sales collapse from 72,000 machines in 2007 to 36,000 in 2009, a spectacular fall that would have driven a listed company to take drastic measures. The group had little choice but to make redundancies in order to ride out the downturn, but took no decisions liable to slow development when the market took off once more. This proved to be a winning strategy as the group now achieves sales 20 per cent above their 2007 level, already a record year at the time. At JCB we can see that the family's entrepreneurial tradition will go on, as the third generation is already at work. Unfortunately such examples are increasingly rare in the West.

Staunch fans of the financial markets like to remind us that although 'old-school' capitalism has made possible the existence of large SMEs like the German *Mittelstands*, private companies rarely manage to raise the financing required to go on to become world leaders. For them, going public is a logical, near inevitable step in a business's lifecycle. No sooner does a company reach a certain size, than it is condemned to take the IPO route.

We can see from examples of groups like Koch Industries that this assertion does not stand up to scrutiny. In 1967 upon his father's death, Charles Koch took the helm of the family company, then known as Rock Island Oil & Refining, based in Wichita, Kansas and renamed it Koch Industries. In little more than 40 years, Charles Koch and his brother David have built Koch Industries up into America's second-largest private company without once having to rely on the markets[5]. Today, with annual revenues of over 115 billion dollars, and a 60,000-strong staff in over 60 countries, Koch Industries has become a conglomerate operating in more than 10 industries including oil, natural gas, chemicals, plastics, fertilisers, cattle breeding, and finance[6]. If it were listed , the group would certainly find itself in the top 20 of the Fortune 500 list of the biggest American companies, ahead of corporate giants like Procter & Gamble or Boeing.

Author of the management bestseller *The Science of Success*[7], Charles Koch willingly declares that his company will only go public 'over his dead body'. In his book, he criticises the dictates of quarterly results, destructive shareholder lawsuits, and the Wall Street obsession for the

Price-Earning Ratio[8]. In Koch's opinion, this culture blinds the market to companies in cyclical industries whose share price is unfairly penalised and who often fail to raise capital effectively when they most need it. There is actually no evidence that these companies are unable to create value for their shareholders. A study carried out several years ago showed that over Koch's first four decades at the helm of his group, the value of Koch Industries increased 2,000 fold while over the same period the Fortune 500 companies' value was multiplied by just 110. This spectacular performance differential primarily reflects the exceptional management talent of Charles Koch, but it also says a lot about the negative impact of the numerous constraints besetting listed companies.

Are men like Anthony Bamford or Charles Koch simply remnants of the past, the final survivors of a capitalism that is doomed to extinction and that today can only inspire nostalgia? Certainly not. They represent hope for Western capitalism, our only chance to stay competitive and regain ground lost to emerging powers. Of course this doesn't at all mean that all listed companies should revert to becoming private or that they should be in some way condemned to underperform. Fortunately, there are still listed companies in the US and Europe in which the founder or his family no longer hold majority stakes but who have nonetheless managed to preserve their culture without falling into the trap of the markets. Volkswagen's rude good health under the leadership of Ferdinand Piëch, the founder's grandson, and despite a car industry going through one of the most difficult periods in its history, is living proof of this observation. Although the founding family holds only 13 per cent of the capital of a group valued at over 80 billions euros, management loyalty to the family tradition is at the core of their strategy. When Ferdinand Piëch decided to buy Porsche in 2009, another company founded by his grandfather, he was not just motivated by the desire to put his hands on one of the most prestigious brands in the car industry. He was rebuilding his family's history. In the same industry we saw how John Elkann, Giovanni Agnelli's grandson was able to turn around the FIAT group with the help of the brilliant Sergio Marchionne. Just a few years back, many thought that the company couldn't survive, but FIAT went back on the attack, entirely revisiting its product range and taking over the American manufacturer Chrysler. It is not just intelligence that got FIAT out of the rut; it is the inner fire, and the courage of those whose very identity depends on their group's survival.

In the UK, the case of Associated British Food (ABF), the multinational food processing and retailing group, is emblematic of this form of family capitalism where, although a company may be listed, loyalty towards the entrepreneurial roots can be turned into a forward-looking management philosophy. Founded by the publicity-shy Weston family, the group now employs 102,000 people throughout the world and is a member of the FTSE 100. George Weston, grandson of the founder, is CEO and now the flag bearer of a culture which shields the group from the worst excesses of financial markets. But how many ABFs are left in the UK today? Very few and it is unfortunate because experience has shown that corporate success is so often a function of the emotional bond linking the key decision makers to their companies and the knowledge that almost all of their personal wealth is in the balance. For them, failure is not an option as there can be no plan B. It is this simple but powerful motivation which, when prevalent in many companies, can carry forward an entire economy.

The emerging countries have not yet entirely taken away from us this wilful, creative, and responsible brand of capitalism but we mustn't get complacent. Even those companies that no longer have a familial presence must instil in their executive teams the feeling that they have been entrusted with a mission that goes above and beyond their personal fates. These business leaders must think and behave like owners. The senior management of listed companies and their boards are of course accountable for what they do. However they should no longer think of themselves as the captains of ships navigating in the winds of financial shareholders who, ultimately, do not care whether or not they will reach port safely. It is up to the leaders of our large corporations to set a target, a destination, and have the courage to stay on course.

---

1 Case studies in American innovation, December 2010, Breakthrough Institute

2 The Entrepreneurial State, Mariana Mazzucato, January 2012

3 Intervention of central banks to increase liquidities in the system, thereby supporting it and stimulating economic recovery

4 Science and Technology Facilities Council, Impact Report 2011

5 Source: Forbes, America's Largest Private Companies

6 Koch Industries Corporate Information

7 "The Science of Success: How Market Based Management Built the World's Largest Private Company", published by John Wiley & Sons, Inc. Hoboken, New Jersey, 2007

8 A valuation metric which compares the market capitalisation of a business to its net earnings

Chapter 3

The new geopolitics of money

The weapons of financial dissuasion

Since the Second World War, we have become accustomed to dividing the world up into two groups: those who have nuclear weapons and everyone else. This distinction has been at the heart of world geopolitics for six decades now, and even the fall of the Berlin Wall, as cathartic as it was, failed to change this state of affairs. A new era is dawning however of a world in which the discerning factor is no longer one's membership of the nuclear club, but rather the measure of one's financial might. Over the coming decades, the dichotomy underpinning the balance of power will be between the great nations who lend and those who borrow. The former will have the resources to fulfil their political ambitions while the latter will look on helpless as their status as a leading power steadily wears thin. Money has become the ultimate weapon of the 21st century.

And yet, while global economic reality has completely changed, the official geopolitical framework has remained frozen. Western powers are still in command of most international institutions, even though they are crippled with debt and their social models are about to implode. This situation is seen as absurd by the emerging powers, especially as they are repeatedly asked to bail out a Europe in disarray.

The emerging powers are now attacking on several fronts: firstly, international organisations. For years now China has been carrying out a strategy of encirclement. By becoming a major source of bilateral financial aid, China has effectively short-circuited the World Bank and the IMF. China instantly grants huge loans to countries but, unlike international institutions, does not ask them for any kind of political concession in return. They insist however on having preferential and near unlimited access to their natural resources. This is how China became in just a few years the leading foreign power in Africa, leaving the former European colonial powers and the US far behind.

As well as deepening the footprint of the largest emerging nations in important regions of the globe, this encirclement strategy allows them to be far more demanding within the very same international organisations with which they compete. Concerned at the daily shrinking of their influence, these institutions feel they have no choice but to accept representatives of countries like China, Brazil, or India at key positions in their ranks. And even if these positions do not yet necessarily grant these countries the power to make decisions, they do confer a genuine, and in many ways, legitimate influence.

Secondly, international trade. The emerging powers have understood that the cost advantage they have had over the West for decades will not last forever. In China wages rise by 15 to 20 per cent per year on average. If we consider transportation costs, quality control, and supply chain issues, many Western importers are now thinking twice about whether it is worth their while to continue sourcing their products from China. To protect themselves from such a potentially harmful disruption to their economy, the Chinese and the other emerging powers have many weapons at their disposal. For instance, currency. China has held its currency at an artificially low level compared to the dollar and the euro. If the yuan were allowed to float, it would appreciate significantly against other currencies and entire sectors of the Chinese industry would suffer or disappear altogether. The other weapon is protectionism. The Chinese, Indian, or Russian public authorities wage guerrilla warfare on a daily basis in order to protect their companies from foreign competition. Amongst other discriminatory measures, they impose technical standards that are extremely difficult to respect for Western firms or they demand local content for any enterprise wishing to submit bids on public contracts.

Third, and probably the most fearsome, the battle for intelligence. Emerging powers, and especially China, are no longer happy to be just the world's workshop. They want to rise up the value chain and gain access to intellectual property, the West's last remaining competitive advantage. China is striving to become a key player in a great many high value-add industries, be they in IT, aerospace, renewable energies, or biotechs to name but a few. And to get there, the country will stop at nothing. For example, demanding Western companies hand over their technologies should they wish to enter into joint ventures with State enterprises; buying stakes or taking holdings in European or American corporations working in strategic industries; or simply tolerating that local companies steal competitors' intellectual property worldwide, especially in software.

Finally, global warming and environmental protection. As some of the world's biggest polluters, emerging countries have unwittingly got caught up in one of the century's biggest issues, to which any resolution will absolutely require their cooperation. These powers are now becoming increasingly aware of their environmental responsibilities, while also understanding far too well what they can get out of it. In their negotiations with the West, China and India expect financial compensation or important technologies in return for their cooperation, as well as concessions on wholly unrelated subjects at the WTO, the UN, or elsewhere. This endless haggling allows the emerging countries to bring to bear all their influence in the casting of roles on the new geopolitical world stage.

For Western countries on their knees at the mercy of the emerging powers to refinance their deficits, it is becoming increasingly difficult to put a stop to this offensive. Our defeatist governments and business leaders have got used to watching the battlements of our capitalism fall one by one in a war where our companies simply cannot fight on an equal footing. While political rhetoric tries to be wilful, in reality, we have become openly passive, thereby reinforcing the emerging powers' conviction that the road is now wide open for them. And yet, as we will see in the coming chapters, there should be no inevitability to all this. By becoming more lucid and less complacent, we have the means at our disposal to fight back, using our rivals' very own weapons.

The assault on international organisations

The emerging powers, led by China, are pulling apart the governance system the West set up after the Second World War. For the BRICS, demanding a greater role and a stronger representation within international organisations is not only a matter of a country's economic supremacy. These emerging powers consider that the Western development model has shown its limitations since 2008 and feel they have nothing to learn from countries which seem to have turned short-term thinking and financial irresponsibility into a system. For these emerging countries, the financial crisis rings the death knell of the Anglo-Saxon style free-market economic system.

Asia bitterly remembers the drastic structural adjustment programmes imposed upon them by the IMF following the 1997 crisis, as well as the remedies that often turned out worse than the diseases they were intended to cure. Emerging countries today reject the underlying philosophy, widely referred to as the 'Washington Consensus'. This philosophy states that IMF and World Bank aid are dependent upon the adoption of methods and priorities inspired by Western economic policy. What troubles the emerging countries even more is that the international organisations have used their financial muscle to go way beyond the field of the economy. To be eligible for assistance, applicant countries must commit to respecting certain criteria of transparency as well as judicial and human rights standards. Many countries consider this as unacceptable interference in their domestic affairs, and a means for Western powers to impose their values in exchange for their cash. Now that the money has changed sides, the new powers have lost all their inhibitions.

China wields a considerable weapon for reforming international organisations: the country literally competes against them. Instead of focusing all of its efforts in a drawn-out and often fruitless multilateral negotiation, China turns directly to countries who could be of use in Asia, Africa, or Latin America and in weeks releases billions of dollars in loans or financial aid. Abdoulaye Wade, former President of Senegal, explained this approach in a 2008 interview for the *Financial Times*[1]:

'China's approach to our needs is simply better adapted than the slow and sometimes patronising post-colonial approach of European investors, donor organisations and non-governmental organisations. In fact, the Chinese model for stimulating rapid economic development has much to teach Africa. With direct aid, credit lines and reasonable contracts, China has helped African nations build infrastructure projects in record time – bridges, roads, schools, hospitals, dams, legislative buildings, stadiums and airports. In many African nations, including Senegal, improvements in infrastructure have played important roles in stimulating economic growth.'

Wade goes still further, saying: 'I have found that a contract that would take five years to discuss, negotiate and sign with the World Bank takes three months when we have dealt with Chinese authorities. I am a firm believer in good governance and the rule of law. But when bureaucracy and senseless red tape impede our ability to act – and when poverty persists while international functionaries drag their feet – African leaders have an obligation to opt for swifter solutions. I achieved more in my one hour meeting with President Hu Jintao in an executive suite at my hotel in Berlin during the recent G8 meeting in Heiligendamm than I did during the entire, orchestrated meeting of world leaders at the summit.' That says it all.

China's ability to utilise its huge currency reserves to support its future economic and political allies without imposing upon them the slightest condition gives it a considerable advantage over Western countries and international organisations. By way of example, in 2006, international organisations made the decision to reduce aid to Cambodia in order to put pressure on the government to address human rights issues. China immediately stepped in and raised its financial contributions to Cambodia. The World Bank pulled out of a pipeline project in Chad at the last minute harbouring fears that project revenue would be used by the government to military ends. Just a few weeks later, China took the World Bank's place. And the list goes on and on.

In addition to China's bilateral activism, the country fosters the development of rival multilateral organisations in the region, such as ASEAN Plus Three, of which the US is not a member. Above all, the Chinese aim to show that multilateralism is possible outside the realm of American influence. In 2009 for example, ASEAN Plus Three approved the setting up of a regional fund of over 120 billion dollars, a sort of Asian IMF, a third of whose financing originated in China. In the same vein China is making its presence increasingly felt within the Asian Development Bank (ADB).

Spinning its web outside of the existing international organisations dominated by the West, and by openly competing with them, China is in a much stronger position to lobby even more effectively within these same organisations. Here, China's main goal is to have its say in the world's economic and financial governance. Security, defence, and peacekeeping are however lesser sources of multilateral concern for the country, considering that these are matters for national sovereignty. As we saw during the Syrian crisis, China had no qualms about using its veto as permanent member of the UN Security Council to block any resolution that could have paved the way to military intervention.

China uses several methods to further consolidate its position within international organisations. The first is to infiltrate them, putting their administration's top people in key positions whenever possible. In 2008, China obtained the appointment of Justin Yifu Lin as Chief Economist at the World Bank, a position previously held by such distinguished figures as the Nobel Prize-winning economist Joseph Stiglitz, or Clinton's former Treasury Secretary Larry Summers and Director of the National Economic Council under Obama. To see such a position go to an eminent member of the Chinese Communist Party, albeit one who had been awarded a Doctorate by the University of Chicago as well as a Masters in Marxist economy by the University of Beijing, shows how far we have come. The other recent noteworthy appointment was that of Min Zhu, first as Special Advisor to Dominique Strauss-Khan when he was in charge of the IMF, then as Deputy Managing Director of the same institution under the leadership of Christine Lagarde.

Since the financial crisis of 2008, Chinese officials no longer hesitate to publicly berate the West whenever the opportunity arises. Governor of the People's Bank of China and one of the most powerful figures of the Chinese economic establishment Zhou Xiaochuan[2] did not mince his words at a meeting of the IMF in 2010. 'The main risk for the global economy comes from developed countries,' he declared before explaining that the worldwide financial crisis was first and foremost the result of 'inappropriate behaviour' from the developed countries' financial institutions and the 'unsustainable fiscal policy' of their governments. Here we are far from the political cant or the muted declarations we usually expect from central bankers or high-ranking international officials. And it is the very same Zhou Xiaochuan who in 2009 suggested replacing the dollar as the world's reserve currency with the Special Drawing Rights (SDR), a virtual currency pegged to a currency basket and hitherto exclusively used by the IMF. Taboos are falling one after the other.

China is not the only one banging its fist on the table for more influence, especially within the IMF. Out of the 400 billion dollars of additional commitments negotiated in April 2012 by Christine Lagarde to double the IMF's resources in its efforts to contain the financial crisis, more than 100 billion dollars came from emerging countries. This amounts to saying that Europe owes a good deal of its survival to the generosity of the countries it never tired of lecturing just a few years ago. And this generosity comes, of course, with a price. Brazil and China today demand a considerable increase of their voting rights within the organisation whose mission has changed so much. Initially set up to direct the flow of financial aid from the Western countries to the emerging countries, the IMF has since become a rescue vehicle for these very same Western countries, using funding essentially from the emerging countries. When the doctor becomes the patient and the patient wears the white coat, a power shift seems inevitable.

Guido Mantega, the Brazilian finance minister, expressed frustration on behalf of the BRICS when he declared recently that it was unacceptable constantly to push back the agreement on reducing European voting rights to the benefit of the emerging countries. He demands that any additional financial contribution be made dependent upon the completion of this agreement which would raise emerging countries' voting rights from 43 per cent to 47 per cent and push China up into third place with 4.42 per cent of the total vote. But even at this level, can we really expect France or Great Britain to legitimately maintain their positions each with 4.29 per cent of voting rights today? And can we really imagine countries such as India or Brazil making do with 2.34 per cent and 1.72% of the vote respectively, thereby accepting to wield less influence than Italy?

This activism of the emerging countries in world governance of course goes well beyond the IMF. The G20 has made a nonsense of the G8. Indeed who could take seriously a summit meeting of heads of State that didn't include China, India, or Brazil? The UN has also become a major hunting ground for the emerging powers. China succeeded in getting Sha Zukang appointed to the position of Under-Secretary-General for economic and social affairs and gets to voice its opinions as permanent member of the Security Council alongside the US, France, Great Britain, and Russia. But how can we continue to justify that India, the world's largest democracy, is not also a permanent member of the Security Council when Great Britain and France still are?

All the emerging powers share the same desire to reduce US power in international affairs and use their growing influence within these organisations to reach their goal. However, beyond this common objective, their priorities diverge. While China puts the emphasis on political and trade policy in order to protect its interests as the world's leading exporter, Russia seems unworried by such matters. Since China became a member of the World Trade Organisation (WTO) in 2001, the country has become a mainstay of all major trade negotiations, skilfully blowing hot and cold on matters of trade liberalisation. This is far from the truth for Russia. The fact that Russia's WTO membership talks lasted 18 years before finally coming through in December 2011 is a sign of the country's mistrust of world's economic governance. Moreover, in stark contrast to China, Russia tends to send lower ranking officials to take up their positions within the international organisations. However, Russia has always been deeply concerned by security matters. As a major nuclear power but nevertheless well aware of the military superiority of the US, Russia uses international forums and treaties to keep its great rival at bay whenever and wherever possible. In 2006, Vladimir Putin and George W. Bush launched The Global Initiative to Combat Nuclear Terrorism; the GICNT now counts 85 countries as members. Russia is also proactive on the subjects of non-proliferation of chemical and biological weapons. The country joined the Proliferation Security Initiative, a group set up by the US with the objective of fighting illicit trade in weapons of mass destruction. On the other hand Russia has gone much further than the US or China, ratifying the Comprehensive Test Ban Treaty and the Missile Technology Control Regime, co-signed by the US but not by China. Russia is also looking to set up an international cooperation framework for the control of, and defence against, cyber-attacks, a subject on which, strangely enough, the US seems, publicly at least, to be dragging its feet.

But let's make no mistake; Russian security initiatives have more to do with their interest in sharing the world's stage as Washington's equals

than they do with a genuine desire to further transparency or cooperation on defence issues. Moscow repeats the need for a multi-polar world
over and over again, when this mantra in fact helps the country to
recruit allies to its cause against the all-powerful US. This of course
doesn't stop Russia from acting unilaterally when such a course of
action is in its own interests. The cornerstone of Russian foreign policy
remains the nation's absolute sovereignty, above all at regional level, be
it for the Caucuses or for Central Asia. As demonstrated again with
Russia's unwavering support of Bashar al Assad's regime, the country is
increasingly keen to defend its vision of world affairs in the Middle East
and beyond. All decisions are subject to the rule of Realpolitik and military might, far from the cosy surroundings of international diplomacy.
In this context, the country's permanent seat on the Security Council is
used as a highly effective weapon to avoid interference in its own domestic affairs or in what Russia considers as the domestic affairs of its key
allies.

China similarly has no intention whatsoever of letting international
organisations dictate its defence policy. Even though the political rhetoric remains centred on China's peaceful, economic rise, this hasn't
stopped the country becoming one of the world's leading military
powers. Military expenditure has seen double-digit growth in the past
few years, rising from 26.5 billion dollars in 2004 to in excess of 106
billion dollars in 2012[3]. Some estimates put China's military budget
ahead of America's by 2035. This arsenal is intended to dissuade the US
from taking part in a possible conflict over the issue of Taiwan. To date,
China has relied on diplomatic pressure to isolate Taiwan but has
understood that it will be easier to achieve its ends if also able to resort
to military force, should it be necessary. In this respect, Beijing is but
employing methods tried and tested by the Americans themselves.

China is particularly concerned by the recent American activism in Asia,
set off in 2011 by then Secretary of State Hillary Clinton. In the space of
just a few months the Americans worked to strengthen their ties with
Vietnam and also with the Philippines with whom they had signed an
agreement covering military cooperation. The US sent warships to
Singapore and several thousand marines to swell the contingent at the
Australian military base of Darwin. Faced with this threat China tries to
impose itself upon its neighbours as the only major power in the region,

using its presence in the South China Sea to reclaim what it considers as its 'historical rights'. China's geostrategic objective is to open up the Chinese island of Hainan where it has based its missile-carrying nuclear submarines, a key element of the country's deterrent force. Through its more than 50 meetings with representatives of the American government since 2009, China has shown its willingness to deal with these issues bilaterally, on a level pegging. However it is out of the question for China to enter into security talks with its neighbours, let alone put up with the slightest interference from international organisations.

Where China and Russia aim (with differing degrees of subtlety) to leverage their influence within international organisations to reinforce their newfound economic and geopolitical power, Brazil makes its voice heard both as a seductive force and as a moral authority. The only major emerging power that has no enemies, Brazil has taken the international lead in matters as important as health, poverty, and hunger. The country played a key role in negotiations leading to the signature of the Tobacco Framework Convention, the first of its kind under the auspices of the World Health Organization (WHO). Brazil is also at the forefront of international policies to combat AIDS, its successes at home giving the country even more credibility. Finally, it is a Brazilian, José Graziano da Silva, architect of his own country's programme to fight hunger, who today heads up the UN's Food and Agriculture Organization (FAO).

Looking at the activism of all the other major emerging powers when it comes to world governance, it is all the more surprising that India, in spite of its economic importance, has remained so discrete within the international organisations. Its relatively passive attitude may be explained by its obsession with the threat of Pakistan at its borders as well as its concern regarding the spectacular growth of its imposing neighbour China both on the economic and military fronts.

With a long established annual growth differential of around 2 to 3 per cent, the Chinese economy is now almost three times as big as the Indian economy. Both countries are engaged in the same mad rush to gain access to raw materials, and their companies often lock horns in Africa or Central Asia. Up until now, India considered itself unable to leverage the international organisations effectively to protect its own interests. This perception however is now changing, and we can expect to see India playing an increasingly important role in international affairs over the coming years.

Confronted by the emerging countries' assault on the world's multilateral organisations, Western powers just don't know which way to turn. Europeans and Americans seem entrenched in their positions of protecting their prerogatives, knowing full well that such an attitude is not sustainable and will end up backfiring. Westerners have no other choice but to make concessions, abandoning little by little the Washington Consensus, which has only increased tension and resentment. They must also continue to share key positions. At a time when Westerners have become the recipients of international financial aid, the voting systems and quotas within international organisations must be thoroughly reviewed. Countries such as Great Britain or France will have to accept that their representatives in certain key instances may be replaced by one representative for the entire European Union. Rather than being forced into this, it would be wiser to face up to the new reality and show openness and a longer-term vision. We should stop wasting time and energy furiously defending yesterday's balance of power. Instead, we should focus on today's challenge: to regain our economic power without which it will be impossible to uphold our diplomatic influence throughout the world.

The dangerous temptation of protectionism

Since the crisis of 2008, protectionism has gained ground throughout the world, particularly within the G20 countries. Behind the forced smiles, the warm handshakes, and the declarations of good intentions at each and every one of the major international summit meetings, hides a shared desire to use every possible means, direct or indirect, to give local companies the advantage over the competition. This is a veritable economic war that is playing out on a global scale and the fiercest fighters are often those, like the European Union, who publicly claim the moral high ground of global free trade. It is all the more surprising that the 'deglobalisation' lobby in France chastise Europe's supposed naivety in such matters and cry out for openly protectionist measures, when the 27-country EU is already the region of the globe where there are the most discriminatory measures[4], just ahead of Russia and Argentina. Great Britain, despite its strong free-market tradition, comes in in fourth place in the league of the most protectionist countries, well ahead of China who for the time being is only in the seventh slot, but is unfortunately getting ever more aggressive on such issues.

The major powers outdo each other in the imagination stakes to get around the rules governing fair trade as established by the WTO. Since the first G20 crisis summit meeting in November 2008, the first source of infringement was government aid for sectors hardest hit by the recession such as the banks, the car and steel industries, and agriculture. The Fire-fighter-State stepped in to put out many a blaze, recapitalising national champions on the verge of bankruptcy, or granting them loans at more than preferential rates. Should we worry? Probably not as almost all the major powers did the same, and if they hadn't they would have condemned many a healthy company to certain death at a time when the banks and the financial markets were frozen. The State, ultimate arbiter of the system legitimately played its role.

More worrying perhaps has been the resurgence of economic guerrilla warfare tactics that have led to unfortunate distortions in competition. A classic in this area has been the technical standards of conformity set up to protect local firms and create an obstacle race for foreign companies looking to sell their products. Countries like China, India, or Indonesia have become masters in the field. Most recent examples include a Chinese certification process for wind turbine production or the highly specific Indian norms for tyre production, making it that much more difficult to import products manufactured elsewhere. Unfortunately such incidents are commonplace and considerably slow down Western expansion into these high-growth markets.

The other widespread technique of the moment used to distort competition is the State's ambition to 'fly the flag' imposing national preference upon all goods and services supplied to the public sector. Supporters of the 'Buy National' ethos include countries such as Russia who passed a series of supposedly temporary measures shortly after the 2008 crisis. Brazil surpassed itself here when it made its 'Buy Brazilian' act of July 2010 permanent, imposing a threshold of 25 per cent minimum on local suppliers for all business contracted with the State. Since the programme 'Plano Brasil Maior' set out by President Rousseff in August 2011, this law now applies to industries as different as IT, healthcare, or communications.

Several emerging powers have also passed laws requiring a minimum local content in the manufacturing of certain goods. Shamelessly, and in total contradiction of the WTO rules, Russia dictated that at least 30 per cent of its cars be equipped with locally manufactured engines or gearboxes. Staying in the car industry, China is about to pass legislation requiring that from 2015 onwards, only Chinese branded electric vehicles will be sold within its borders. Bearing in mind the potential of this market, we can easily comprehend the threat that such restrictive measures would mean for Western companies.

Beyond the discriminatory laws mentioned above, the reign of the arbitrary is a constant threat to Western investments. The Strategic Sectors Law passed by Russia in 2008 allows the State to cap the level of any stake held by foreign interests amongst a list of sectors considered sensitive. A special commission chaired by the Prime Minister himself must authorise each investment. In the same vein, Chinese measures taken in the field of mergers and acquisitions involving Chinese companies or assets, give cause for concern. Each transaction must be submitted for official approval, and evaluated in terms of its impact on 'national security', a sufficiently vague notion that opens the door to all sorts of abuse.

The Western corporations that have managed to break into these markets in spite of all the obstacles find themselves the victims of campaigns of red tape. Most of the time they choose to keep quiet and carry on regardless but the impact of such dissuasive measures must not be underestimated. In this way China's retail sector has become a bitter battlefield between on the one hand the leading foreign retailers like Auchan, Walmart, and Carrefour and local players like China Resources Enterprise. The former have managed to dominate the sector thanks to their extensive experience while the latter find it hard to accept such Western supremacy on their own soil. These local companies use their ties with municipal and regional public authorities to put a spanner in the works for their Western rivals. Before China joined the WTO in 2001 the situation was far more straightforward: retailers, insurance companies, and banks simply didn't have the right to do business in most Chinese cities. Today the Chinese try to discourage foreign competition in rather more roundabout ways. For instance, anti-trust inquiries have become a formidable weapon to intimidate foreigners. Tetra Pak the leading packaging company was one of the latest victims of this policy in 2013. This followed investigations about the pricing policies of pharmaceutical companies and baby formula makers. In the retail sector, Walmart and Carrefour were accused of employing deceitful pricing policies in 19 of their stores and even of selling products beyond their sell-by date. Both groups had to pay big fines and publicly apologise even though nothing was ever proved. The retail sector is not the only target. In 2011, Unilever also had to pay a fine and apologise publicly, simply because they had announced a forthcoming price increase and involuntarily provoked a rush on their products. Was there anything illegal in their actions? Nothing in the slightest, but no matter, the Chinese authorities clearly wanted to make an example of them.

So how should we react? The lack of significant progress through trade negotiations in Doha under the auspices of the WTO show that it is near impossible to settle such matters multilaterally. Several years of heated discussions failed to enable nations with such divergent interests to reach a consensus. Europeans and Americans couldn't imagine dumping their systems of subsidies and domestic support for their agriculture. This was nonetheless an explicit demand from the Cairns group comprised of major agricultural countries such as Brazil, Argentina, Australia, and India. On the other hand, emerging countries refused to allow improved access to their markets for manufactured goods without concessions from their richer rivals. It became a complete stalemate. Members of the WTO were already talking at cross purposes well before the financial crisis struck but since then, they have fallen back on even more entrenched positions. Under these circumstances, reviving hopes of major international trade talks like the Doha Round has become totally unrealistic.

A more pragmatic approach to settling these issues is not via multilateralism but rather through promoting what we can refer to as 'multi-bilateralism'. The European Union has the size and credibility to negotiate on equal terms with Beijing without having to squeeze into the often unproductive framework of the WTO. We should develop a trade doctrine based on the concept of 'gradual response'. Russia and China must be made to understand that each time they take competition-distorting measures at the expense of Western companies, they should expect equivalent measures from the other blocs, be it Europe or the US. Rather than lodging a complaint with the WTO, we should engage in direct discussions with the offending country, strong-arming whenever necessary, to dissuade, making them understand the boomerang effect of the discriminatory measures envisaged. This is not about taking the slippery slope of protectionism or trade wars but rather putting an end to our naive, bureaucratic optimism that undermines our credibility when up against countries that understand only strong, unambiguous voices. Today Europe and the US produce 40 per cent of the goods and services in the world, while consuming 55 per cent. It is high time we recognise the power this gives us over our partners to achieve greater fairness in international trade. Concessions will then have to be made on both sides, as much by the emerging powers as by the West.

Currency wars

In the arsenal of economic weapons, the manipulation of exchange rates is both one of the most widespread and one of the most dangerous. Acknowledging this, the US Senate approved the Currency Exchange Rate Oversight Reform Act in October 2011. In the event of a currency being held at artificially low levels, this law allows the US to consider such manipulation as an illegal State subsidy against which America would be entitled to demand penalties and compensation. It does not take a genius to understand that it is China in Capitol Hill's sights here.

By decreeing the yuan's exchange rate rather than letting it float according to trade and the markets – as is the case for all the major currencies – the Chinese public authorities have set off an imbalance which cost the West hundreds of billions of dollars and contributed to rising unemployment. Every month the US buys around 30 billion dollars of Chinese goods and services but only exports around 10 billion dollars of American goods and services to China[5]. This 20 billion dollar deficit creates a demand surplus for the yuan, which, if allowed to float freely on the markets, would automatically strengthen against the dollar. The yuan's appreciation would, in turn, have a stabilising effect by making Chinese products more expensive and thus reducing imports, allowing American companies to legitimately sell their products at more competitive prices both at home and abroad. It is because they have been unable to do this that tens of thousands of firms have been forced out of business or resorted to layoffs, provoking a massive deindustrialisation of the American economy.

Europe has also been affected by the same syndrome, although the consequences have been even more dire. Under pressure from the Germans for years now, and even during one of the most severe economic crises since the War, the European Central Bank's orthodox monetary policies have kept the euro at a level far above and beyond its actual intrinsic value. The contrast with the US and Great Britain here is striking. Through their policies of quantitative easing, these two countries have pumped trillions into their economies and succeeded in devaluing their respective currencies thereby helping their exporters. No such thing was possible in Europe, and even though things are gradually evolving under Mario Draghi's leadership, the damage has already been done. When factories close because of currency dumping, the harm is lasting, as even if the euro were to weaken, production capacity and jobs would be hard to recover.

China presents an extreme case as the yuan's exchange rate is centrally administrated, however the country is now in good company. Around 10 big central banks in the world have reverted to direct and often massive intervention on the currency markets in order to influence their currency's value. Depending on one's point of view, their approach may be qualified as manipulative, or as pragmatic, but the tendency is rife. The Bank of Japan for example is doing everything in its power to weaken its currency, thus dissuading the markets from continuing to buy the yen as a safe-haven currency. The central bank sells yen by the trillion, making no secret of its offloading, and finally succeeded in depreciating it against the main other currencies. In early 2013, Prime Minister Shinzo Abe launched a massive programme of stimulus and quantitative easing aimed at dragging the country back to growth. The so-called 'Abeconomics' programme also includes a growth strategy aimed at increasing the country's competitiveness. Whether the reforms will be enough remains to be seen. The Swiss National Bank worried by the stratospheric levels reached by the Swiss franc at the peak of the euro zone crisis and the resulting damage to the country's exports, managed to shock the markets when it pegged its currency to the euro in 2011. The franc lost 6 per cent of its value in just one day and has since fluctuated in the narrow band the central bank was aiming for. But this liar's poker is a dangerous game. One day, when the markets call the Swiss National Bank's bluff, the bank will need to have the resources to keep its commitments, and this is doubtful when one considers the limited firepower a central bank has at its disposal compared to the sea of speculation on the currency markets. The Brazilian Central Bank has met with similar issues. Overwhelmed by the real's strength, the central bank did not stop at an intervention on the currency markets. The bank also resorted to a tax on incoming capital flows, a weapon that no one had dared to use any more for quite some years.

This headlong lunge towards competitive devaluation throughout the world is not without consequence. We mustn't forget the massive, relentless devaluations of the 1930s that resulted in an unprecedented contraction of the world's trade and investments. Customs barriers were set up on both sides of the Atlantic and only worsened a situation which was already disastrous.

The worrying rise of protectionism since the 2008 crisis is largely the result of this cold war played out daily on the international money markets. The wheels of trade will not keep on turning freely if States and corporations are under the impression that exchange rates are being manipulated. In this kind of environment, withdrawal and isolation become tempting options. So what is to be done? Could we really go back to a post-war international monetary system à la Bretton Woods with administered exchange rates for all currencies and the gold standard for the dollar? Impossible. There were good reasons for this system's collapse in 1971 and it would be neither desirable nor conceivable to bring it back today.

There are two conditions to be met in order to restore a bare minimum of trust. The first is better policy coordination between the major central banks. We saw how effective were the actions agreed between the Fed, the ECB, the BNS, and the Bank of Japan at the darkest hour of the 2008 crisis following the bankruptcy of Lehman Brothers, or more recently during the sovereign debt crisis in Europe. We mustn't underestimate the practical and psychological impact of such concerted action, as it is credibility rather than sheer firepower that matters in the markets.

The second condition is harder to meet, but nevertheless essential. A clear distinction must be made between administering an arbitrarily decreed exchange rate on the one hand, and on the other, how a central banker may step in to influence his currency's exchange rate while respecting market decisions. The former should be opposed vigorously as it undermines the foundations of our international monetary system and creates structural imbalance in favour of the offender. The latter, as controversial as it may be, is inevitable in an environment where financial speculation can create absurd and damaging situations for the real economy.

What China is doing today is totally unacceptable. We cannot let a country that will soon become the world's leading economy use currency manipulation as a weapon to bring down industry in the West. However China may yet understand that undervaluing its currency in fact fuels its runaway inflation and this will end up eating away at its competitive advantage over the West. But this will take years and we just don't have enough time any more. The US has so far applied pressure too weakly upon China and it is now urgent to replace words with actions. As far as Europe is concerned and despite being China's number one trading partner, the Continent's voice has yet to be heard on the subject. It is high time we realised that behind this currency war lies a very real battle for the survival of our Western models of society.

How to buy a continent: the example of Africa

For decades Africa remained the exclusive hunting ground of the former colonial powers, but more recently the continent has succumbed to Chinese rule. Where Europe and the US seemed resigned to the inexorable slide of a continent weakened by corruption and political instability, China saw the opportunity of the century, the chance to conquer politically, economically, and ideologically an entire continent rich in natural resources. According to certain estimates, almost one million Chinese live and work in Africa today, attracted by projects in energy, mining, infrastructure, and telecoms. Perhaps the most surprising aspect is the sheer speed at which China succeeded in taking over the continent when we consider that until the late 1990s, the country had virtually no presence in Africa. Then, driven by their seemingly unlimited requirements for raw materials, the Chinese authorities clearly identified the weakness of the Western approach and drew up their highly effective two-prong strategy for Africa: huge financial support on the one hand and diplomatic cooperation on the other. All of this unconditionally and without the slightest interference, which allows Chinese companies to work closely and shamelessly with some of the most corrupt and least democratic regimes on the planet.

First the financial support. As we have observed above, most African countries wear themselves out negotiating in vain with Western countries and international organisations for loans that inevitably come with conditions on domestic governance. The Chinese, on the other hand, turned up at these same countries, whose subsoil abounds in natural resources, with the most basic of proposals: multi-billion dollar condition-free loans refundable in raw materials produced by the recipient country. In this way China granted Angola loans totalling five billion dollars and thus enabled the Chinese oil company Sinopec to become one of the country's biggest players in the industry, pushing aside Westerners like Total. The Democratic Republic of Congo provides another good illustration, securing a nine billion dollar loan against copper supplies of which China is the world's top consumer, and a commitment to let Chinese companies build the country's infrastructure. Most of these funds come from the Export-Import Bank of China (China Eximbank), an institution that plays a key role in the Chinese approach. At a time when Western banks are slashing their activities and withdrawing to home turf, China Eximbank allows itself the luxury of lending huge sums of money at well below market rates.

Angola and the Congo are particularly striking examples given the colossal amounts involved, but they are not isolated: more than 20 other African countries have also fallen under the realm of Chinese influence. China has become a force to be reckoned with in Nigeria, in the Republic of Equatorial Guinea, and in Gabon, primarily in oil, but also in Zambia, Tanzania, or Mozambique for metals. Sectors like infrastructure are also becoming top priority as we have seen in Ghana where China lent almost 600 million dollars to have a hydroelectric dam built by the Chinese state enterprise SinoHydro. China is involved in around a dozen dam projects in Africa with a construction cost of five billion dollars, of which over 60 per cent are Chinese funded.

Even North Africa is steadily falling into the net of the Chinese, particularly in the field of telecoms. Chinese companies like Huawei Technologies or ZTE Communications have succeeded in signing major contracts in Algeria, Tunisia, Morocco, or Egypt.

The entire Chinese Statentrepreneurial machine has been involved for over 10 years now in the country's African conquest. It all begins with the secret services, embedded deep in the Ministry of State Security (MSS), the infamous *Guoanbu*, whose Second Bureau, specialised in industrial espionage, analyses the political and economic environments of the target countries and coordinates field activities of the many Chinese companies engaged locally. The Ministry of Commerce (MOFCOM) works closely with the MSS in industrial intelligence and reports any sensitive information to State representatives at all levels of the hierarchy both in China and abroad. There is no clear dividing line between business leaders and intelligence operatives. The CEO of a Chinese State enterprise could very well be fully engaged in the business world while maintaining a near-official reporting line with the MSS or the MOFCOM. This unlikely, but nonetheless effective, combination has been put to good use in Africa.

Having placed its pawns on the African map, the State machine can then leverage its banking system to facilitate negotiations between its enterprises and the local regimes. As well as the aforementioned China Eximbank, Chinese efforts are supported by the China Development Bank (CDB), the Industrial and Commercial Bank of China (ICBC), the China Trade and Investment Corporation (CITIC), and the China Export and Credit Corporation (CECIC). These institutions provide export credit and project funding but also acquisition financing at rates that undercut any competitor on the market. This allows Chinese companies who already benefitted from a clear labour cost a head start to add yet another advantage, that of financing costs. Needless to say, their Western competitors are unable to keep up. Mining ventures requiring additional infrastructure investments will easily find their funding in a Chinese consortium, when their British or American competitor would struggle just to fund the mining project itself. In such circumstances, the Chinese steamroller becomes unstoppable.

The Chinese institutions even allow themselves to play at being venture capitalists thus giving their investments a development aid dimension which goes down particularly well with local governments. For example, the CDB set up the China Africa Development Fund (CADF), a five billion dollar investment fund. This fund invests in priority zones for economic development throughout Africa, particularly in Nigeria, Ethiopia, Zambia, Zimbabwe, and Algeria. In such zones the fund finances company creation and development and joint ventures, locally supplying products and services of all kinds and thus reindustrialising the region in question. Europeans have beaten about the bush for so long with similar ideas without ever carrying them out. Thanks to the Chinese, these plans have been made reality. A new fund of one billion dollars has also been set up to finance African entrepreneurs who wish to set up their businesses in these priority zones.

All of these initiatives form part of a concerted and extremely well thought out institutional and diplomatic effort. At the core of this effort is the Forum on China Africa Cooperation (FOCAC) that came together for the first time in the year 2000, uniting 100 African and Chinese ministers from over 45 countries as well as representatives of over 17 regional and international development organisations. Needless to say, the Westerners have only minor roles to play. The Forum has met five times since its creation and each time has turned out multi-year action plans that outline the contours of the new 'Chinafrica'. China has set itself up as a major economic as well as diplomatic power in the region, as it doesn't stop at promoting its own interests. In 2009 during the fourth meeting held in Sharm el-Sheikh in Egypt, China announced it would donate enough funding to build 30 hospitals, 30 malaria prevention and treatment centres as well as a training programme for 3,000 doctors and nurses and 20,000 additional professionals in other sectors of the economy. The Prime Minister at the time Wen Jiabao also committed to setting up 50 schools to celebrate 'China-Africa friend-ship'. In a continent where the average age is extremely low, an entire generation of Africans will grow up believing that China is synonymous with opportunity and development. Even the United Nations World Food Programme's Director Josette Sheeran, despite being a competi-tor of China's in these matters, publicly congratulated China for its progress in the fields of food safety, agriculture, and infrastructure. During the forum's last ministerial congress in July 2012, the President at that time, Hu Jintao, announced that he would double Chinese credit to Africa pushing it up to 20 billion dollars, specifying that these new loans would be allocated to infrastructure, agriculture, and manufac-turing industries, but also to the development of SMEs.

So has Africa closed its doors to the West? Should we resign ourselves to abandoning the 'lost continent' to the hands of the new Chinese empire before the Africans have even had a chance to be masters of their own fates? I don't think so. The economic reality of the 21st century is one of a world where possession of and access to raw materials are preconditions to remaining at the forefront of the world stage. This will force us to return to Africa once more, armed with intelligence but also the pragmatism that has been sadly lacking in recent years. It is point-less to continue to dream of imposing our development and govern-ance models upon nations that have rich pasts and cultures. We must stop trying to export our brand of democracy to peoples whose social structures and secular traditions should be respected. Let us accept that in many cases, economic progress will precede political change and not the opposite. We must not fall back into the naivety of the Washington Consensus, which has already done us enough damage.

But going beyond our own well understood interests, our historical ties with Africa in fact burden us with a sort of moral debt: to help the continent avoid unwittingly falling into a neo-colonial trap. The conti-nent's subsoil is becoming, directly or indirectly, Chinese property. The least the Chinese could do is to employ the millions of jobless young Africans locally, instead of importing their own labour force. The price of development must not be the loss of economic sovereignty. This is the card the West must play, particularly the Europeans, if they really want to regain a foothold on this continent of such strategic importance.

Intellectual property: the last bastion of the West

In becoming the world's leading manufacturing force, while simultane-ously securing access to the natural resources required to sustain its extraordinary growth, China has already succeeded in reaching two of its main strategic objectives. All that is left to do is to go after the last remaining bastion of the West: innovation and intellectual property. The stated goal is that the 'Made in China' label becomes increasingly synonymous with 'manufactured *and* designed in China'. The public authorities have understood that it is only when China will no longer make do with being just the world's workshop that the country will finally dominate the economic and geopolitical world stage of the 21st century.

China has come a long way already, its progress as impressive as it is worrying. In 2012, the China's State Intellectual Property Office granted 1.26 million patents, more than any other patent authority in the world[6]. And this is only the beginning as the official objective is to grant more than two million patents a year before 2015. This figure includes patents covering new inventions but also 'improvements' on existing technologies. These improvements constitute one of the biggest sources of controversy when we consider the habits of Chinese companies who illegally copy the intellectual property of Western companies then camouflage them just enough to cover their tracks. In absolute terms, Chinese R&D spending is second only to the US at roughly 197 billion dollars in 2012 with an increase of 53 billion dollars expected in 2013[7].

The most worrying aspect is that these 'breakthroughs' are not usually the result of inventions obtained legally nor fairly. According to a report from the US International Trade Commission, Chinese counterfeiting and piracy cost the American economy 2.1 million jobs and some 48.2 billion dollars in 2009 alone. Almost three quarters of this figure are attributed to a net loss of revenues on products or services that could have been sold if they hadn't been copied, and the rest from a shortfall in earnings from royalties and licence revenues. The primary targets are the big Western corporations who spend fortunes on lengthy and uncertain legal procedures seeking to defend their rights. However,

SMEs are by no means sheltered from such attacks and data hackers, particularly in the field of software, are now using the Internet as a weapon to steal intellectual property wherever it is. The impact on SMEs is all the more serious, as they generally can't afford to pursue and prosecute offenders. And so the crime goes unpunished.

When we think how much wealth creation in the West is dependent on technological innovation, it is easier to understand why the Chinese threat is of a truly existential nature. According to the US Department of Trade, technological innovation has accounted for three quarters of the annual growth in America since the mid-1940s. The same is true in Europe. If we were to lose this last remaining growth engine when we have already sacrificed our capacity to produce what we consume, the whole edifice of Western capitalism would be in danger of collapse. If our very human resources are at stake, if the intelligence of our research-ers is no longer protected, what on earth do we have left?

The Chinese attack on this front is particularly well thought-out as it is not simply dependent on pure theft. The other method used is a weapon called *zizhu chaungxin*, or the policy that imposes local content from any company bidding for public-sector contracts. In a 2006 memorandum drawn up by the public authorities entitled 'The national medium and long-term orientations for the national programme for science and technology development (2006-2020)', the State put in place a near-official system of discrimination to favour local businesses. In order to be eligible to compete for a part of the gigantic State and regional authority procurement market, but also for State-owned companies, a market worth an estimated 90 billion dollars per year[8], bidders must respect a certain number of criteria, essentially technology transfer and local content for innovation.

As we have seen earlier, this is the same principle that forced GE to hand over its in-flight electronic systems to its joint venture with the State enterprise Aviation Industry Corporation of China (AVIC). It is also the hope of gaining access to the Eldorado of high-speed rail transport in China that pushed Siemens to give up its precious technologies to the joint venture set up with its Chinese partner. All the Chinese companies have to do then is draw on some creative inspiration from this imported know-how and put these technologies to use in other ventures. In this way they can claim to have developed the innovative technologies them-selves and sell them throughout the world under their own brand with-out paying the slightest royalty. The worst aspect of this racket is that our companies are well aware of the dangers they risk but continue to dive in headfirst in this fool's game. Once again, the short-term thinking of Western CEOs and the lure of immediate profits that they hope to bring back from their Chinese adventures leads them to sacrifice their long-term future while they bolster their own competitors.

In theory, WTO rules should allow the West to put a stop to this organ-ised pillaging, although the reality is quite different. Indeed it was under the auspices of the WTO that a specific public tender agreement intended to impose transparency and fairness in the way public bodies purchase goods and services was negotiated: the 'Plurilateral Agreement on Government Procurement' ('GPA'). Unfortunately, contrary to the usual practice, this agreement is not automatically binding for all WTO members, but only for those signing. Unsurprisingly, and in spite of the pressure exerted by its trading partners, China has so far refused to ratify the agreement.

It is because we have accepted China using the yuan as a weapon to artificially support its industry while also possessing one of the world's least expensive workforces that we have opened the door to the offshor-ing of our production facilities, the deindustrialisation of our econo-mies, and the closing of thousands of SMEs. It is with the same casual indifference that we are now letting the Chinese get their hands on Western technologies which will enable them to outpace our compa-nies in the few remaining high value added sectors where we still have some competitive advantage. Today more than ever, intelligence and its necessary corollary, intellectual property, have become the very founda-tions of the wealth of nations.

Of course, no one can claim to have a monopoly on such matters, and every day Chinese scientists demonstrate their extraordinary talent for innovation. These scientists and their employers should be the first to understand that their discoveries will not become tomorrow's business successes if they are incapable of protecting copyrights on their crea-tions without fear that others will make them their own. As China rapidly becomes a major scientific power, it should become increasingly sensitive to the importance of such questions. The problem is that we don't have the luxury to hang around much longer.

Intellectual property protection must not be a WTO reserved power and must not limit itself to just the fight against theft and counterfeiting. Within the framework of their industrial policy, governments should watch over their national champions, making sure they no longer have to sell off their technologies cheaply with the sole aim of cutting a lucrative deal. Our listed corporations should for example be able to count on their governments to save them from the blackmail of Chinese local content directives. Were the State to become once more a sort of 'industrial coach', it would play a vital role at a time when collusion between the public and private sectors is increasingly being used as a weapon of conquest by the major emerging powers.

Environmental protection: might makes right

When the 15th United Nations Framework Convention on Climate Change (UNFCCC) failed in Copenhagen in December 2009, a turning point in international relations had been reached. For six decades, the world's centre of gravity was to be found somewhere in the middle of the Atlantic Ocean and yet the Copenhagen Summit Meeting was dominated and sabotaged by the Chinese-US team. The ultimate humiliation came when Europe was not even invited to the heads of States meeting to draft the agreement's final wording. Presidents Obama and Wen Jiabao, together with the Indian, Brazilian, and South African leaders simply considered it unnecessary to bother inviting the German Chancellor or the French President to their final discussions. This attitude speaks volumes when one considers how environmental policy has become one of the most important issues of the century. As Norbert Röttgen, German Minister for the Environment, so rightly stated, 'Climate change is not a subject in itself. It is an issue that forms a vital component of the new world order.'

By becoming the world's second biggest polluter, China has acquired the status of unavoidable arbiter in all climate change talks. Before

2030, China will be single-handedly responsible for almost one quarter of all the world's greenhouse gas emissions. This level is unquestionably high in absolute terms but, when considered per inhabitant, 'only' amounts to half that of the US. Without China's active participation it is, therefore, completely unrealistic to imagine reaching the greenhouse gas reduction target of 50 per cent by 2050[9].

When it comes to environmental issues, the West and developing countries can find little to agree about. On one hand the West voice concerns about the existential threat posed by global warming and lecture the new polluters, trying to shoehorn them into a highly restrictive framework of measures. On the other, they point to the irony of a situation, which sees the major Western powers, chief polluters of the past and those initially responsible for global warming, take the moral high ground, insisting that economic development cannot come at just any price.

While Westerners can afford the luxury of worrying about the dangers of economic growth, developing countries are more concerned about overcoming poverty and raising their people's standard of living. The famous principle of 'common but differentiated responsibilities', cornerstone of the Kyoto Protocol, has remained far too vague to settle the debate. Developing countries are willing to make concessions but only on three conditions: that the transition to clean technologies be paid for principally by the West; that the corresponding technology transfer take place; and above all that emission reduction objectives be expressed in relative, rather than absolute, figures, as required by the West. Developing countries would thus be ready to accept the same limits as the West on emissions per inhabitant or by GDP growth unit, well aware that with such criteria they still have considerable room for manoeuvre.

If we look more closely, the fault line goes beyond the traditional West/developing countries division. America is not so unhappy to see developing countries, particularly China, playing the bad guys at international summit meetings. As enthusiastic as he may be about environmental issues on a personal level, Obama has understood that he is powerless when up against a Congress dominated by Republicans who are largely hostile to any major environmental concession, and subject to the omnipotent energy and industry lobbies. Beyond Washington, Americans in general don't seem to care any more about environmental issues, issues which were practically non-existent in the debates leading up to the previous presidential election. In a recent survey, only 40 per cent of respondents in America believe that they will be personally harmed by global warming[10]. In developing countries we can observe the opposite trend. A 2010 study revealed that 70 per cent of respondents in China, India, and South Korea were willing to pay more for their energy if this could mitigate their impact on climate change. In the US, only 40 per cent of those polled declared themselves ready to make such an effort.

Although we have got used to the idea of emerging powers not taking environmental issues seriously, the reality has changed considerably. In China, the last two five-year plans feature concrete measures on environmental policy. For example, the eleventh plan (2006/2010) fixed a target of a 20 per cent reduction in energy consumption over five years as well as a 10 per cent reduction in pollutant emissions. The objective in cities is to treat 70 per cent of waste-water and 60 per cent of waste. Moreover, China has developed an ambitious programme to replace its multiple, small but highly polluting coal-fired power stations with much larger, more efficient plants. The twelfth five-year plan (2011/2016) confirmed this priority, insisting on the importance of developing renewable energy technologies for China.

India has also made progress in such matters, even if the country isn't moving as fast. India has used the carbon credit exchange mechanism established by the Kyoto Protocol[11], but launched much later in 2005, in order to voluntarily reduce its greenhouse gas emissions, selling them to producers in developed countries. In addition to this, several encouraging projects have been implemented such as the bio-fuel trains in the Gujarat region or Mumbai's bus network transitioning from diesel fuel to compressed natural gas. Unlike China, where public authorities are able to impose their objectives via their State enterprises, in India SMEs usually use obsolete technologies that account for 70 per cent of industrial pollution but only 40 per cent of production[12]. Even if India has the will, it is very difficult for the government to change the habits of the 4.5 million small businesses spread out across the country.

There can be no doubt that the real turning point in environmental policy was the Durban Summit of 2011. While China had hitherto made its presence felt through thinly veiled resistance to European pressure, the Durban Summit allowed China to take advantage of the general confusion, particularly disagreement between Europe and the US, to literally take control of environmental issues. To everyone's surprise, and for the first time, China chose to dissociate itself from the US on these issues, declaring its readiness to sign a legally-binding global agreement with a detailed time-frame to reduce greenhouse gas emissions. The Chinese delegation had even tried to rally support from the Indians prior to the Summit.

Why the sudden *volte-face* in China's position? Chinese leaders are beginning to understand that, as the world's rising economic giant, it is now in their interests to promote sustainable development. As the biggest global consumer of raw materials, particularly agricultural produce, China cannot help but be concerned by the resurgence of flooding and droughts throughout the world. Awareness that economic growth and environmental protection go hand in hand is gathering momentum in Beijing and resonates with the people's concerns. Along with a more acute sense of their responsibilities, the Chinese authorities have realised that they could leverage environmental policy to increase their influence in many parts of the world, notably in Africa, where the early consequences of global warming are all the more visible.

This environmental Realpolitik reveals China's increasing desire to play the card of 'smart power' while the US seems caught up in an outmoded dialectic of international relations. In so far as Europe is capable of speaking with one voice, the environment offers an unexpected chance to revive its influence and play the role of the world's third major power. As the US and China cross swords on an ever-growing list of strategic issues, Europe has the opportunity to set itself up as an unavoidable arbiter.

1 "Time for the West to practise what it preaches", *Financial Times*, 23 January 2008

2 Zhou Xiaochuan was ranked as the world's fourth most influential personality in the list of the Top 100 global thinkers published by the presitigious journal *Foreign Policy* in its December 2010 issue.

3 "Misconceptions about China's growth in military spending", Carnegie Endowment for International Peace, May 2013

4 10th GTA report, November 2011

5 U.S Department of Commerce, U.S. International Trade in Goods and Services Highlights

6 "China's Great Leap Forward in Patents", IP Watchdog, 4 April, 2013

7 "Research Outlays to decline next year", *Wall Street Journal*, 17 December 2012

8 "Can China's government procurement market be cracked?", Matechak, Jason and Brett Gerson, China Business Review online, 2010

9 Compared to emission levels in 1990

10 "Climate Change in the American Mind, Americans' Global Warming Beliefs and Attitudes", April 2013, Yale Project on Climate Change Communication

11 Through the Clean Development Mechanism ("CDM")

12 "China and India's participation in global climate negotiations", Walsh, Tian, Whalley, Agarwal, June 2011

Part Three

Rebuilding upon the ruins of Western capitalism

Chapter 1

First step: bring down the myths

Emerging countries are winning the economic war, but can they reign?

The advance of emerging countries to the forefront of the world's political and economic stage has been so dramatic, that many Westerners consider the decline of their countries to be inevitable. As if it were somehow written in the course of history, the myth of emerging powers' invincibility is steadily winning over hearts and minds. For the most defeatist among us, we simply have to put up with it and avoid making any waves in the hope that the new conquerors will bring their capital to our Western economies. For the more hawkish, we should be brandishing protectionism a weapon capable of protecting our jobs, our values, and, ultimately, our way of life. But between these two extremes, no one seems to be asking themselves the only truly relevant question. The emerging powers certainly showed themselves capable of filling the void left by the implosion of Western capitalism, but will they know how to reign? Will they be able to maintain their influence over the long-term? Nothing is less certain.

From Pax Romana to Pax Americana, the history of empires shows that while economic domination and military strength form the basis of conquests, in order to achieve a lasting rule, two conditions must be met. The first is that the new power should establish a certain social and political equilibrium within its borders. The system established to achieve this balance may well be at odds with the democratic principles defended by the West, which we wrongly assume to be universal. However, as imperfect as it may be, this equilibrium must be built around a form of consensus, as well as a shared vision of the future. This is particularly true at a time when State propaganda is so easily swept aside by the viral power of social networking, as we have seen from Tahrir Square to the streets of Tehran.

The second condition is that outside its borders the empire should go beyond the most rudimentary form of power, offering a culture, a philosophy, or simply an ideal with which millions of individuals across the world can identify. America's domination of international affairs since the mid-20th century owes as much to the Pentagon and Wall Street as it does to Hollywood or pop music. These elements that cut across borders and cultural origins give great nations a form of 'soft power' at certain points in their history without which the more traditional 'hard power' would not be able to last.

Applying these two criteria, it is clear that the emerging powers are some way from establishing a truly sustainable model of power. In countries like China or Russia, the domestic equilibrium remains precarious as these regimes have not established the conditions to achieve social consensus on their direction. Neither do they offer their people the impression that power is exercised in their best interests. Nepotism, corruption, and personal gain observed at the highest echelons of the State undermine the legitimacy of governments, particularly seen through the eyes of a population becoming both better informed and better educated. Added to the general sense of unfairness, is frustration engendered by the chronic inefficiency of State bureaucracy. A pervasive State is increasingly considered as the enemy within, and this is particularly true for the middle classes. And yet a great power cannot prevail today without responding to the needs of this middle class who will most certainly become the world's biggest political and economic force in the coming years.

The political leaders of emerging powers have yet to grasp the full scope of this new challenge. The middle classes account for 1.8 billion of the world's individuals today. This figure will rocket to five billion tomorrow, with almost all of the growth coming from developing countries. In less than two years, more than 1.2 billion people will have access to the Internet in the five biggest emerging powers (China, India, Indonesia, Brazil, and Russia)[1] and will not only be able to get information but also to share that information amongst themselves and join forces. This combination of factors can only have profound consequences, not only economically but also politically.

By way of illustration, the Bo Xilai affair came to light in China during the spring of 2012 and revealed the cancer that seems to be eating away at the Chinese regime from the inside, weakening it in the eyes of an increasingly lucid population who now see the limits of the system. Governor of the People's Congress of Chongqing, and one of the 25 members of the all-powerful politburo, Bo Xilai used his enormous power to amass a personal fortune of hundreds of millions of dollars. For many years amongst the main beneficiaries of systemic racketeering and bribery in his region, this man whose father was one of Mao's Eight Elders and an eminent member of the Communist Party, was arrested along with his wife who was accused of the murder of a British businessman. But for every Bo Xilai caught red-handed in the sort of scandal that shows up the system's failures, there are countless others, family members of the Party's or State enterprises' leaders who, without going as far as committing criminal acts as such, continue to share the bounty of the 'Chinese dream'. While millions of Chinese youth leave the countryside to cram into dormitory towns on the outskirts of cities in the hope of finding work that is more often than not insecure, a few thousand mandarins take up the key positions and live opulent lifestyles. This dichotomy between the fate awaiting the 'ant tribe' to use the expression of the Chinese sociologist Lian Si, and the accumulated privileges of the new nomenklatura is a time bomb just waiting to explode.

China's dynastic power sharing is in itself nothing new. What is new, however, is the scope and visibility of the wealth accumulated by the beneficiaries of a system at all levels of the State apparatus; from the central bodies of the Communist Party down to the smallest of the regional municipalities. The list of dignitaries' offspring occupying key positions in the country's biggest corporations is long and ever more embarrassing for the regime especially since the foreign press[2] started to look more closely at the most blatant cases. Former President Hu Jintao's son, Hu Haifeng, was the all-powerful representative of the Party at Tsinghua Holdings, a holding company with a large number of strategic stakes, particularly in the technology sector; Wen Yunsong, son of the former Prime Minister Wen Jiabao, is chairman of China Satellite Communications, an important State-owned enterprise; Jiang Mianheng, son of the former president Jiang Zemin, is one of the largest shareholder of Shanghai Alliance Investments, a group known for its joint venture with Microsoft; Li Xiaolin, the daughter of ex-Prime

Minister Li Peng, is chairman of China Power International, one of the top five electricity producers in the country. His son, Li Xiaopeng, was at the helm of another State-owned enterprise in the same sector.

Beyond the social tensions building in the system, the incestuous ties between political power and businesses – what the Chinese refer to as *guanxi*, or their culture's deep-rooted system of networks – slow down reforms in entire sectors of the economy that remain closed to competition, be it domestic or foreign.

It is undeniable that the country's overall standard of living has vastly improved, that a new middle class is emerging, and that the new millionaires are most often entrepreneurs who have managed to work their way up to the very top of Chinese society solely on the strength of their individual merit. But the frustration of those left behind is all the greater for it.

When average Beijing house prices climb steeply every month, how many can still dream of putting a foot on the property ladder? According to the IMF, seven of the 10 least affordable housing markets in the world are now located in China, with median house prices in Beijing soaring to over 22 times the median wage[3]. The 250 million Chinese born since 1980 no longer have the fatalistic patience of their elders. This increasingly vindictive generation no longer reads the official newspapers but gets its information browsing the Web where Chinese youth spend more than 34 hours a week[4]. Young people are denied Facebook and Twitter, still banned in China, but have their own type of social media, *weibos*, or micro-blogs whose short, viral messages enable them to express themselves freely. It is through these uncensored media that they are able to denounce abuse.

Is it really possible to lastingly build up a major power on such a fragile social foundation? There are legitimate reasons to have doubts here. The regime could mend its ways and evolve towards a new system where people have the feeling that the fruits of the Chinese miracle are shared out more fairly. Unfortunately, such a prospect seems a long way off.

Having been unable to establish a true social balance to bolster its political power at home, China doesn't seem to be in a better position to win over hearts and minds beyond its borders. The Beijing Olympics in

2008 were supposed to show the face of modern China and bring the country to the forefront of the world's collective consciousness. But even there, the only objective achieved was to open the eyes of the world to China's extraordinary economic power, not playing on the feel good factor at all. The reality today is that China frightens the rest of the world.

In order to better understand the limits of China's geopolitical positioning, we need look no further than the regions in which the country already has important strategic interests. Take Africa, for example. China's success in Africa is often misleading. The country has managed to put its huge financial resources to use, resulting in several African regimes finding themselves locked into multi-year contracts to supply raw materials. But these agreements don't do enough for the local populations who look on helpless. Tens of thousands of Chinese workers turn up, no sooner than the contracts have been signed, despite the surplus labour force created by sky-high African unemployment. The million Chinese living today in Africa are not perceived as the ambassadors of a nation proudly exporting its values and culture, but rather as the anonymous soldiers of a colossal power, driven only by its economic interests and desires for geopolitical hegemony.

The assassination of Wu Shangzai, the Chinese manager of a Zambian coal mine, by African workers during the summer of 2012 revealed the extent of the malaise. A recent Human Rights Watch report on the working conditions of African workers employed locally by Chinese companies paints the picture of a veritable powder keg. The dark calling cards of colonial exploitation seem to have returned; meagre salaries coupled with punishingly long working days and ill treatment of workers, to name but a few.

So is China more successful at home in Asia? Not in the slightest. Countries like Indonesia, Vietnam, South Korea, and Japan are all trying to stay in the Americans' good books to counteract China's growing ambition in the region. This movement has not gone unnoticed by President Obama who sees a historic occasion to shift the centre of gravity of American foreign policy from Europe to Asia-Pacific.

China is not alone amongst the major emerging powers in not knowing how to navigate the final stages of their race to economic success.

Putin's Russia suffers from the same inability to build up the kind of social balance without which citizens find it hard to imagine a brighter future for themselves. Anti-Kremlin protests rallied over 100,000 people in December 2011 and continued until the elections in the spring 2012. Such movements demonstrate the frustration of the new middle classes who no longer wish to put up with the oligarchy running their country.

Ironically, Putin is largely to thank for improvements in this educated, digitally literate population's lot. He was the one who put the country back on track after the chaotic privatisations of the 1990s. This, however, is no longer enough. This well-informed middle class has grown up in the post-Soviet era and is unlikely to keep tolerating the endemic corruption, the bureaucracy, the arbitrariness, and the distribution of the country's wealth amongst a dozen individuals whose main merit is to be able to count on the Kremlin's unfailing support.

The country has a long tradition of State authoritarianism, but in the end, the country's leaders will be judged on results, not promises. Behind the impressive growth figures of these last years and the 500 billion dollars of currency reserves hide many substantial weaknesses.

The country's economy is still highly dependent upon oil and gas, which means that in a downturn, recessions are all the more brutal. In 2009 for instance, GDP plummeted by almost 8 per cent and Russia experienced the worst recession of all the G20 countries. Furthermore, the Russian economy continues to suffer from chronically poor productivity and inefficiency, which leaves little hope for medium-term perspectives. GDP per inhabitant is still 70 per cent lower than in the US. Russian infrastructure is also in a disastrous state. The 2012/13 World Economic Forum Global Competitiveness Report ranked Russia 136th out of 144 for the quality of its road network, behind countries like Angola or Tajikistan[5]. No wonder the average Russian doesn't get the feeling in his daily existence that the extraordinary wealth in the country's subsoil has been shared out fairly. And this is what will end up weakening the regime and thwarting its ambitions to be a major power on the global stage.

Neither does Russia's foreign policy seem in line with its international aspirations, as it maintains a confrontational approach on the diplomatic front. By taking a stance reminiscent of the Cold War during the

Snowden affair or in Syria, the Kremlin is playing a dangerous game which, ultimately, may undermine its credibility. The same applies in the Caucuses or the former Central Asian republics where Russia has been unable to establish a positive zone of influence. The country's power is entirely built on its military might or its economic muscle. However as we have seen, and as important as they may be, these factors rarely form a sustainable power base.

Unlike China and Russia, India and Brazil have never had ambitions to play a central role on the international political stage. They certainly aspire to a position of greater influence but have never claimed to be either willing or able to offer an alternative to American supremacy. Nevertheless they remain major emerging powers, whose companies have become formidable competitors for the West's biggest corporations. It is, therefore, important to take a closer look at their development prospects.

After many euphoric years, India is now at a juncture. While the country's GDP growth hovered at around 8 per cent during 2000-2010, growth for 2012-13 fell to 5 per cent[6]. The business community is reluctant to openly criticise India's long-standing Congress Party for its inertia and inability to lead the structural reforms the country so desperately needs. The State machine's cumbersome bureaucracy, corruption amongst the political classes, and arbitrary regulatory regimes are all evils that hold back Indian enterprise from realising its full potential. The government has also been incapable of capitalising on the recent years' successes to reduce inequality within the population. India is still home to almost one third of the Earth's poor. Between 2006 and 2011, the Gini coefficient, commonly used to measure inequalities in wealth, went up from 38.1 to 39.9[7]. Education in India also remains poor, with one third of women and one fifth of men unable to read or write. India's spending on public health care is 1.2 per cent of GDP, compared to China's 2.7 per cent, leaving the poor often with little choice but to turn to expensive, unregulated private providers[8].

While many Indian companies have become world leaders in their industries over the last 20 years, the wage share of added value has plummeted from 70 to 50 per cent. Suffice to say, the Indian miracle has not had the same resonance with everybody.

Far from the hi-tech image reflected in the glass and steel towers of Bangalore, India, in fact, suffers from inadequate or inexistent infrastructure. The country doesn't produce enough energy to cover its own needs; roads are in a calamitous state and logistics for the transport of goods are still so primitive that it is often easier for certain companies to export their produce rather than delivering them within the country's borders.

Although these subjects feature prominently in candidates' manifestos at each election, coalition strategies between the two major parties – the Congress Party and the Bharatiya Janata Party or BJP – and their smaller regional counterparts end up paralysing political life. Key decisions are simply not being taken. India will most probably play an increasingly important role on the world stage over the coming years, but the country cannot count on the achievements of its private sector or its entrepreneurial genius alone to get them there. If the State continues to play the card of inertia, the country will forever remain a fallen angel of the emerging world.

Can we find, in the Brazilian model, more reasons to believe in the BRIC's future and their supposedly inexorable rise towards world domination? With an estimated annual growth rate of only 2.5 per cent in 2013[9], Brazil is now beginning to question its own model. Even though it has been one of the national priorities in recent years to promote innovation and reduce the relative share of raw materials in the economy, exactly the opposite has happened. China, being the number one customer for Brazilian natural resources, has meant that when the Chinese ogre sneezes, all of Brazil catches a cold. However, Brazilian problems do not end there. As with most of the other BRIC countries, State bureaucracy has become a major handicap for the private sector, particularly for SMEs. The State has also increased its presence amongst major corporations, using corporate giants like Petrobras or Vale to pursue its own agenda without worrying too much about minority shareholders.

Brazil's successes over the last few years have been so spectacular that they almost make us forget decades of hyper-inflation and political instability, which held back the economy up until the 1990s. The country has since been able to restructure and ride on Asian growth to create wealth. Brazil has also harnessed its huge agricultural resources to put itself up amongst the leading producers of clean energies. However, the country did not manage to build up a knowledge-based economy focused on innovation and able to diversify its sources of revenues. In these matters, the contrast with China and its obsession with intellectual property is striking. The consequence is that although Brazil is now undoubtedly a considerable regional power, the country still has a long way to go before it can genuinely count itself amongst the world's great powers.

Given these structural weaknesses across the spectrum of emerging countries, it is tempting to think that the BRICs were nothing but an amusing acronym invented by an ambitious economist from Goldman Sachs to capture the imagination of investors hungry for dreams and profits. Can they really continue to grow at the same rates as in the last few years? Shouldn't we in the West secretly rejoice at the challenges faced by these models, which we once perceived as an existential threat for our economies, responsible for mass unemployment and deindustrialisation? Is it payback time at last?

Thinking this way would be a big mistake. It would lull us into believing that the status quo is a viable option for the West, or even that the delicate phase emerging countries are going through is our chance to regain the initiative. And yet nothing could be further from the realities of the globalised economy in which we live. Were Chinese growth to suddenly stumble, the slowdown of the world's second economic powerhouse behind the US would be a disaster for the entire planet. China and the other emerging powers have financial reserves at their disposal, which would enable them to get through another crisis relatively unscathed, whereas such a downturn would be fatal for the over-indebted West with almost no prospects for medium-term growth. It is, therefore, clearly in both European and American interests that the emerging economies continue to make progress.

Those who revel in this kind of *Schadenfreude,* upon seeing emerging countries falter, forget how quickly these countries are able to adapt and turn around their economic, political, and even social models in order to seize opportunities. Who would have predicted in 1998 as the Asian crisis took hold, that the continent would pick up again so fast as to become the epicentre of world growth once more? And who could have anticipated scarcely 20 years ago that China would become the world's greatest capitalist force while ostensibly under a communist regime? Who could have foreseen that the integration of Hong Kong into the People's Republic would go through so easily? If the Chinese regime suddenly decides that in order to consolidate and sustain its powerbase it has to become more flexible, more democratic, and less corrupt, it will make all this happen in the blink of an eye and take Western observers by surprise. This pragmatism has enabled China to get where it is today, and it is this same pragmatism that will drive it to evolve in the future.

As far as India is concerned, roadblocks on the way to development are many. But who would have thought that this country of 1.2 billion inhabitants would become, and remain, the world's biggest democracy? Who would have imagined that some of the jewels in the crown of the former British colonial power, notably in the car and steel industries, would fall into Indian hands, and that the new Indian owners would be successful where Western shareholders had failed?

Ultimately, the biggest danger for the Westerners when faced with competition from emerging powers is our lack of lucidity; we rarely seem to see them for what they are. We overestimate them when succumbing to panic or defeatism in the face of countries that often produce more, better, or cheaper goods than we do. But we forget that they, too, are faced with serious issues and that countries like Germany have shown that it is possible to be a major exporter and leader in heavy industry while still bearing high labour costs.

On the other hand, we seriously under-estimate these countries by interpreting the slightest downturn as a leading indicator of a hard landing for economies we like to think of as overheating, especially when comparing them to our own. Emerging countries' robust growth is here to stay; it corresponds to a social and demographic reality, and it is high time we learned to see this phenomenon as an opportunity rather than a threat. In this way it will be easier for us to overcome our inhibitions and regain confidence in our ability to measure up to the great emerging powers on their own turf.

The economic Maginot Line fantasy: one man's wealth is not another man's poverty

To the myth of emerging powers' invincibility we need to add a necessary corollary, that is, the need to erect a Maginot Line around our Western economies. Anti-globalisation activists emboldened since the 2008 crisis, are the torch-bearers of a philosophy, whose logic is the same as the protectionist refrains from the 1930s. Emerging countries challenge our very values and way of life when they precipitate factory closures and mass unemployment. It is therefore only fair to impose trade barriers as well as a 'national preference' or at least a 'buy European' ethos. To hell with our competitiveness issues or our inability to create a knowledge-based economy even though we have a considerable head start in this area.

It is difficult to deny that globalisation has benefitted Western prosperity as much as it has emerging country growth. When wages stagnate for years in the US and Europe, what on earth would have happened to households' purchasing power if they hadn't been able to stock up at Walmart or Tesco with goods made in China at a fraction of the price of local produce? Our local manufacturers have certainly lost jobs, but the economic shortfall is nothing compared to the advantages gained through the trade.

It has become fashionable to criticise the English economist David Ricardo. At the beginning of the 19th century, he argued in favour of free trade between nations and the resulting mutual benefit, provided that each learns to concentrate on what they do best. But it turns out that Ricardo was right. It is protectionism that deepened and lengthened the Great Depression from the Wall Street Crash of 1929 up to the Second World War.

Conversely, it is the opening up of world trade that brought about the unprecedented prosperity we have known ever since. Given that the most open economies boast annual GDP figures of around 24,000 dollars per inhabitant, which is more than a dozen times the level of the most protected economies, it is clear that free trade is a vital factor in economic growth. Just take Singapore or Hong Kong, which were fishing ports 50 years ago. It is by transforming themselves into quasi free trade zones and by developing centres of excellence that they have become economic giants.

In addition to European and American consumers, our big corporations have also benefitted hugely from globalisation. L'Oréal, Procter & Gamble, BMW, Nestlé, and EADS are just a few of our corporate giants for whom emerging countries have become their main driver of growth and, in many cases, their main source of revenue. When we ask our Western companies what they think about 'buying national' or 'buying European' their reply is not long coming. They are convinced they have much more to lose than they have to gain by flying such flags. At the end of the day, it is only politicians in election season or publicity-hungry economists who dare defend the idea, were it practical, of artificially protecting our industry by putting up trade and tariff barriers.

The other fallacy about globalisation is that our own companies take advantage of it to close down their historical plants so as to maximise profits by off-shoring production facilities and thus manufacturing goods at lower costs.

For some of the hardcore supporters of the economic Maginot Line, all we have to do is to outlaw off-shoring or make it so expensive that companies would think twice before considering it. However, the tragic example of Peugeot, the French car manufacturer, came back to remind them that in the many sectors where competition is fierce, keeping production facilities artificially open is pointless when the very survival of the company is at stake. Peugeot, a company that in July 2012 still manufactured 50 per cent of its vehicles within French borders, announced historic losses and the inevitable closure of its Aulnay plant. By contrast, Renault achieved a profit of 1.73 billion euros in 2012. Ninety per cent of this profit was made abroad, thanks to Nissan and the entry-level Dacia brand. This fact would seem to validate charismatic group CEO Carlos Ghosn's internationalisation strategy. As the instigator of this strategy, Ghosn has been unfairly lambasted for his lack of economic patriotism. The verdict now seems clear. It is, in fact, globalisation combined with the foresightedness of its leaders that saved Renault. And it is misplaced economic patriotism, coupled with lacklustre leadership, that condemned Peugeot. Which type of company do we prefer to have in the West?

Protectionist pleas are becoming increasingly urgent on the other side of the Atlantic, too. The most recent illustrations are the car industry's Congress-endorsed battle against Chinese imports or the conflict opposing American solar cell manufacturers and their Chinese competitors. These manufacturers accuse China of subsidising local manufacturers to the tune of billions of dollars, and succeeded in obtaining from Congress customs duties often exceeding 50 per cent of imported goods' prices. The hypocrisy of this decision cannot fail to surprise when we consider that the renewable energy industry in the US is, itself, one of the biggest beneficiaries of State subsidies in the world.

American solar panel manufacturers received over one billion dollars of financial aid from Washington in 2011. California-based Solyndra alone benefitted from more than 500 million dollars of federal grants since its creation but even that was not enough to stop it going out of business in September 2011. What separates Americans and Chinese in this case is not the level of State intervention but rather the ability to draw up and roll out a winning strategy in a fast-growing sector of the market. The former use their technological know-how to create innovative products and hope that demand will follow. The latter wait for the demand to show up, then adjust their aim with an offering that perfectly corresponds to customer wants and needs both in functionality and price.

Blaming globalisation for one man's success and another man's failure is a dangerous short-cut. The influx of Chinese-made solar panels into the American market has reduced the unit price by more than 65 per cent over the last four years, thus making this clean energy source considerably more accessible. Moreover, the critics tend to forget that these panels amount to only 40 per cent of the installation's total cost, meaning that the remaining 60 per cent of the equipment and service is more often than not supplied by American companies, thereby creating jobs and paying taxes. The tariff barriers recently imposed by Washington will, therefore, end up backfiring on those they were set up to protect.

Our aim here is certainly not to condone a laissez-faire attitude when confronted with the serious breaches of the rules governing fair competition by countries like China, India, or Russia.

While the average customs duty levied on imports in the developed countries has fallen from 10 per cent in 1980 to less than 5 per cent today, it is unacceptable that over the same period tariffs imposed by emerging countries should have only gone down from 30 per cent to some 15 per cent[10]. While this remains a positive trend in both cases, the differential has become unjustifiable, much more so than it was 30 years ago. In recognition for opening up our markets, we should demand that the favour be returned and adopt the policy of a 'gradual response' as suggested earlier in this book. However, it would be totally counter-productive for the West to dive headlong into a huge trade war with no other objective than to appease industrial wrath. Particularly when the real problem of such ill-tempered industrialists is their reluctance to adapt their companies to the new challenges in their sectors. Resorting to protectionism would mean remaining in a state of denial. Globalisation is only the enemy of the West if we stay on the defensive, looking to protect rather than conquer. Instead of hoping for better days and turning to their governments, begging for financial aid and trade tariffs, our industrial leaders would be better fighting on with the weapons they already have to hand: initiative and intelligence.

---

1   "The internet's new billion", BCG, September 2010

2   "China's power families", *Financial Times*, 10 July 2012, and "Wen's family hidden billions", *New York Times*, 27 October 2012

3   "China Has The Most Unaffordable Housing in the World", *The Atlantic*, 1 July, 2013

4   According to a study conducted by the consulting firm Accenture

5   World Economic Forum, Global Competitiveness Report 2012/13

6   Source: government statistics

7   Source: Euromonitor International: "Special Report: Income Inequality Rising Across the Globe", March 2012. The Gini index is a measure of the degree of inequality in the distribution of revenues in a given society, developed by the Italian statistician Corrado Gini. A score of zero on the Gini index indicates perfect equality (everyone has the same revenue) and 100 per cent means total inequality (one person has all the revenue)

8   "(Why India Trials China)", *New York Times*, 19 June, 2013

9   Source : IMF

10 Source: WTO

Chapter 2

Turning the apparatchik CEO back into a real entrepreneur

Reconciling our listed companies with the long term

Once we have got rid of our favourite scapegoats, we will have to own up to a simple truth: Western capitalism is not the powerless victim of the greatest miscarriage of economic justice in history, but is in fact entirely to blame for its own misfortune. By replacing our great entrepreneurs with overpaid, risk-averse managers, the financial shareholders who dominate our big corporations have ended up sucking the very life force out of our capitalism. The problem is that this phenomenon which started over 20 years ago happened at a time when emerging countries had grasped the potential of our entrepreneurial capitalism and decided to adopt both its values and methods.

Our challenge today is to relearn this capitalism in a thoroughly different context from the one in which we discarded it. It is neither feasible nor desirable to go back and attempt to recreate the lost world of the post-war boom, the period when most of our major groups came into existence. We won't be able to bring back to life the golden age of the Sainsburys, Weinstocks, or Rockefellers. Our duty, however, is to enable tomorrow's captains of industry to develop and grow, and to change the behaviour of the CEOs of listed companies so that they act like responsible business owners rather than mere administrators. As we have seen, this attitude comes most naturally to those who are both owners and managers of their companies. It is nevertheless possible to replicate similar behaviour within a listed company, provided, of course, that their boards become aware of the urgency for governance reform.

In order to fight short-term thinking, the first thing to do is revise top executive pay for listed companies. It is not the absolute level of their pay packages, but rather their structure which has become irrelevant. We must, however, steer clear of the demagogical trap set by those who call for executive pay to be capped at a multiple of the minimum wage, or to overtax them so as to reinstate 'social justice'. They forget that there is nothing easier for the CEO of a large corporation than to quit and take on a similar job, but this time in a country where such limits don't exist. And imagine if, having already lost our business creators, we began to lose the brains behind our largest companies; what would we have left?

On the other hand, we should also recognise that stock options, share awards, and performance-related bonuses, have done nothing to better align the interests of senior executives and their shareholders. In fact, quite the opposite, as these are calculated over excessively short periods of time, the resulting compensation has often enabled executives to get rich quick while their company's stock price and results stagnate for years. However, the worst is that these manifold performance incentives have provoked managerial myopia amongst their fortunate beneficiaries. Why bother thinking about next month when the market hammers home the message that only next week counts? Why would a chief executive make risky R&D investments when he knows full well that the return on these investments will at best benefit his successor's pay check, and at worst, expose himself to scathing attacks that he has misused his group's available cash?

We must, therefore, use our imagination and find other methods, bearing in mind that reforming our executives' compensation structures is a necessary, if not sufficient, condition to making our companies more competitive. As long as asset managers – mutual funds, hedge funds, and the rest – remain incentivised on the basis of their short-term performance, they will do nothing other than encourage the leaders of their portfolio companies to continue to worry only about their quarterly results. It is therefore the entire investment chain that needs a thorough overhaul, so as to give each stakeholder, including the intermediaries who dominate the financial system today, a good reason to start thinking long-term. As we will see later, the solutions are very much practical and not just philosophical.

The regulator can also play an important role here by putting a stop to the ever-increasing burden in terms of the frequency of financial information expected from public companies. The diktat of quarterly results is slowly but surely destroying our economies. Our business leaders have been transformed into public relations officers who spend all their waking hours in road shows, where their every word is read and re-read by lawyers on the lookout for any potential misunderstanding, and emptying any phrase of its substance. One of the City's best equity managers confessed to me that he had given up visiting the companies he planned to invest in, as he could no longer put up with their management teams' political cant. A terrible waste of time, in his opinion. The problem is that our business leaders so wear themselves out by spouting empty words that they forget that they are paid to act. And therein lies the rub of modern capitalism in the West.

The investor has every right to be kept informed and to call on or confront the chief executive of his portfolio company, if need be. But being a shareholder of a listed company does not confer unlimited prerogatives, and certainly not the right to distract a company's management from its fundamental mission by bullying and harassment. The regulator's mission is to protect the investor and make sure that he has all the necessary information at his disposal to be able to knowingly take the right decisions. But it is also the regulator's duty to make sure that the best interests of the company are respected, and that an individual shareholder is not able to threaten the common good through his own improper actions. Going public must no longer mean replacing business strategy with tactical communication and all those concerned should remember this: first and foremost, senior executives, but also directors, should learn to be more daring, as well as the regulator.

In listed companies, as in every political system, too much direct democracy often ends up jeopardising democracy itself. The annual shareholder meeting should remain a forum for discussion and free expression. Shareholders elect company directors who are thus mandated to fix strategic priorities and appoint a CEO who will take the day-to-day decisions required to implement the direction the board has set. The CEO will in turn appoint, at his discretion, the right management team to enable him to get the job done. Upsetting this balance, for example by allowing shareholders to short-circuit the board and hound the CEO with their views, is tantamount to risking corporate paralysis, especially in a society that has become as litigious as our own. At the other extreme, the chief executive ruling by divine right, using his fellow directors as a mere sounding board, can as easily lead to perpetual turmoil.

Let's look at the example of executive compensation. Given the dysfunctional nature of the current situation that allows certain business leaders to be rewarded for their failures, governments on both sides of the Atlantic have tried to legislate such that shareholders brought together at the annual general meeting could decide on the level and structure of their top management's pay. The idea is to go beyond the existing framework that already allows shareholders in the US[1] and Great Britain to vote and express their points of view on executive compensation, while falling short of being legally binding. The current plan would make this vote binding, thereby removing one of the board's hitherto most important prerogatives.

Such reforms could be dangerous, and the fact that many corporate boards have carried out their roles so badly in the past does not justify emptying them of their substance. What would we think of a political system where parliament were cut back to the bare minimum and all the major laws were voted by referendum? Transposed to the business world, where decisions require a minimum of sector expertise and a clear understanding of a company's competitive environment, such an approach could be very damaging.

Rather than giving up all hope that listed companies' directors may at last fulfil their mission, particularly on matters of remuneration, we would be better repairing what is repairable. We must make them more accountable, ensuring that they are competent and convince them, for instance, that benchmarking their CEO's pay against that of other chief executives in the industry is simply not enough.

The leaders of our largest corporations are undeniably going to have to change. As difficult as it might be, they should sometimes imagine that their company is a small business which they have created and which they would love to hand down to their own children. If they could adopt such a mindset they would certainly worry far more about the future.

But if we are unable to count on our CEOs' bent for introspection, we will have to help them see themselves as veritable entrepreneurs in whom our expectations go well beyond their ability to manage everyday affairs. And yet such an ambition can only be collective. Shareholders should be engaged but more loyal; directors should be alert but a bit braver; and regulators should be more sensitive to the need of keeping companies safe from the noise of Wall Street and the City.

CEOs must think like business owners: 'put your money where your mouth is!'

Capitalism is usually explained to children as the system which enables those who take risks to make a profit and that it is this profit that creates jobs and pays the taxes without which no collective would be able to function properly. We teach them that at the heart of all human activity lies the wise old adage: 'nothing ventured nothing gained'.

We forget to tell them, most probably because we are ashamed, that Western capitalism version 2.0 invented a new concept, which defies economic gravity: profit without investment. It has in fact become possible to take no financial risk in the strictest sense, and yet still accumulate fortunes of hundreds of millions of dollars. How? All you need is to be a brilliant manager sought after by the world's biggest multinationals, and negotiate your employment contract to include a golden handshake, a loyalty incentive, and a golden parachute. Once signed, such a contract will allow you to secure your family's financial future for the next three or four generations without ever having even put a foot on your future employer's premises. But that isn't all, as these multiple bonuses mentioned above only whet the appetite of these big cats of modern capitalism. For good measure, such special employees require the same potential for financial gain as a business creator. And this is where the stock options, stock grants, top-up pension plans, and other financial gadgets come in.

In order to benefit from such fabulous treatment, have we at least asked our *über-capitalist* to demonstrate his faith in the company that is about to welcome him by investing some of his savings in its shares? And yet

such a proposal should seem irresistible, as the company about to benefit from his managerial genius could only be an exceptional investment
prospect. But no. Nothing. Nothing is ever asked in return for the
financial sacrifices made up front and the prospects of additional earnings to come. Perhaps the most surprising aspect is that the chosen one
almost never tries to become a shareholder independently of his stock
options or share windfalls.

Over lunch with the CEO of a major listed British company, at which he
extolled the virtues of his company, I dared ask him how many company
shares he had bought himself. He began by explaining that as a director
it was difficult for him to find the 'right window' to buy stock without
violating market regulations before confessing that he found it unwise
to 'put all his eggs in one basket'. The eggs, in this instance, being his
career and his personal wealth. A home truth that spoke volumes about
the disconnect that exists today between the trajectories of decision-
makers and the destinies of their groups.

It was during the 1980s in the US that the manager-deification process
began. We got used to comparing their compensation with the potential increase in their companies' stock price – thus comparing an individual's compensation to a company's market capitalisation! – considering it logical that the one who presides over a group worth tens of
billions may get a payback as substantial as that of a major investor and
his capital gains. Notwithstanding the remarkable contributions of
certain star managers, what is the underlying logic behind this philosophy that has steadily taken hold across Europe and the entire developed
world? Emerging countries haven't dived headlong into this mad rush
for managerial talent. There, as in the West up until the 1980s, fortunes
are still made by entrepreneurs who are prepared to take real risks to
build up those groups that they still manage today.

If we really want our managers to start behaving like owners, things will
have to change. Becoming a shareholder after exercising one's options in
no way has the same psychological impact as investing one's own savings
in that company; least of all when the option-holder's salary already
guarantees him significant personal wealth. There is nothing wrong in
offering high salaries to managers who have ensured the long-term
success of their companies while at their helm. But let's ask them to

invest more than just their time and energy. They should be expected to leave their comfort zones and put themselves in danger for once. Directors of listed companies should demand prospective CEOs invest a substantial part of their personal liquid net worth in the company upon arrival. Each entrant should contribute according to his means as it is not the absolute amount that counts but the relative effort. If necessary, companies should consider lending the required sums of money while requesting personal guarantees from their managers.

What would the right level of investment be initially? At least 10 per cent of the executive's liquid net worth. At this level, the investment is high enough to ensure the executive's personal commitment over the long term without discouraging good candidates from such careers. Over time, this approach should be extended to all executive committee members.

Naturally, it is not up to the regulator to interfere in such matters, which clearly lie within the board's remit. Independent directors should make the effort to think out of the box and propose creative solutions that reconcile both shareholders and management, but also senior executives with their own companies. A listed company that publicly proclaimed such executive investment policies would be rewarded by the markets. Private and institutional investors would applaud such an approach, as it would align their interests with those of their portfolio company's management. These investors would come to understand what they have to gain from a new management philosophy focused on the long term.

A business leader investing at least 10 per cent of his personal fortune in his company upon arrival would waste far less time justifying his pay at each successive AGM. Investors are not necessarily shocked by the fact that CEOs get rich, but rather by the mercenary spirit that so often pervades senior appointments. A new CEO investing his own savings in his company's stock would implicitly send a very strong message to both his investors and his troops. It would be tantamount to saying, 'I believe in this, follow me'. Even customers would appreciate the gesture, as they would interpret this as a sign of trust and continuity.

If we really want to make our businesses competitive again we need to rebuild a virtuous circle. It is not intelligence that has been lacking in the West over the last 20 years compared to Chinese or Indian companies, but rather a sense of responsibility and accountability. We have forgotten something obvious which is at the heart of the capitalist model: our desire to win is even greater when we know we have something to lose. Not lose what we could have gained – as is the case with stock options and share awards – but lose something that we had before attempting a new venture. Put another way, the gains of senior executives must be proportional to the real risks they have dared to take.

Beyond the issue of senior executive compensation, the State could play an important role in encouraging employee stock ownership in every company, listed or not. Governments could for example offer a reduced tax rate for capital gains on shares held by company employees, or even make interest charges on loans contracted to buy one's own company's shares tax deductible. Such a policy would be neither right wing nor left. In being more proactive in such matters, governments could kill three birds with one stone. They could attract future entrepreneurs and encourage them to set up their own businesses; they could help companies motivate their employees; and most of all, they would make a big step towards stabilising a listed company's shareholder base. Such shareholder stability would free up executives from the pressures exerted by nomadic financial investors and would enable them to think in strategic rather than tactical terms – a critical aspect in the battle for competitiveness.

One of the English language's least elegant, but perhaps wisest sayings is: 'Put your money where your mouth is'! Most of the Western world seem to have forgotten the virtues of this, most basic of principles. And the price of this oversight? Nothing less than our ability to create and to put our faith in those bearing the ideas of tomorrow. And without them we will find it near impossible to build ourselves a future.

Appraise and compensate business leaders over time

In the age of instant information we have invented the concept of instant management. We believe that 50,000-strong groups can be managed like small businesses. Business schools around the world teach their students that a chief executive has but 100 days to take in the realities of the company he now heads up and start to turn it around. Beyond this milestone, the company runs the risk of inertia.

No sooner has a new CEO been appointed, than the markets expect him to have reviewed and amended group strategy and set the corporation out on his chosen new direction. Financial analysts have become masters in the art of forecasting figures for those companies they follow. They are even beginning to believe that the growth of a a company's revenues may be decreed with the same ease that they manipulate their Excel spreadsheets. As a direct consequence of this, all it takes is for the actual results to miss their forecasts by just a few percentage points for the axe to fall, and for the company to see its value slashed by several billion in a matter of hours. The worst of it is that CEOs play the game, turning up at analysts' meetings with stomach cramps, despite the fact that in reality these analysts have at best a purely theoretical understanding of the company's operational reality.

This reckless pursuit contaminates management boards who tend, in turn, to treat their newly recruited executives as saviours capable of turning around situations in the blink of an eye. And if this were the case, wouldn't it be right to compensate them rapidly for their supposed success? This is how compensation plans in most listed companies are set out over periods ranging from one to three years. Over these timeframes, substantial payments are made at regular intervals according to the results achieved. These payments take the form of bonuses, stock options, or share awards whose accumulated worth will enable the talented, or lucky, CEO to build up a fortune comparable in scale to that of a very successful entrepreneur. Over such a short period of time, a thousand factors over which the CEO has little or no control might have come into play, influencing the share price or results of the company and therefore their paypacket. But who cares? While they have the job, they take whatever they can get.

The gap between the time horizon over which a listed company's CEO is measured and compensated and the time horizon required to build up a genuine and lasting corporate success is one of the greatest scourges of Western capitalism today. When one thinks of the number of years it takes the pharmaceutical industry to develop a new drug or the automotive industry to develop a new range of vehicles, how could one possibly consider annual or even tri-annual incentive schemes? To use a sporting analogy, it is as if the boards in question were to attribute the medals in a marathon based on runners' split times at the halfway stage. Why should our athletes bother finishing the last 13 miles? The problem for us, is that in this economic race against emerging powers, our Chinese and Indian competitors have just one thing in mind: the finishing line on the 26 mile mark.

So what can we do? We can't wait until the end of an entire economic cycle to compensate our senior executives. But would it be unreasonable to hold out just five years before the stock options, shares, and other incentive schemes kick in or are fully vested? Five years is no magical threshold but it is probably enough time to be sure that success has not come purely by chance. It is also the time-frame for senior executives to see for themselves that they have not been appointed just to please the market's quarterly expectations. If we really want them to take the decisions that will shape the future of their companies for many years to come, let's make sure that at least their personal finances are aligned with the mission they signed up for.

Once the time-frame issue is resolved, we must define the relevant criteria to incentivise the senior executives of listed companies. Share prices today still play an overly important role in their compensation, particularly when we take into account the exceptional market volatility of recent years. If it is the declarations of Janet Yellen or Mario Draghi that determine the major shifts in the world's stock markets in the short term, then is it really appropriate that the majority of our executive pay be indexed to these movements?

Naturally, over a longer period, the random nature of share price evolution is mitigated somewhat, giving us another good reason to adopt the five-year timeline suggested earlier. But in any case, if we really want to foster long-term thinking, shouldn't we favour the use of other indicators besides the stock market to appraise and remunerate our executives? First and foremost in an entrepreneur's mind is revenue growth and profitability. Why not reintroduce these basic criteria and put them at the heart of a CEO's compensation structure? In addition to giving senior executives the right incentives, it would probably limit the amount of time spent by boards on sterile calculation related to share buybacks and other balance sheet restructuring manoeuvres that may give an artificial and short-lived boost to the stock price but contribute nothing of substance to the business itself. Another key performance indicator could be the return on invested capital over a long period of time, which would push for greater investment in research and development or production facility improvements.

Today it is becoming increasingly urgent to get back to basics. The goal should be to shield the manager from the temptation of fawning to the demands of financial shareholders, whom, despite being nothing more than short-term tenants, often display the behaviour of bad-tempered landlords. While we cannot take this right away from them, CEOs benefitting from the full support of their boards must remain cool-headed and act in the best interests of their companies. A hedge fund using the media to wage a smear campaign against a listed company to provoke its restructuring should not have any more power than a pension fund shareholder that has remained loyal for the last 20 years. That too is shareholder democracy.

A listed company that made intelligent use of the media to increase awareness of its long-term incentive policy would eventually be applauded by the markets. The five-year rule would restore trust and give a CEO the peace of mind without which it is almost impossible to manage a group effectively. This kind of serenity is vital, as without it, agitation quickly replaces collective ambition.

Re-energise corporate boards and redefine the 'standards of good governance'

The standards of good governance to be found in capitalism version 2.0 have finished up castrating the boards of our biggest groups. We wanted to protect ourselves from the dangers of the CEO of divine right by appointing independent directors, but we ended up turning him into a sort of functionary. We had hoped that these directors hailing from so many different sectors would bring a critical, dispassionate viewpoint as well as complementary skills compared to those of the most senior executives. However, we forgot that these directors first had to have a perfect grasp of the industry in which their company operates. We dreamed of rationalising the decision-making process but we fell into the trap of analysis-paralysis and knee-jerk risk-aversion.

By transforming the directors into arbiters we made them forget that they should be first and foremost a cohesive team whose mission, apart of course from supervising, is also to support the senior executive in his role. Though their primary role is to constitute a check and balance, that does not mean that directors don't share responsibility for results. I have lost count of the number of times that, in my former life as investment banker, I found myself in the strange position of having to enlighten directors of a company on the competitive dynamics of activities within their own group and whose very existence they were almost unaware of. In order to make them feel more responsible, a few simple measures should be envisaged.

First of all, the totality of directors' attendance fees should be settled in restricted share units locked up for the entire duration of their mandates. This compensation should also be made variable according to company results whereas today attendance fees amount to a guaranteed income, no matter what happens.

Before taking up their positions, those independent directors who don't consider themselves sufficiently expert in their company's industry should undertake a short period of induction training. A few in-house sessions with the group's main operational managers, and some additional seminars with external strategy consultants specialised in their industry would enable them to better comprehend the company and its competitive environment. Once in the job, they should also be able to commission audits or external independent studies allowing them to keep track of potential risks and helping them to form an opinion on major strategic issues in the sector.

Finally, as with the CEO, the directors should commit to a multi-year plan with clearly defined targets. They, too, should be appraised and compensated at least partially according to company performance. Keeping their pay as a fixed fee amounts to giving them an objective reason to shy away from allowing the company to take the slightest risk. They already live in fear of shareholder lawsuits but if, in addition, success makes no difference to their pay packet, then why would they bother challenging the CEO to risk branching out in new directions? Over a reference period of five years we could imagine doubling their compensation if the company objectives presented at the AGM are met, but halving their pay if they are missed.

One cannot be overly prescriptive with implementation guidelines as the situation in each company is so different, but the spirit of the proposed reforms must remain to re-inject a good dose of entrepreneurship in the way corporate boards operate. This is no easy task as old habits die hard. However, if we don't do this, we will find it increasingly difficult to compete on a level playing field with foreign rivals who have shown that they are willing and able to make major strategic decisions sheltered from the whims of market vagaries.

Rebuild bridges with shareholders and increase their loyalty

Having a stable shareholder base is a considerable asset for a business, and, by extension, for the economy as a whole. However, as we have seen, the major Western corporations no longer belong to their founders. The vast majority of these companies are listed, and their shares held by financial intermediaries. Small shareholders, insurance companies, and pension funds who, up until the 1980s, used to form the bedrock of the shareholder base have since been replaced by fund managers, hedge funds, and high-frequency traders who treat their portfolio companies' securities as mere means to an end. There is no loyalty left between a listed company and its shareholders and patience is a virtue that has completely disappeared from the system.

The battle would not be entirely lost if we only used our imaginations to increase shareholder loyalty. Several options should be considered. First of all we should leverage the extraordinary resource that is the employee shareholder scheme. With support from governments providing a more favourable tax treatment of these schemes, companies could afford to be far more ambitious in this area. Of course, we are not suggesting here to fall into the stock options trap again which proved ineffectual as an incentive. It is more about paying a part of an executive's salary and bonus in company stock. Top-up and financing schemes would make this an attractive investment provided that the employee commits to holding on to his shares for several years.

Above and beyond staff, companies should offer their shareholders loyalty bonuses. A named shareholder who had held on to his securities for a period of at least two years could, for example, receive share awards in a ratio to be defined, and these shares would in turn be locked up for a minimum holding period. The potential dilutive impact[2] of such measures would be counterbalanced by the advantages, both for the company and for the overall shareholder community, in a greater stability of capital.

By far the most emblematic measure to stabilise our listed groups' shareholder base would be to reform the capital gains tax regime. Not by brutally shifting to a system where capital gains and income are taxed at the same level; a measure which unduly penalises the entrepreneur and his financial backers. However, we could for instance imagine a sliding scale where tax rates applied to capital gains would be lower and lower the longer you held on to your shares. Even in the US where the tax rate applied to short and long term capital gains is already different, the gap could be widened. This measure would have a twofold impact: first, it would rebuild bridges between companies and their shareholders; second, it would reduce overall market volatility.

In the West there is a direct correlation between the ephemeral nature of our corporations' shareholders, the short-term thinking of our business leaders and our general loss of competitiveness. As long as we fail to break this chain, we will be unable to regain the initiative. The solution lies not just in changing the behaviours of our CEOs and their boards. We will also have to put finance back in its place: at their service.

---

1 The "Say on Pay" rule which, since the Dodd-Frank bill, allows shareholders at AGMs to vote periodically and non-bindingly on executive compensation in a listed company

2 By creating new shares to be distributed to loyal shareholders, the company's results per share would be, all else being equal, reduced or "diluted"

Chapter 3

Transforming finance from an end to a means

Retool but don't punish finance

It is near impossible to open a newspaper today without seeing the world of finance lambasted in turn by politicians, business leaders, or the public at large. At the epicentre of this tsunami of criticism are, of course, the banks, but also the 'shadow banking' sector, which includes hedge funds, and, more generally, all those structures operating essentially beyond the supervisory scope of the regulators. According to the Financial Stability Board, the global 'shadow banking' sector amounted to 67 trillion dollars at the end of 2011 with the US shadow banking system accounting for 23 trillion dollars of the total amount[1].

The list of grudges held against the financial world is a long one. The 2008 crisis showed how bankers had taken advantage of the financial vulnerability of American households and lent them astronomical sums of money, then cobbled together the resulting bad debts into complex financial products and sold them across the globe, thus bringing about the ruin of institutions and savers worldwide. In so doing, banks were directly responsible for the worst credit crisis we had seen since the 1930s, a crisis that threatened to blow apart the entire financial system and, with it, the global economy.

Since the beginning of the European sovereign debt crisis in 2010, we now know that it was once again the banks that enabled Greece as well as several other countries to borrow amounts that they would never be able to pay back and to cover up the magnitude and scope of the problem through the use of sophisticated financial instruments.

Public anger and calls for reform are both understandable and justified. But the scale and violence of the attacks make us run the risk of punishing a sector that historically has made a significant contribution to the prosperity of our Western economies. Public authorities and the regulator are right to consider drastic measures in order to stabilise banks and the world of hedge funds to avoid them becoming a permanent threat to the system. However, by falling into the trap of cheap populism they are in danger of throwing the baby out with the bathwater, thereby losing what was once one of the main competitive advantages of our capitalism compared with emerging powers.

A few figures to begin with. Financial services amount to around 8 per cent of GDP in the US, 9 per cent in Great Britain, 5 per cent in France, and 4 per cent in Germany[2]. Wall Street and the City are clearly of strategic importance in their home countries, but even in continental Europe, millions of jobs are involved. Those who strongly suggest shrinking the financial world when we are already victims of chronic unemployment should be asked how they intend to counterbalance the adverse effects of their proposal. Unfortunately, the idea that the economy works in a 'push-down-pop-up' mode where jobs lost on one side will miraculously spring up on the other in industry or services is simply not realistic. And even if we could decree such a job shift, these sectors simply aren't taking on enough workers either because they are also not doing so well. And it won't be by sanctioning banks that we will make things better.

If we really want to change things and avoid excessive measures, we will have to educate our populations. To the man on the street, a financier looks just like Gordon Gekko, the main character in Oliver Stone's cult film *Wall Street*. Red braces, slicked-back hair, somewhere between his sports car and his private jet; the financier is supposed to see the world through his trading screens with no consideration whatsoever for the companies he invests in or for the men and women who work there. Scandals like the one involving Jérôme Kerviel, the Société Générale trader who managed to violate internal control mechanisms and place speculative bets worth tens of billions of euros, have done nothing to improve the sector's image.

Even if it is impossible to deny that banks have gone off the rails in recent years allowing casino capitalism to proliferate, it is dangerous to categorise the entire sector in this way as politicians and commentators are fond of doing. The financial sector was the enabler that allowed the

start-ups that were Microsoft and Facebook to find the financing necessary to make some entrepreneurs' dreams come true and to create
hundreds of thousands of jobs across the globe. Finance is also home to
the many professionals who organise and underwrite companies' Initial
Public Offerings or bond issues, which in turn allow them to raise the
cash that they require for their future development. By now, we are used
to hearing the media talk negatively about how finance paves the way
for globalisation. But do we ever hear that globalised finance has
enabled companies like Lagardère or Vodafone to levy funding from
Californian pensioners, Quebecer teachers or Chinese entrepreneurs?
Should we really be complaining that our greatest corporations can
now count on investment coming from the four corners of the earth?
Investment bankers specialised in mergers and acquisitions helped
make companies like WPP, GE, or LVMH world leaders in their industries by external growth. Are they really that unworthy?

But even in such stigmatised professions as trading, we tend to forget
that the lion's share of capital flow does not come from banks speculat-
ing with their own capital. Most transactions are the result of intermediation where supply and demand meet. Whatever the financial product, be they stocks, bonds, currencies, or commodities – held directly or
through derivatives – banks' trading departments are there to enable
those who wish to take on risk to find others wanting to get rid of that
risk. If this role didn't exist it would be necessary to invent it, as it is
these very activities that for example enable a German machine tool
manufacturer looking to export to the US to cover his exchange rate
risk. It is this same activity that allows a major French food company to
protect itself from wild swings in commodity prices for foodstuffs it
needs to make its products.

And yet such basic explanations of finance's true role are never discussed
when the subject is raised in public. Indeed, banks have improperly
used their privileged position at the intersection of supply and demand
for personal gain. They are buyers, sellers, and, in certain cases, makers
of the risk that they are supposed to intermediate. They claim to be
advisors or intermediaries when, in truth, they are in fact themselves
the transaction's counterparties. It is these unacceptable conflicts of
interest that we must get rid of in the future, but we need to do this
without abandoning the professions themselves.

The other huge misunderstanding regarding finance has something to do with the nature of its participants. We wrongly imagine that the finance industry is the sole preserve of gigantic institutions, banks, or insurance companies, employing tens of thousands of people across the world. In fact the reality is very different. The financial sector includes thousands of firms like Stanhope Capital, the group I co-founded in 2004 and have run since, with staff of no more than a few hundred and who together pack a considerable collective punch in the world's main financial centres. In London and New York, but also in Paris and Frankfurt, these companies, often set up by former employees of the big banks, act at all levels of the value chain from asset management through to client advisory and intermediation. These firms' culture is not dissimilar to the one that made the City great before the Big Bang in the 1980s or the one prevailing in Wall Street before the big partnerships became behemoths quoted on the stock exchange. The dawning of this 'new' finance is a silent revolution that has been, for the most part, overlooked when it holds so many solutions for the entire sector's future.

As was the case in the past, those who manage these firms are still the ones who own them. It is their capital which is at stake, not just their jobs. What is more, in the field of asset management, these entrepreneurs generally invest their personal wealth in the fund they manage alongside their clients'. And they don't do this just to please them, but because they believe in themselves and what they are selling. Here we couldn't be further from the obsessive bonus culture that makes mercenaries of the major financial institutions' staff and pushes them to take more and more risk, whatever the consequences. If casino chips were no longer bought but handed out to gamblers free of charge, we can easily imagine what would happen. The gamblers would bet everything in minutes as they have nothing to lose and everything to gain. Something similar takes place in the big banks, although here the losses are very real and are incurred first by the client, then by the bank, and ultimately by the taxpayer. If the brilliant mathematicians that rule the major banks' trading floors had mortgaged their houses so as to invest in the increasingly sophisticated products they are asked to come up with, it is highly likely that many a self-destructing product launched over the last few years would never have seen the light of day.

We often forget that systemic risk is not plucked from thin air. It is the sum of individual behaviours, of micro-decisions which, if only driven by greed, become collective time bombs. The bad news is that the planet's main financial institutions have become too big to manage. It has become near impossible for them to control their own risk. The good news, on the other hand, is that the last decade has seen the creation of a growing number of smaller independent firms who collectively act as the system's natural safeguard against excessive risk-taking.

The world of finance is far from being as monolithic as one might expect and we should bear this in mind when considering reform. As we were coming out of the 2008 crisis, I had the feeling that the populism of the time was rapidly turning into a witch-hunt. The banker was 'going to have to pay', the banker in question being anyone who directly or indirectly worked in the financial sector. Finding this both unfair and destructive, I felt compelled to set up The New City Initiative (NCI) in 2010. NCI is a think tank that brings together the sector's main independent firms in London and Paris, with the objective of enabling financial entrepreneurs to help governments and regulators reform the financial system, drawing on the responsible methods and values that underpin their professional lives. The entrepreneurial firms that form the NCI's membership, together manage assets in excess of 350 billion euros and, for the most part, did not exist 15 years ago. Today they represent the future of the financial industry.

'But what is the real size of this entrepreneurial financial sector? Most probably marginal, I suppose?' This was how, Vince Cable, the British Secretary of State for Business, Innovation and Skills, and a man known for his straight talk, began a meeting with NCI members. Somewhat stunned by his remarks, my NCI colleagues and I commissioned a study[3], the conclusions of which ended up astonishing us all. Half of the City's employees work in companies of fewer than 200 staff. Light years from the caricature of a City monopolised by the five big retail banks (Barclays, HSBC, RBS, Lloyds, Santander) and a handful of American investment banks, Europe's biggest financial centre is also the capital of financial SMEs. During the crisis, these small businesses cost the taxpayer nothing at all, and yet continued to recruit in order to meet the increasing demand from clients who had abandoned the big banks, hoping to find a more humane vision of finance. NCI has published several studies showing that better aligning the interests of financial advisors and investors with those of their clients would greatly contribute to reducing the sector's inherent risk and doing the real economy the world of good.

In Paris, financial SMEs don't yet figure as prominently as in London, but do form one of the rare segments to show robust growth in recent years. Investment management companies such as Carmignac or Comgest handle over 50 and 15 billion euros of client assets respectively and are now both well-known and respected industry players globally. Strangely enough, the French are probably the only ones not yet in the know that Paris has now established itself as the second most important financial centre of the European Community and one of the most dynamic, thanks to these very same financial entrepreneurial firms.

And yes, of course, it is urgent to reform finance so that it rapidly recovers its original vocation and before it endangers the economy again. I have been fighting this battle for years with many other professionals from the industry. This is a prerequisite to ensure that our corporations are no longer the victims of volcanic markets threatening to erupt at any moment and find once more the serenity they require to build for the future.

There are three conditions to help us get there: first we mustn't confuse reform with punishment. Punishing, or cutting back finance, amounts to depriving ourselves of what should be a considerable asset to help us compete globally.

Second, we mustn't forget that financial regulation is a weapon to hold back those who try to overstep the mark, but it cannot be the only one. Experience has shown that rules and regulations can always be interpreted or circumvented by any malevolent bright spark. They cannot replace sound management and a strong sense of responsibility. Nothing will fundamentally change if bankers and asset managers do not return to a more direct, almost personal, interest in meeting client requirements. This is the only way for their businesses to sustain the test of time. The average employee of a big bank must stop seeing himself as nothing more than just a tiny cog in a gigantic machine over which he has no control. As we will see over the coming chapters, ideas abound to make each employee individually accountable, and transform them in turn into quasi entrepreneurs.

Third, and finally, regulation must take into account the extraordinary variety that exists within the world of finance. Although reforms designed to prevent further damage from the big banks are certainly justified, we should not lay down the same rules for much smaller, independent financial firms whose balance sheets could never amount to the slightest systemic risk. Were we to commit such an error, we would eventually stifle competition within the sector and kill off entrepreneurship in the financial world even though it is precisely what is sorely needed in order to re-establish a degree of stability in the system as a whole.

Putting the client and the economy back at the heart of banking

Across the globe, governments and regulators alike are on the look out for every possible way to avoid a repeat of the last financial crisis last whose impact we are still feeling. Approaches differ, revealing practical and cultural specificities that vary from one financial centre to another. In New York and London there is a will to repair the world of finance whilst keeping in mind the danger of going too far and killing the golden goose. There, the objective is first and foremost to secure the banking industry and avoid jeopardising savers' deposits through the riskier practices of proprietary trading[4] and investment banking. There is also a desire to reform the world of alternative funds[5] without lumping them into those being scape-goated for the 2008 crisis, and rightly so, as this was above all a banking crisis. On the other hand, Brussels still defends the integrated banking model without imposing overly rigid structural barriers between different activities within any one institution. Here, the focus is more on prudential ratios or on ways to impose new rules on compensation. Brussels prefers to use its regulatory might to chastise alternative funds and shadow banking firms, which are variously branded as opaque, greedy, and dangerous shirkers of the regulatory bodies and public authorities. The danger with Brussels' anti hedge-fund crusade is that it distracts us from the real issues still affecting a highly vulnerable European banking sector.

And, as for the financial centres in emerging countries: they seem happy for the moment keeping score and have no plans for significant reform of their legislative framework in the foreseeable future. Centres like Singapore or Hong Kong wait patiently for American and European financial institutions to throw in the towel and finally resolve to relocate to more lenient tax and regulatory regimes. However, contrary to what is often claimed by industry, it is not so easy for a sizeable financial institution to relocate either its headquarters or its main activities. It is therefore important to keep watch on the competition from emerging countries in the area of financial services while not giving unwarranted credence to the occasional threats to relocate hailing from certain big banks.

After over three years of prevaricating on these questions, it is now clear that we have not gone far enough. New regulations are still too timid and, even more importantly, we have barely scratched the surface of the central issue of the governance and management of our banks. It hasn't been said often enough that beyond their inadequate regulatory framework, banks were first and foremost victims of their incompetent senior management and their powerless boards. Dealing with the former issue without confronting the latter is tantamount to doing up a building without first testing for asbestos or termites.

Let's look first at the regulatory issues. The Dodd-Frank bill in the US puts forward some excellent ideas but doesn't cross the Rubicon. The legislation sets up an independent consumer protection agency to fight abusive mortgage and credit card practices. American financial institutions will have to provide their clients with clear, precise information on fees charged on products sold as well as the potential risks involved, which is something of a breakthrough. The new law also looks to put an end to the 'too big to fail' mentality which allows those institutions considered a systemic importance to benefit from taxpayer bailouts when in difficulty. As we have seen, this implicit guarantee from the authorities was the same as handing senior executives a blank cheque to be used in the event of getting themselves into difficulty. From now on, these institutions will have to submit to greater scrutiny and discipline: the drafting and regular updating of 'financial wills' allowing an orderly liquidation procedure if and when required, limited debt levels, and broader and more frequent communication with the supervisory authorities to name but a few.

The new framework also allows for additional measures that can inspire only praise, such as the creation of an independent supervisory council for systemic risk, restrictions on the proliferation of sophisticated financial instruments that are often incomprehensible, or tighter rules on senior banking executives' compensation. But by far the most emblematic measure of the Dodd-Frank bill is the Volcker rule, named after its famous instigator and former Fed boss Paul Volcker. This rule drastically limits the amount of their own capital that American banks can now commit to proprietary trading. As we know, for many years these same activities built the fortune of institutions like Goldman Sachs but they also ruined hundred-year-old banks like Lehman Brothers or Bear Stearns. This 'casino finance' is what the Volcker rule aims to put a stop to, but will it succeed?

The Dodd-Frank bill clearly marks a significant step forward on the road to restructuring the US financial sector, but it comes up short. Even Sandy Weill, architect of the giant Citigroup, who fought through the 1990s to repeal the Glass-Steagall Act which mandated the total separation of investment and retail banking activities, found himself suddenly calling for its return. Without going quite so far as to bring back the straitjacket of a law that would mean breaking up all the major banking groups, new regulation could have at least suggested forcing so called universal banks to split their capital between the two activities. In the end it was the overwhelming campaign led by the banking lobbies in Washington that got the better of the Obama administration and their good intentions.

It is certainly the British who have proven the most courageous in these matters. The Independent Commission on Banking, headed by Sir John Vickers, submitted a report to Chancellor of the Exchequer George Osborne in 2012. It recommended separate boards and balance sheets within the universal banks for investment banking and retail banking rather than a clear split between them. In so doing, these institutions would no longer be able to endlessly dip into the meagre capital that guarantees clients' savings in order to finance much riskier market activities. The critics of this idea point out that the bankruptcy of British banks Northern Rock and Bradford & Bingley in 2008 had nothing to do with such inter-activity confusion; these retail banks collapsed simply because they had set out on a mad rush for mortgage loans. Universal banks are by no means automatically destined for disaster. But what would we have to say to the tens of thousands of households who would lose their savings if trading at BNP Paribas, Barclays, or HSBC had resulted in such losses as to force these banks out of business? Do we really believe that the French or British governments could afford to pay them back their deposits? Instead of living with the sword of Damocles hanging over our heads, wouldn't we be better asking these institutions to ring-fence their capital, splitting their balance sheet and thus strictly protecting the capital set aside to guarantee deposits?

I met with members of this Commission on several occasions to help provide input on their thinking. And it was then that I realised what a difficult task it was to reform the City despite their valiant efforts, and that it was very much to their credit that their conclusions did not end up dragged down by inertia or by pressure from the powerful banks that still rule the Square Mile. It is now up to David Cameron's government to implement these measures as quickly as possible and not wait the proposed seven years before starting.

In Europe, where putting the blame on financiers is commonplace, voices have remained curiously silent on these questions of balance sheet segmentation. It would seem that European banks found a more sympathetic ear in Brussels and that the Liikanen Report[6] is unlikely to change things a great deal.

The official view is that these matters should be dealt with through the Basel agreements and the prudential ratios banks must respect. Since Basel believes that a minimum capital ratio of 7 per cent[7] is sufficient to guarantee the future of banking, then why worry about anything else? We pretend not to know that this ratio is manifestly inadequate – twice this level would only begin to address the issue – and that banks remain chronically undercapitalised. As things stand, those who could resist another financial crisis are few and far between. For obvious reasons this undercapitalisation is even more worrying for universal banks who choose not to segment their capital between volatile market activities and their retail banking deposits. On these issues, Brussels has chosen to bury its head in the sand. In this context, the new law proposed by the French government in November 2012 was both unexpected and welcome. Pierre Moscovici, the Minister of Finance, declared during a press conference that his intention is to push for the creation of special-ised subsidiaries within the large banking groups. Banks would be expected to transfer to these units 'the market activities which are not essential to the financing of the economy'. French banks which were until then used to a somewhat more cosy relationship with Bercy felt let down, but they are slowly coming to grips with the new reality. Large financial institutions have to be protected against themselves.

By contrast, the European authorities have been rather shy on these issues but joyfully jumped on to the bandwagon of pay reform in the world of financial services. The Commission's work stems from the right observations on the root causes of systemic failures but has taken the wrong approach to putting them right. They observed that bonus culture often makes bankers put their own interests before their clients' or their shareholders' and that this culture encourages them to take ever-escalating risks. European authorities issued a directive[8] to fix this, according to which at least 40 per cent of a bonus – and at least 60 per cent for the highest earners – should be deferred for a minimum period of three years. Furthermore, half of all variable pay should take the form of stock or similar instruments. We cannot but support this direc-tive, as to get bankers thinking long term is indeed a worthy cause. But, by imposing such a rule, is the Commission really playing its rightful role? We can imagine that a bank bailed out by the taxpayers should abide by strict guidelines on pay, but for all the others, is it really right for a public authority to interfere in shareholders' and management's roles in order to dictate the way employees should be incentivised?

These new regulatory measures have done nothing to improve matters, as the banks were quick to find a remedy that helped them sidestep the effects. Many immediately doubled or tripled their executives' basic salaries, turning a huge part of their variable income into fixed remu-neration. An ironic twist of fate when that which was supposed to align bankers' and clients' interests ends up increasing the bankers' guaran-teed income regardless. Perhaps, even more serious, is that Europe implicitly removes accountability from these banks' boards and senior management teams by taking away from them one of their main powers. The Americans weren't to make the same mistake, as the Dodd-Frank bill deliberately avoids dealing with such issues. The British are also philosophically opposed to such State interventionism in the day-to-day running of private businesses, but they will of course not be able to absolve themselves of their duties vis-à-vis European regulation.

And yet it is our banks' governance and management systems that need to be placed back at the heart of the debate today, if we really want them to serve the economy once more. The tragedies we have seen occurring in the banking world over the last five years find their origins first in the inability of executive teams and their boards to identify and manage risk. The worry of being 'too big to fail' has been replaced by the fear of being 'too big to manage'. The unexpected loss of over six billion dollars by one of the world's best-managed banks JP Morgan in 2012 shows just how difficult the task has become. The biggest financial institutions have become such sprawling behemoths that it is near impossible for them to centralise all the information necessary to keep track of risk in real time. Now if the banks' management struggle to keep up then it is easy to understand that independent directors feel completely lost. Not only do they rarely have the relevant information at their disposal concerning the state of their institutions' affairs, but in many cases they don't even understand it. Grasping a bank's balance sheet and risks requires a certain degree of sectorial expertise that most directors simply don't have. The British financial regulators have understood the importance of this issue and now meticulously check on skill levels of all candidates for the job of bank director. However, this is not the case in the rest of Europe.

But we need to go much further down this path, equipping banks' boards with the tools they need to supervise risk while keeping the general public informed. In the future, independent directors should have the power to mandate external banking risk specialists without needing a green light from senior management. These consultants would then draft a "Risk Report" in a language that is readily understandable by all parties, including amongst other things a simplified stress test showing the probable impact on the bank of a potential financial shock. I put forward the idea to Sir John Vickers and his Independent Commission on Banking that this 'risk report' be made public in the same way as these institutions' audited accounts statements, then made available in every one of their branches. And this newfound triangularity between independent directors, the banks' management, and the general public would enable us to kill two birds with one stone. We would stop these institutions hiding behind the complexity of their activities to conceal risk, and we would also reduce the likelihood of senior executives manipulating their boards over such matters.

Once we have sorted out banking governance, we still have to deal with their management system. If they have become 'too big to manage' over the last 20 years it is largely due to banks' excessive centralisation policies. This, in turn, has deprived individual teams of their prerogatives and in so doing stripped them of any sense of responsibility they once had. Previously each department, down to the branch managers, retained a good deal of managerial freedom. They managed their own resources, could recruit and even adapt their sales strategies to meet local customers' specific needs.

Teams often operated as small businesses under the umbrella of a much larger institution. Today, the steep hierarchies to be found in banks have killed all notion of entrepreneurship. Disenfranchising the individual inevitably leads to dehumanising customer relationships. This is how we killed off any sense of loyalty. Both bank employees and clients are willing to move at the first opportunity. What makes matters worse is that the centralisation designed to improve risk control and service quality actually produces the opposite effect. In practice it is impossible for a vast banking giant to keep track of the risks taken by thousands of its employees every day if they are not incentivised and made accountable for their acts. These staff members must be able to reap the benefits of their successes while also accepting to bear the brunt of the consequences should they fail.

Handelsbanken's success demonstrates how relevant a participative model can be in the financial sector. Sweden's second largest bank with assets totalling over 250 billion euros, Handelsbanken distinguishes itself from its competitors by devolving almost all powers out to the field. Ninety-six per cent of all decisions on loans are taken by local branch managers with headquarters stepping in only to support, providing development resources where necessary. In order to incentivise employees, Handelsbanken chooses not to pay the huge bonuses expected by those working in the industry, but what they consider a competitive salary and a stake in the Oktogonen foundation, which retains one third of the bank's profits when exceeding average perform-ance in the sector. Every single member of staff, from the CEO to the cashier, gets an equal share. Oktogonen's accumulated funds are rein-vested in Handelsbanken shares and locked up until their beneficiaries' retirement. And the result? The institution got through two financial crises in 1992 and 2008 unscathed, and its British subsidiary remains one of the country's most dynamic banks[9] in a mature, saturated market.

Without going as far as Handelsbanken, many options could be tried out and tested in order to reconcile banks with their customers. All we have to do is take into account the variety of professions to be found in such groups, and build in their particular characteristics. By way of example, for retail bankers working in mortgage or consumer loans, why not calculate their bonus based on repayment rates rather than on the overall volume of loans granted when we know that the latter is a recipe for disaster? If we had adopted these methods several years back, the British taxpayer wouldn't have had to save RBS from bankruptcy to the tune of 45 billion pounds sterling. In asset management or depart-ments in charge of selling financial products, why not lock up part of their employees' bonuses, investing them in the very funds or products offered to clients? These bonuses would be gradually released over peri-ods of several years. In once applying our inelegant adage from earlier, 'put your money where your mouth is', we could have avoided some of the biggest financial disasters of recent years. Would bankers have invested their own savings in the subprime debt products they were sell-ing so frenetically up until 2008?

In literally every single department of a bank, defining compensation structures that better align staff and customer interests is both doable and desirable. It is primarily up to senior management to instigate changes, not the regulator who is condemned to offering one-size-fits-all solutions that will not achieve the real and lasting effects we need. Better market regulation is vital, but we will fail to put an end to the sector's chronic instability if we don't dust off and reinstate the age-old concept of individual responsibility, both in words and deeds alike.

Making non-bank finance accountable too

Recognising that the banks, and not the independent asset managers, were the driving winds of the hurricane that almost swept away our savings does not mean that non-bank finance is in many respects just as dysfunctional. Many investment funds, driven solely by short-term gain, pulled our biggest groups and their boards into a death spiral of what we referred to earlier as instant management. Fund managers' short-term thinking became second nature, and a dangerously contagious nature at that.

The reasons for this short-sightedness are not difficult to understand. Fund managers, particularly those in hedge funds, have managed to set in stone a fee structure that has now become so widespread that to utter the words 'two and twenty' is enough for everyone to be on the same page. Two and twenty has in fact become the 'open sesame' of modern finance, the magic formula that allows fund managers to amass fortunes often exceeding those of their rich investors. How could this be possible? Very easily indeed. For their services these professionals charge a 2 per cent annual management fee on the value of the assets they look after as well as performance fees amounting to 20 per cent of profits[10], realised or not. The annual net asset value is most often used as the basis on which performance fees are calculated and paid out to the fund manager. If at the time of the calculation, it is above the entry-level value for a particular investor, then 20 per cent of the difference will be skimmed off in fees. No matter that the capital gains may disappear the following month if the markets were to turn, or that the supposedly liquid securities may turn out to be the opposite and therefore hard to price. If the difference is positive any one year, the fund manager hits the jackpot. Should it be negative, then he can console himself with the 2 per cent management fee he had already received. Is he asked to hand back his 20 per cent performance fees to investors if the latent capital gains suddenly morph into hard cash losses the following year? Of course not.

It is this logic that enabled the legendary John Paulson, who famously gambled on the subprime bubble's exploding in 2008, to build up a personal fortune estimated at 12.5 billion dollars by *Forbes* magazine. In

2010 alone, when one of his flagship funds Paulson Advantage Plus chalked up a 17 per cent latent capital gain, John Paulson shattered all hedge fund records, personally earning over 5 billion dollars[11]. Unfortunately for his investors, the capital gains didn't remain latent very long. In 2011, this same fund shed 51 per cent of its value and in 2012 lost a further 19 per cent. Investors could legitimately hope that the billions of dollars of performance fees billed in 2010 be handed back to them. Although nothing of the sort happened.

In the heat of the 2008 crisis, when hedge funds suffered huge losses and yet prevented their investors from pulling their money out, I remember a conversation I had at the time with a star fund manager who explained that clients should 'get to learn the virtues of patience again, against their will if necessary'. His comments smack of irony when considering that this very individual had raked in gargantuan performance fees in the good years that were calculated, billed, and settled promptly every quarter. . .

In practice, the performance fees that were supposed to align investor and fund managers' interests have in fact driven a wedge between them. It is not performance fees as such that are to blame, but the fact that they are calculated over periods that are far too short to make any sense. We forget that investment cycles are long and that it is only after a certain amount of time that one can really pass judgement on a fund manager. Three years are necessary to establish that he is not bad, and five years to be certain that he is really good.

Brussels is looking to play a part in resolving such issues and is once again proposing a regulatory framework that promises to be excessively rigid and uniform. In fact, the financial sector itself should be taking charge of this, defining standards of good practice that participating stakeholders should be encouraged to adhere to. Those who don't should run the risk of alienating their investors.

A few simple measures would be enough to reverse the trend and bring back a semblance of trust. As with listed companies' CEOs, for example, we might also expect asset managers to invest a considerable part of their own personal liquid assets in the funds they look after. The previously mentioned minimum threshold of 10 per cent would seem reasonable. Furthermore, for fund managers charging their clients performance fees, the reference period should be extended to at least three years and the capital gains calculated on the net asset value on fund exit after deducting a minimum return to investors. Finally, if a fund manager were to choose not to wait the full three years before billing his performance fees, it would be advisable that he reinvest a significant part of his fees in his own fund, say 50 per cent, and that these amounts be locked up for several years. However, these measures should not have an adverse tax impact on fund managers willing to align their interests with those of their investors. Governments should, for instance, consider waiting until fund exit to tax them on deferred remuneration, that is, when it is actually paid to them rather than when allocated.

What is at stake here is not of a purely technical nature. It would be dangerous to believe that the remuneration of bankers, fund managers, and listed-company CEOs is only a matter of concern for the sector's already over-paid professionals. We could dream of a better world in which all economic stakeholders from the Wall Street financier to the FTSE 100 CEO acted unprompted and exclusively for the common good irrespective of their individual interests, but what would be the point? We would be better off aiming to create an environment in which individual interests become compatible with the common good. Compensation and incentive schemes are inevitably at the heart of the issue. As well as being fair, solutions must also be measured and adjusted to fit roles and specifics of each profession. Much to the dismay of this debate's demagogical multitude, getting the sick man that is, Western capitalism, back on his feet is more a matter for the neurosurgeon than for ER. We will need to show patience and discernment and avoid quick but unsatisfactory fixes.

To stabilise the financial system, encourage competition, and bring back the partnership mindset

In the world of financial services, competition is the hard done by customer's best friend. Unfortunately, since the crisis of 2008 we have witnessed a wave of consolidation in the banking industry, giving unprecedented powers to the sector's survivors. In the US where the assets of the three biggest institutions historically add up to between 10 and 15 per cent of the total held by all commercial banks, their share today is over 40 per cent. Giants like Bank of America, JP Morgan, or Citigroup dominate almost all professions, from retail banking to investment banking through to asset management. In Great Britain the four leading banks boast a combined market share of 73 per cent[12] and in France, more than 86 per cent.

This is a worrying situation on several counts. First the balance of power between banks and their clients has become totally one-sided. Individual customers and small businesses have counted themselves amongst the first victims of the draconian measures adopted by banks to strengthen their balance sheets. In recent years and throughout Europe, thousands of SMEs saw their lines of credit dry up overnight, leaving them in financial distress without ever having defaulted on their commitments. And yet these very same banks bend over backwards to lend to big corporations who are overflowing with cash. There can be no doubt today that the attitudes of the banks contributed to spreading and further deepening the crisis. Paradoxically, many of these banks were bailed out by the taxpayer, and yet the shareholder State could do nothing to change their behaviour.

The other concern is that the biggest banks take advantage of their dominant position and pile pressure on to both public authorities and the regulator. The intense lobbying in Brussels, London, and Washington to slow down reform is literally unprecedented. These institutions' holy cause is to avoid calling into question any aspect of their universal banking model, although we have seen that better segmenting their various activities and associated risks should be their priority. With the notable exceptions of the United Kingdom, European and American banks would seem to have won the war.

The last problem, but by no means the least, is that banks should serve as an essential and cooperative conduit for the implementation of monetary policy. When central banks decide to cut interest rates to stimulate consumption, the banking system is supposed to pass on rate reductions and maintain or even increase overall lending. However sector concentration creates a bottleneck that blocks up credit flow. And this is exactly what we saw with Mario Draghi's LTRO programme[13]. Over one trillion euros was lent to banks over a three-year period at an extremely low 1 per cent, a world first, but to what effect? Instead of lending to individual customers or enterprises, banks deposited their windfalls at the European Central Bank or invested in Treasury bonds. And they did it with a clear conscience, knowing full well that with their dominant position they were in no danger of losing market share in the process.

There are two prerequisites to increasing competition in the sector. The first of these is to increase transparency, a vital condition indeed. For every loan request customers make, their bank should provide them with a comprehensive list of the rates offered by the main competitors. Websites put together these comparisons, however, only the most worldly put them to good use. The regulator should demand that banks communicate simply and clearly on these questions. Another possible reform concerns loan closure. Banks wishing to put an end to, or modify the terms of, a business relationship with a borrower, even when they have always honoured their contractual obligations, should be forced to give enough notice for them to fall on their feet. The arbitrary nature of such decisions should no longer be tolerated.

Second condition: leave enough room for new entrants to the banking sector. The near incestuous relationship between the main financial institutions and public authorities has created a situation approaching *numerus clausus*. For example, in France the senior civil servants who land top banking jobs are countless. Besides a few recently established online banks whose market position remains negligible, have we observed a single new institution of any importance see the light of day? In Great Britain, Virgin Money or Metro Bank are rare exceptions. The only new players able to challenge the banks on their own terms are subsidiaries of retail giants like Tesco or Carrefour. But even for them, there is still a long way to go, and the road to get there will be fraught with numerous obstacles.

This competition should also be encouraged beyond retail banking, extending it to the realms of asset management and investment banking. Earlier, I mentioned the dynamism of financial SMEs who already make up a significant number of the City's jobs and constitute a new force to be reckoned with in other European capitals. And yet nothing has been done to help them grow; in fact, quite the opposite is true. These small businesses have far more limited means than traditional banks, but nonetheless have to put up with increasingly costly and restrictive regulatory and legal red tape. A survey conducted amongst members of the New City Initiative revealed that financial SMEs devoted on average 5 per cent of their revenues dealing with such matters. At these levels, many firms who were already fighting for survival in the shadows of the bigger banks are more than tempted to throw in the towel. And as far as the new entrants are concerned, barriers are beginning to get the better of their entrepreneurial drive. Public authorities and regulatory bodies should no longer get away with laying down the same rules for everyone regardless of their size or the nature of their business. Should they continue on this dangerous path, they will end up intensifying sector consolidation at the customer's expense.

The regulator should make a clear distinction between financial institutions using their balance sheets to act as counterparties to their clients and those that act purely as intermediaries or in a client-advisory capacity. The former can provoke systemic risk that should be dealt with at the source, while the latter present little or no risk to the system. But even for firms included in the first group, there should be criteria governing size and materiality so that they aren't necessarily subjected to the same rules as the sector giants. European financial regulations have coined the concept of 'proportionality' in order to make the new directives more flexible, leaving national authorities the freedom to adapt as and when required. Unfortunately, and despite its importance, this principle is almost never applied. The regulator must understand that sometimes 'more' does not mean 'better'. What is needed today is a two-speed regulatory framework. This does not mean making exceptions for anyone, but simply creating an environment where regulations do not end up killing off initiative and new ideas in a sector that so badly needs them.

The financial services industry could become an engine for economic growth again, provided we encourage competition, we return to values of individual responsibility, and that we establish a more balanced regulatory environment. In fact this means nothing less than reviving the spirit of the old-fashioned partnerships that used to dominate Wall Street and the City. Their unfailing respect for a sense of continuity and customer service is the secret for success applicable to the entire industry, above and beyond the world of partnerships. This return to traditional values will give the big banks a chance to go back to their roots and offer newcomers the opportunity to write the next chapter of financial history.

1 Global Shadow Banking Monitoring Report 2012, Financial Stability Board

2 Bank of England, Measuring Financial Sector Output and its Contribution to UK GDP, 2011

3 Study carried out by IMAS

4 When a bank trades on its own account, rather than for a client, for speculative purposes

5 An activity of hedge funds and private equity funds (venture capital, LBO)

6 Report from the experts' commission on European banking reform headed by Erkki Liikanen, Governor of the Bank of Finland, submitted in September 2012

7 Ratio Tier 1

8 Directive CRD3

9 With 97 branches and over 800 staff

10 This part of the manager's compensation is called performance fee or carried interest

11 Source: Forbes

12 "Competition and choice in retail banking", House of Commons Treasury Committee, Ninth Report of Session 2010-11

13 Long Term Refinancing Operation

Chapter 4

Repositioning the business-creator as the cornerstone of capitalism

No entrepreneur, no capitalism

In order to revitalise Western capitalism, we must mend every link of the capitalist chain, focusing on the weaknesses that caused it to splinter. We must wake listed company bosses from their slumber and restore their sense of initiative and long-term thinking. Energise corporate boards and involve them in their company's success. Put businesses and private clients back at the heart of banking. Increase shareholder loyalty in listed companies to give their senior executives time to think. Finally, we must ensure that financial intermediaries become responsible agents and move away from the 'heads I win, tails you lose' mentality. But none of this will be enough to provide a lasting solution for our problems and our loss of competitiveness without putting the business-creator back at the epicentre of our capitalism.

Twenty years from now, the companies that make up the Dow Jones or the FTSE 100 should no longer be dinosaurs of Western capitalism but companies that haven't even been dreamed up yet. Their future founders must find the desire and the resources as well as an environment conducive to building businesses. These men and women should no longer succeed *in spite of* the system around them but *thanks to* that system.

Given the sheer size of the implications, the issue should be a matter for consensus, far removed from the political arena. Unfortunately, to defend free enterprise and the entrepreneur today is to be accused of unbridled liberalism, and suspected of wanting to let market forces decide everything. So the old political dividing lines reappear again at each election. The left talks of solidarity and sharing without admitting that if we no longer create, then there will be nothing left to redistribute. The right talks of individual responsibility and initiative but does next to nothing to encourage this once elected. Paralysis is always the winner in these futile debates when we can no longer afford the luxury of waiting. The wealth created by the post-war generation is about to dry up.

Politicians' inability to acknowledge the problem and overcome their inhibitions on business-related questions is all the more harmful when considering the role that the State should be playing to put the entrepreneur back in his pivotal role. As we will see later, public authorities could develop a more favourable fiscal framework to help start-ups get off the ground. The State could also be more proactive in making higher education a veritable springboard for business creation instead of simply swelling the ranks of the unemployed. Finally, if we agree that shareholder stability, inherent in family-owned businesses, can have a very positive impact on competitiveness, then the State should help entrepreneurial families pass on their businesses to the next generation instead of penalising them.

But the State cannot do everything. Big corporations also have a good degree of responsibility in encouraging the emergence and development of new players in their respective sectors of activity. It is now fashionable for listed companies to appoint a senior executive to the position of Director of Corporate Social Responsibility ('CSR'). These professionals do their best to embody their employers' concern for doing social good, involving them in projects whose relevance and impact are often questionable. And yet what better proof of this social responsibility than if these big groups were to help out entrepreneurs? They could be former employees or simply individuals looking to benefit from their logistical, financial, or sales support, even the halo effect of their reputation.

Banks must also make an effort, not waiting until a company has already met with success before offering them their services. Shouldn't it be obvious to these banks that if they continue to lend only to established businesses there will be fewer and fewer established businesses, and ultimately, fewer and fewer customers? We must think up incentives to encourage banks to lend to small corporations. However, using coercion as is often suggested would make no sense at all.

And lastly we must enable venture capitalists to raise more funds from both institutional and private investors. By bringing enough seed funding to the table to develop start-ups, these investment funds play a fundamental role that is neither fairly recognised nor promoted in Europe. In recent years we have seen LBO[1] funds taking the lion's share of private equity allocations. These LBO funds can certainly play a useful role in contributing to mature enterprises' expansion, sector consolidation, or activity rationalisation. However, we have also seen how often these funds resort to loading up the companies they buy with debt, thereby risking their suffocation. It is now time to move the emphasis away from this segment, and back to venture capital instead.

We need to rally all those concerned – the State, our universities, big corporations, banks, and venture capital funds – and in just a few years change the face of entrepreneurship in the West. Once more, everyone must be convinced that this is a strategic priority, first and foremost governments themselves.

Fiscal and administrative moratoria for young entrepreneurs

The countless mechanisms set up to help SMEs in Western countries have proven, for the most part, to be incomprehensible and ineffective. Hiding underneath the plethora of programmes and institutions launched in recent years are labyrinthine depths of bureaucracy that discourage more than the faint-hearted entrepreneur.

For years, Great Britain has attempted to come to the aid of its entrepreneurs. The Regional Growth Fund is one of the key mechanisms, with 2.4 billion pounds sterling to be allocated over the period 2011/2015, with a focus on companies or projects in regions where public spending cuts have hit hardest. The UK's coalition government also aims at doubling the share of small businesses in the provision of goods and services to the administration[2]. In order to make this happen, the tendering process will be simplified and requirements for small companies relaxed. Although the British approach has been somewhat more pragmatic than that of other European governments, the results have so far been quite disappointing.

In France, the *Banque Publique d'Investissement* ('BPI') has become the umbrella company in charge of helping SMEs. Under the stewardship of the State and the Caisse des Depots, BPI is supposed to provide them with both debt and equity financings as well as guarantees. BPI now regroups the resources of OSEO, a network of regional development agencies and FSI, the French sovereign wealth fund. In addition to that, SMEs can turn to the APCE (*Agency for Business Creation*[3]) whose mission is to 'further the spirit of enterprise'. Quite a challenge indeed. Then follows the NACRE (*New Support for the Creation and Buyout of Businesses*[4]) jointly run by the Labour Ministry and the Caisse des Dépôts with the primary aim of helping job seekers set up their own companies. Is this maze of well-meaning institutions really effective? If France is so concerned about its entrepreneurs' well being, then why is it that they rank their country last amongst the G20 when asked whether their local business environment encourages the spirit of entrepreneurship[5]?

Europe is not to be left behind in trying to stimulate business creation. Through the Small Business Act of 2008 and the Market Access Strategy programme measures, the European Commission has singled out exporting entrepreneurs as its top priority. This focus stems from the observation that these small companies do not always have the necessary information or resources to go after overseas markets. In collaboration with member States the Commission is working to reduce these obstacles, however here too, and after several years of these measures, one struggles to quantify any tangible impact they might have had. As usual, we float somewhere between our declared good intentions and an impenetrable bureaucratic language.

The reason why all of these efforts have come to so little is that they don't seem to take into account the underlying reality of an entrepreneur's existence. The budding business creator is no helpless welfare recipient who goes out cap in hand in search of public funding. Nor is he a legal expert able to keep up with the twists and turns of civil servants' brains and their aid programmes without ever having put a foot inside a company themselves. The first thing an entrepreneur requires is to be left in peace. He wishes to stay focused on his project and sheltered from the fiscal and administrative assaults that await him no sooner has he registered his company.

This expectation may be met with a simple, powerful, and easily understandable measure: a three-year fiscal and administrative moratorium starting from the day the business is created. During this critical period, when start-ups are fighting for their survival, the fledgling business would be exempt from any tax or payroll charges and would be authorised to hire and fire, being subject to a lighter legal framework.

Such a measure would have as powerful an impact on attitudes as it would on behaviours. Employers would have the feeling that they had at long last been understood and that the State was willing to help clear the way ahead. Brand new start-ups could take on more staff secure in the knowledge that they would not have to bear the brunt of payroll taxes for a given time. And most of all, this measure would allow them more workforce flexibility. We can no longer accept that young businesses forced to lay off workers in order to survive are then required to to empty their coffers for severance payments and in so doing precipitate the untimely demise they were trying to avoid.

The cost for the State of this fiscal and administrative moratorium would be marginal. The shortfall in corporation tax would be minimal as profits generated by start-ups over their first three years of existence are unfortunately not high. And as far as payroll taxes are concerned, any loss would be more than counterbalanced by the positive impact on job creation.

All European capitals tremble at the prospect of seeing the Continent plunge into a Japan-style recession. Ten lost years of economic misery with no growth, and deflationary damage. We seem to forget that the key to avoiding such a scenario is neither in Mario Draghi's hands, nor with the big corporations. It is small businesses that will enable Europe to find its way back to growth, and it is by freeing up the most fragile of them from stifling fiscal and administrative constraints that the State can play a genuinely useful role.

Facilitate the transmission of family-held businesses

It is no accident that those countries whose economies are strong today are the ones who have upheld strong family shareholder bases. Countries like Germany, the Netherlands, Austria, Switzerland, Denmark, or Finland, which are less sensitive to pressure from the financial markets, have built up centres of excellence in industries where competition from emerging countries has not yet managed to overtake them. Despite cost differentials, the family groups who dominate these economies have locally maintained both production facilities and jobs. They have stayed competitive by focusing on high value-added segments where they take market share not by price-cutting, which they couldn't afford to do anyway, but by way of specific products manufactured to a high quality.

Without the emotional bond of family shareholders to the historical activity of their company and their patience, many of these businesses would have given up long ago. They would have sold out to the highest bidder or would have offshored their production facilities to countries where labour costs are lower. If we in the West would only recognise the link between shareholder stability, the level of an economy's industry, and its overall prosperity, we would be far more aware of the need to preserve family groups, and one way to do this is by facilitating their transmission.

Are we aware, for example, that in France less than 10 per cent of companies of fewer than 10 employees are passed on to the next generation whereas this figure is 58 per cent in the Netherlands and 55 per cent in Germany with a European average of 44 per cent[6]? In Great Britain, too, the level of transmission falls well below the European average. Getting rid of this problem involves eliminating inheritance tax when a family-owned private company is passed on to the next generation or to its staff. If inheritance tax is not removed all together, then we should allow it to be settled over a longer period of time, say 10 years.

The subject of transmission is also highly important in the financial sector, particularly in the Anglo-Saxon world, in which we have seen partnerships acting as a stabilising force for the system as a whole. If the objective of reform is to avoid excessive risk-taking and yet create a stronger alignment between financial service providers and their clients, then we should favour the partnership model. Partners in these structures are far more concerned with the continuity of their company's operations and customer base than with the size of their bonuses. With this in mind, they are far more likely to weigh up risk on behalf of their clients than their counterparts in the banking world. Tax structures more favourable to capital transmission or redeployment within these structures would doubtless bring about more virtuous behaviour within the sector as a whole.

Make entrepreneurship commonplace from student age onwards

The first hurdle a young business creator has to get over is neither financial nor practical, but psychological, especially in the Old World. Why dare risk the entrepreneurial adventure when one lives in a society where company bosses are berated every day by politicians and the media? How can one find the courage and energy to set up a business when all ones university classmates aspire to is job security in a big corporation or the civil service? Of course amongst the most talented we still find a handful of ambitious go-getters, but of what do they dream? Of instant fortune. They long to create the next Facebook and be worth several billion dollars by the age of 30, or to earn their place on the trading floor and make a killing before the next crash. And so, where are the real entrepreneurs, the ones who aspire to more than just making a quick buck, but prefer to build up a company that will end up employing hundreds of people and that they will nurture throughout their professional careers?

If they are so few and far between, it is because the prevailing culture encourages extremes. Old fashioned, unimaginative conservatism in the vast majority of cases, and delusional fantasy in others. But the issue today is that a country's wealth is created somewhere in between. The emerging powers, and even certain European countries, are there to remind us every day that economic success is built on a foundation of tens of thousands of medium-sized companies whose CEOs look nothing at all like either Mark Zuckerberg or Larry Page. Western capitalism today needs to embed entrepreneurship in our minds but also in our words and deeds. To succeed here, the process must begin as early as possible at university.

Although progress has been made within academia, European universities remain closed and inward looking. Ties between universities and businesses need to be strengthened considerably, be it with multinationals or SMEs. But above all, university can and should become a genuine breeding ground for budding entrepreneurs, providing them with the training, the confidence, and the contacts to get started. With the notable exception of business schools, which are, for obvious reasons, already in close contact with private enterprise, the world of academia is still reluctant to make the move. Germany, however, has lost any inhibitions it might once have had and for years now has taken advantage of close ties developed between its universities and businesses. Just a few years ago the heirs of the pharmaceutical giant Merck made a donation of 25 million euros to the Heinrich Heine University in Düsseldorf, two thirds of which was used to fund salaries and R&D expenses for more than 18 scientists. At the University of Lübeck, companies like Siemens and Phillips finance applied research projects, particularly in the field of medical equipment. The chemicals giant BASF is about to open a laboratory in the campus of the University of Münster. The University of Munich prides itself on having raised almost 120 million euros over seven years to pay for 21 professorships.

Of course, these groups use the academic environment to commercial ends. For the most part these groups leverage university facilities to reinforce their R&D efforts and keep ahead of the game in their respective fields. But everybody gets to benefit, the universities themselves who get to stay on budget and the student and would-be entrepreneur who early in life becomes familiar with the world of business and makes extremely useful contacts for his future career.

Great Britain is becoming more active in such matters. Several universities have even gone as far as to set up business parks or business innovation centres on their own campuses. In this way they aim to attract businesses by giving them access to their laboratories, by organising workshops or studies in their subject matter areas, or even organising training programmes for their employees. The Babraham Institute in Cambridge has shown the way. Specialised in biochemistry and biotechnologies, this institute has invited 40 SMEs and start-ups on to its campus which can thus interact with students and research scientists on a daily basis.

On a much bigger scale, Sofia Antipolis in France provides a success story that we can all learn from. Set up 40 years ago in conjunction with the University, the technology park now accounts for over 50 per cent of the Alpes Maritimes department's GDP, an annual figure of six billion euros. The 2,400-hectare park is host to over 1,400 enterprises employing 30,000 people, with world-renowned centres of scientific excellence in the fields of telecommunications, chemistry, and biotechnologies.

Sadly, such success stories are still relatively rare occurrences. Universities are not sufficiently proactive while corporations are still too centralised and fail to develop much of an interest in provincial universities. As for the State, it still hasn't figured out that doling out subsidiaries is not enough to get projects off the ground. In the future, attitudes and mentalities will have to change, and a better coordination of efforts between businesses and the regions should allow universities to play a central role in developing entrepreneurship in Europe.

Rebuild bridges between large corporations and SMEs

Once upon a time, a big company would find itself at the heart of a local ecosystem bringing together a multitude of small businesses, both suppliers and customers, working closely with local authorities to improve infrastructure or housing. Notwithstanding a few notable exceptions, this is now a bygone age. Corporations no longer have local but global supply chains. They have often chosen to offshore their production facilities and in so doing, destroyed the local industrial fabric. In addition to this, they put almost unbearable pressure on their suppliers for deliveries, payment terms and conditions, inventory financing, or product quality. In a word, local SMEs who are lucky enough to still be able to work with a major group don't see them as a benevolent family member they can admire and try to emulate, but as a necessary evil, the source of all their hassles but without whom they wouldn't survive.

What these big companies don't seem to realise is that although they believe they have gained in terms of efficiency, they have lost out in reliability. It is hard to quantify the value of loyalty when analysing one's supply chain, but the German example is there to remind us again that in times of crisis, the geographic and emotional proximity that can exist between big companies and their network of SMEs can prove to be a major asset. This closeness allows them to rise above the strictly legal character of a business relationship in order to make a special effort when necessary, while waiting for better days to come. The small business is no longer just a reference number in a catalogue but a true partner with whom one can be demanding, but who in turn does not deserve to be stretched to their limits. This is the mentality we should aim to revive in Western capitalism, not as an act of charity, but because it is in our own interests.

There are countless ideas to make this happen. The first is to ask big companies to sign up to a charter for small and medium businesses. This charter would contain a clause stipulating that the corporation pay its suppliers within the contractually agreed time-frame when today late payments are endemic, used effectively as a cash flow management tool. In Great Britain, United Utilities observed that in 2008 only 60 per cent of its suppliers were paid on time. In an effort to improve business relationships with them, the company launched a campaign within its ranks, which pulled this percentage up to 93 per cent in 2012. Many other groups would be well advised to follow suit.

To enable these corporations to make peace with the field and once more become local development powerhouses, we should increase efforts to build industrial clusters. Since the beginning of the 1990s, through the work of Harvard professor Michael Porter, the concept has become popular although not always generating the success expected of it. It involves bringing together business expertise in a given sector, university research facilities and financial resources from banks and the authorities to develop geographical centres of excellence supported by the best possible infrastructure. These clusters are suited for companies, whether large or small who understand, even if they are competitors, the mutual benefits they can enjoy in this collaborative environment.

In Europe, the Nordics and Germany have turned their clusters into veritable machines of scientific or industrial innovation as well as export platforms to go after markets abroad. Medicon Valley is a particularly good example of this. Situated in the Oresund region of Denmark on the Swedish border, Medicon Valley has become in just a few short years one of the world's leading centres of excellence in the fields of biotechs and pharmaceuticals. The Medicon Valley network employs over 40,000 people and counts amongst its members around 150 biotech companies, 70 pharmaceutical groups including Novo Nordisk or AstraZeneca, 26 university hospitals, and 130 medical technology companies.

In Germany, where the leading industrial groups have remained faithful to their local roots, the *Kompetenznetze* have also worked wonders. Throughout the country there are now 130 huge clusters divided up into 30 regions and specialised in 18 innovative areas in industries as widespread as energy, microsystems or medical equipment. In order to be a part of a *Kompetenznetze*, companies must first go through a rigorous evaluation process, but once on board are allowed to brandish a quality label when entering in discussions with customers, business partners, or banks. This is a win-win situation both for the small businesses and big corporations who thus secure a way to leave their mark on an entire industrial network.

Despite efforts to emulate the German model, results in Great Britain and in France have been disappointing. In Great Britain, eight regional development agencies were charged with taking ownership of the subject but were subsequently wound up in 2012, having not understood that the main mission of the clusters should be to strengthen ties between small business and big corporations.

The problem differs little in France where the *Systèmes Productifs Locaux* (SPL), or local production mechanisms, and the *pôles de compétitivité* or competitiveness clusters have not managed to establish the virtuous circle that we have seen elsewhere. The first barrier is that these clusters *à la française* are first of all playthings of the State and place big corporations at the system's centre rather than SMEs[7]. Local small businesses feel wholly unsupported by these big groups whose nerve centre is inevitably Paris, and who too often see in the clusters the means to obtaining additional public subsidies for their research and development. The second barrier to success is that the higher education system is neither sufficiently interested nor involved in cluster initiatives by local businesses.

Instead of letting public authorities take the lead, big companies should choose to be far more proactive in matters of regional development and innovation. And while clusters offer an important vehicle for progress, corporate venture capital provides another. Big groups are often overflowing with cash to the point of not knowing what to do with it all, so why not allocate more funds to innovative companies who develop products or technologies linked to their field? This form of venture capital has become second nature for major corporations like Intel who has made investments in excess of 10 billion dollars in start-ups since 1991[8]. More often than not, these groups provide more than just cash. They open their doors to the young CEOs of their sponsored companies and help them draw up their business plans. They also enable them to boost their development no end through the credibility they bring in the eyes of their customers and suppliers. This is the type of helping hand that SMEs are most in need of today.

In addition to the example of Intel, many other leading corporations like Johnson & Johnson, Dow Chemical, Siemens, SAP, Philips or Procter & Gamble have also grasped the extent of the benefits they can draw from such interaction, and have even gone so far as to create their own incubators. The harsh reality however is that these examples still remain far too isolated, especially in Europe. We can hope to bring big groups around to seeing that it is in their interests to invest in such start-ups, but the State can also play a useful role by encouraging such behaviour. Through the Corporate Venture Scheme, the British government has introduced corporate tax breaks amounting to 20 per cent of sums invested in start-up capital, and even in certain cases to defer taxes on any capital gains made. Many other European countries should take note of such ideas.

Another way for the big corporations to help small businesses locally would be to reallocate certain amounts of their CSR budgets to socially responsible projects creating jobs in their own regions. It is altogether laudable for a food giant to finance the opening of a dairy in rural Senegal, but we mustn't forget that misery is also to be found in communities just a stone's throw from the outskirts of Europe's big cities. Here, it is vital to encourage the emergence of entrepreneurial careers, even if they aren't thick on the ground. Many big Western companies support microcredit in Africa, Asia or Latin America while forgetting that there are quite literally thousands of micro-entrepreneurs on their doorsteps who are unable to secure financial backing for their projects no matter how little they require. CSR should not be allowed to remain just a public relations gimmick.

Working more closely with the world of small business could provide big corporations with a two-fold opportunity. It would stimulate economic activity in their regions, which can only be in their interest over time. They would also build strengthened and lasting relationships with their business partners, be they suppliers or customers. As economic cycles become increasingly brutal, the environment of flexibility and trust resulting from these close-knit ties will prove to be a Godsend.

Incentivise banks to lend to SMEs

In spite of the trillions of dollars pumped into the global economy by the world's central banks to relieve the financial system and the economy, the results have not been forthcoming. The arteries of Western capitalism remain hopelessly blocked when banks prefer to restructure their balance sheet rather than play their key role in the transmission of monetary policy. In Europe, when the ECB lent banks one trillion euros at the modest annual rate of just 1 per cent over three years, what did they do with all this cash? They immediately re-deposited it at the ECB or reinvested part of it in the government bonds of the already debt-burdened States. The money is simply going around in circles in a macabre merry-go-round that does nothing at all for the real economy.

SMEs who were already badly off before the crisis are now almost entirely excluded from the world of credit and can only rely on themselves to cope with customer pressure, customers who, *crise oblige*, settle their bills later than they should. Small businesses can in no way be held responsible for the financial sector's misguided behaviour, yet they have found themselves nonetheless among the principal victims. And what a tragic paradox it is to think that many of these banks owe their survival to taxpayer generosity, the same taxpayer they refuse to lend to today.

So what should we do? We can no longer get away with standing by and watching this destructive spiral take hold. Thousands of companies continue to go out of business every day. This is because they cannot obtain the lines of credit they need despite having the customers and excellent prospects for their future success. On the other hand, we cannot force banks into lending, despite what some suggest. The burden of responsibility would be too great to bear for the public authorities if the banks suddenly freed up credit flow again regardless of their customers' solubility. We should however leverage incentives more actively. For example, rather than central banks simply no longer paying interest on bank deposits, they should charge on bank deposits so that financial institutions think twice before deciding to hold on to too much cash while the real economy is bled dry.

Central bankers should be more demanding regarding the ultimate use of these funds extended to banks. When the ECB launched its LTRO programme in 2011, they could have asked applicants to commit to lending on a certain percentage of these funds directly to SMEs. Now if the ECB chose not to do this, it is because it confined itself to an overly restrictive vision of its role, considering that it is not its job to support the economy. It has however, become urgent to break out of this orthodoxy and face up to the fact that monetary policy is meaningless if it doesn't contribute to broader economic policies aimed at stimulating activity and job creation.

States should also be far more proactive in encouraging banks to increase small business lending. For instance, they could imagine, on an exceptional basis, lowering corporate tax rates for banks that lend to SMEs above and beyond a certain minimum threshold over a three-year period. Naturally, such a measure would create controversy, giving tax breaks to institutions that have already more than taken advantage of State generosity. But it does not really matter. If we really want results, we should leave room for pragmatism. France's creating a public super-bank for SMEs – the *Banque Publique d'Investissement* – bringing together Oséo, the *Fonds Stratégique d'Investissement* and certain activities of the Caisse des Dépôts is a sound idea but is ultimately no game-changer. Small business financing should not be confined to just one provider but should be made an objective for the entire banking system. The creation of a British Business Bank in the UK will have to face up to the same challenge.

Great Britain's Project Merlin showed that the country has understood the need to directly involve the major banks in this approach but has so far failed to implement the corresponding tools to encourage them to keep their promises. In 2011 the five biggest British banks committed to lend 76 billion pounds sterling to SMEs, and despite their promise to the government, the agreement did not contain any sanctions in the event of failure nor incentives in the event of success. And obviously, the objectives were not met. More recently, the government added the National Loan Guarantee Scheme (NLGS) to its SME assistance programme, offering SMEs the opportunity to borrow at rates 1 per cent lower than normal. But once more the system is entirely dependent on the banks' good will when it should have been made worth their while to take part in the programme.

Lending to small businesses is not about charitable hand-outs. Most SMEs who knock on their banks' doors are not about to set out on madcap speculative schemes but simply wish to finance their working capital or further develop their production facilities. If only headquarters paid more attention to information fed up to them from their branches, they would realise that small business lending is less risky and more profitable than they imagine. Were they to support these SMEs, banks would find a way to become better corporate citizens without challenging the precautionary principles to which they should of course continue to adhere.

Boost venture capital

As if hostile banks were not enough to discourage our start-ups, the world of venture capital is in a sorry state, especially in Europe where it is on life support and barely breathing. Whereas in 2007 European venture capital funds managed to raise 8.2 billion euros, an amount considerably lower than that required, they managed a mere 4.8 billion euros in 2011 and the trend seems to be forever downward[9]. Faced with the waning interest of both private and institutional investors, public authorities do the best they can to fill the void left behind, financing their own specialised institutions. The European Commission uses the European Investment Fund to stimulate the sector while France invests considerable sums in tech start-ups by way of its sovereign fund, the FSI, although this was not at all its original purpose. If we look at Europe as a whole, today one third of all the money allocated by venture capital funds actually comes from public sources whereas this figure was only 10 per cent prior to the last crisis.

In addition to the financial resources deployed, there are also a number of large development projects underway. The British Prime Minister David Cameron stated his intention to transform the London Olympic site into a mini Silicon Valley, building on the capital's leading role in both the hi-tech and venture capital businesses. It is, in fact, in London that the major American venture capitalists have headquartered their European subsidiaries and that the rare European funds with an international reputation are still to be found.

France also wishes to capitalise on the reputation of its scientists to put itself amongst the sector's leaders, but it risks meeting many obstacles on the way up there. In spite of several remarkable success stories, French venture capital funds still struggle to attract the major international institutional investors, when local private investors have practically thrown in the towel. And so the French State comes once more to the sector's rescue, proposing to invest more than a billion euros to set up a gigantic technology park in Saclay where engineering schools and start-ups can come together. It is, however, unlikely that, as ambitious as it may be, the project at Saclay will be able to reverse the current trend.

But while Europe's biggest corporations shine in cutting edge sectors such as semi-conductors, software, telecoms, or biotechs, why is it that start-ups fail to emulate their elders' success? All the critical success factors would seem to be present: young, first-rate engineers; markets where customers are at least as tech-friendly as in the US; and governments who spare no effort to facilitate their development. The reality is, that in spite of public authorities' determination, structural barriers are still omnipresent. The first and by far the most important is the rarity of entrepreneurial vocations. Young European engineers are gripped with fear at the thought of going out on their own and being faced with failure. They believe that their career before the age of 30 will shape the rest of their existence, and that it is therefore in their best interests to follow the straightest, safest path forward in a well-paid job at a big corporation. The only way we will be able to get over this psychological barrier is by demystifying business creation as early as possible in a young student's life.

The second problem is that European start-ups are somewhat fainthearted. Unlike in the US where fledgling companies manage to raise tens of millions of dollars over the first few years of their existences, European companies' fund-raising rounds always seem to come up short. At best they cobble together a few million, then when they begin to run out of cash, the initial investors lose interest. Despite their brilliant ideas, these start-ups are incapable of pre-empting new markets or technologies. The few who do make it are rapidly bought out by their American competitors who are inevitably more aggressive and better capitalised.

This unfortunate state of affairs is as much the consequence of overly shy entrepreneurs who underestimate their financial requirements for fear of putting off backers as it is the failure of fund providers to step back and see the big picture. In all fairness to our venture capitalists, they have enough trouble raising funds from their own investors to allow them to be overly generous in turn with their portfolio companies.

It is high time to break this deadlock. European States have neither the finances nor the will to stand in for the private sector and help start-ups get airborne. However, indirectly, public authorities could have considerable impact by encouraging private and institutional investors to put their money to good use in SME capital. Current schemes are hopelessly inadequate in most of Europe. Tax breaks for individuals investing in small businesses are capped at such a low level as to render them near useless[10]. And as for institutional investors, no fiscal incentives have been offered to increase their small business spending despite their considerably greater financial clout. Tax credits offered to each stakeholder must be much higher in absolute terms, but must also take into account the maturity of the company in question. Taking part in early capital rounds for a brand new start-up deserves more of a helping hand than investing in a 10-year-old SME with an established staff and customer base. Fiscal incentives should be better differentiated in order to maximise investments and results.

Reviving the world of venture capital should be a strategic priority for us. Recent years have seen decisive action from public authorities save the sector from certain death, and we should be thankful for this. But we should also acknowledge that the State alone cannot shoulder the immense responsibility of supporting our fledgling companies. This would be both unhealthy and dangerous. If we really want to breathe new life into our business creators, we will need to recreate a genuine ecosystem around them and encourage those who should be working beside them to take the necessary financial risks. Their good health will determine the future of our economies.

---

1 Leveraged Buy-Out

2 Market estimated at over 191 billion pounds sterling

3 *Agence pour la Création d'Entreprises*

4 *Nouvel Accompagnement pour la Création et la Reprise d'Entreprises*

5 "Entrepreneurs speak out", Ernst & Young, 2011

6 Source: Report drawn up by KPMG for the French Finance Ministry in 2007

7 A survey commissioned by the Comité Richelieu in conjunction with the Economy Ministry showed that 71 per cent of respondent SMEs declared that they lacked consideration within their competitiveness cluster

8 The corporate venture capital represents approximately 9 per cent of venture capital spending in the US. Source: National Venture Capital Association

9 Source: European Private Equity and Venture Capital Association

10 In France, income tax breaks are limited to 5,000 euros annually for a single person and 10,000 euros for a couple. In addition to that there is a reduction in fortune tax of 50 per cent of the amount invested, capped at 45,000 euros

Conclusion – Reinvent the magic triangle

To bring about a return to growth and cease to be the powerless spectators of a world beyond our control, we will have to fundamentally rethink the balance of power between the markets, the entrepreneur, and the State. Business creators must once more take up their rightful place as the cornerstone of Western capitalism. Markets should be used differently, returning to their original purpose of supporting wealth creators by freeing up capital flow and encouraging risk-taking. The State must stop playing the role of nanny and start playing the role of coach by creating an environment that allows private initiative to flourish and meet with success. In order to do this we must abandon the unproductive discussions between those in favour of 'less State' or 'more State'. We would be better off fighting for 'better State'.

The State remains effectively the only tool we have at our disposal to define long-term national economic priorities and to mobilise public and private sector resources to achieve those goals. This mission is vital in sectors where research requires the bringing together of a large number of stakeholders and huge, high-risk capital investments that the private sector alone is often unwilling to cover. State support is equally useful in more mature industries where our companies are up against hybrid groups. As we have seen already, emerging powers have become masters in the art of pooling all their resources – financial, political, logistical, and diplomatic – to come to the aid of their businesses, both public and private, in their conquest of overseas markets. If we leave our companies to their own devices, they will go to war with these competitors like lambs to the slaughter and sooner or later they will lose.

It is therefore pragmatism and common sense that force our hand to reinvent the magic triangle: Entrepreneur – State – Market. Emerging powers' successes have freed us in the West from a great burden: that of having to make an ideological choice. The new economic world order, coupled with the more than questionable behaviour of the markets over the last few years have propelled us into the post-liberal age. We should have no qualms about believing that it is essentially down to the individual and private initiative to build a nation's wealth, and sing the praises of capitalism, while recognising that the State has a key role to play. No longer the *Welfare* State, which has proved to be the ruin of Europe, but the *Coach* State.

For those fatalists who are convinced we can do nothing against the all-powerful markets and that we have already lost the war, we should remember that up until the eighties Western capitalism had a sure-fire recipe for success. It was no perfect world but everybody was in their rightful place. The business creator created and the financier financed. This relationship must be adapted to today's environment which is certainly different, but where the priorities should remain the same.

Restoring the balance, of course, means regulating, but if we stop at this, nothing will change. In a few years another financial crisis will hit and sweep away all our efforts, showing us once more that our impregnable sea wall was in fact terribly fragile. If we really want to safeguard our capitalism and make its main stakeholders accountable, then it is behaviours and motivations that we should set about changing. And in order to achieve this we will have to return to a good old-fashioned guiding principle: we always take better care of that which we own. Chief executives should invest their own savings in the companies they run; bankers and other financial intermediaries should invest their bonuses in the very products they sell and be compensated based on their results long term; financial shareholders should be rewarded by their portfolio companies for their loyalty. But most importantly, business creators should be left to do what they do best, sheltered from the fiscal and administrative harassment they are still subjected to today.

In Europe we dream today of growth rates in excess of 2 per cent. In our collective subconsciousness, we try to persuade ourselves that abandoning any hope of real growth is the price we have to pay for the relative comfort to which the Welfare State has accustomed us to. Implicitly we accept the notion that if we simply share what we have, then we will no longer need to create. But what will happen when our finances run out and we have nothing left to share out? That is the existential question that we need to answer if we want to prevent the unravelling of our social fabric, the rise of demogogues and potentially the return of conflicts we haven't experienced for over six decades.

And the answer? In order to survive we will have to learn to create again.

Acknowledgements

The most wonderful encounters in my life have always been the result of happenstance, and this book is once again a fine example of this. I owe a great deal to my friends Sylvie and Léon Bressler who over an improvised dinner held in a magnificent villa overlooking the Gulf of Ajaccio introduced me to Odile Jacob and Bernard Gotlieb. With the recklessness that can go to one's head on a beautiful summer night after a few glasses of a fine wine, I drummed up the courage to talk to them about my project which, at that stage, was just a collection of thoughts. You can imagine my surprise when, as the time came to part company, Odile turned to me and in her own inimitable fashion, threw me a "We are with you!".

That was the first step on a long journey, through which Odile and Bernard guided me with patience and intelligence. Their legendary publishing house released the French version of this book in February 2013 under the title "Le Choc des capitalismes". They also introduced me to Bloomsbury, my British publishers. I am immensely grateful to them.

I would also like to thank those who helped me successfully complete this project. Jonathan Pearson, a brilliant Cambridge University graduate and highly regarded think tank professional, who assisted me in my extensive research. Andrew Simpkin, a man of many talents, who read my manuscript and made a number of excellent suggestions. Many thanks also to the team at Bloomsbury. Stephen Rutt, the project editorial director and Alana Clogan, the commissioning editor, who supported me and showed a tremendous amount of enthusiasm throughout the process. I am also indebted to Sophia Blackwell who ensured that the book would reach a broad public.

Needless to say, I am very grateful to my family – my wife Alexandra and our children Arielle and David - who stoically put up with my uncivilised working habits and gave me the stamina to carry on in spite of everything. Finally, I cannot end without mentioning my mother,

Odette Pinto, a model of strength, courage and joie de vivre. She is the one who instilled in me the somewhat insane faith of the entrepreneur. This book is also the expression of the values she shared with my late father Isaac Jack Pinto who often reminded me that one should always see the world for what it is but without ever losing hope of changing it.

London, 26th October 2013

Index